TECHNOLOGIES OF KINSHIP

Technologies of Kinship

*Asian American Racialization
and the Making of Family*

LiLi Johnson

NEW YORK UNIVERSITY PRESS
New York

NEW YORK UNIVERSITY PRESS
New York
www.nyupress.org

© 2025 by New York University
All rights reserved

Library of Congress Cataloging-in-Publication Data
Names: Johnson, LiLi author
Title: Technologies of kinship : Asian American racialization and the making of family / LiLi Johnson.
Description: New York : New York University Press, [2025] | Includes bibliographical references and index.
Identifiers: LCCN 2025002391 (print) | LCCN 2025002392 (ebook) | ISBN 9781479833351 hardback alk. paper | ISBN 9781479833368 paperback alk. paper | ISBN 9781479833375 ebook | ISBN 9781479833399 ebook other
Subjects: LCSH: Asian Americans—Ethnic identity | Ethnicity—United States | Families—United States | Technology—Social aspects—United States
Classification: LCC E184.A75 J64 2025 (print) | LCC E184.A75 (ebook)
LC record available at https://lccn.loc.gov/2025002391

LC ebook record available at https://lccn.loc.gov/2025002392 This book is printed on acid-free paper, and its binding materials are chosen for strength and durability. We strive to use environmentally responsible suppliers and materials to the greatest extent possible in publishing our books.

The manufacturer's authorized representative in the EU for product safety is Mare Nostrum Group B.V., Mauritskade 21D, 1091 GC Amsterdam, The Netherlands.
Email: gpsr@mare-nostrum.co.uk.

Manufactured in the United States of America

10 9 8 7 6 5 4 3 2 1

Also available as an ebook

For my mother,
Kay Ann Johnson

CONTENTS

List of Figures   ix

Introduction: Technology, Race, and Kinship   1

1. Paper Families and Family Papers: Government Bureaucracy and Family Formation in the Era of Chinese Exclusion   29

2. The Making of the Model Minority Family: Immigration Policy, Cultural Narrative, and Asian American Racialization   63

3. Photographic Conceptions: Kinship Formation in Transnational Adoption from Asia   91

4. Making Racial Choices: The Digital Profile Interface in Economies of Family Formation   117

5. 23andMe and the Racialization of Genetic Ancestry Testing   153

Conclusion: Futures of Kinship   181

Acknowledgments   189

Notes   193

Bibliography   211

Index   227

About the Author   241

LIST OF FIGURES

Figure 1.1. Reference sheet, May 24, 1935. Box 363. Case file 125/68, Moy Sue. Chinese Exclusion Act Case Files. National Archives, New York.   42

Figure 1.2. Photograph submitted with testimony, October 25, 1927. Box 363. Case file 125/68, Moy Sue. Chinese Exclusion Act Case Files. National Archives, New York.   53

Figure 1.3. Affidavit, 1938. Box 538. Case file 171/76, Wong Tung Yee. Chinese Exclusion Act Case Files. National Archives, New York.   56

Figure 3.1. *The two Cha Jung Hees*. Courtesy of Deann Borshay Liem.   112

Figure 4.1. Public donor search webpage from California Cryobank. October 2024.   118

Figure 4.2. One of twelve tables with OkCupid QuickMatch Scores on Racial Preference. "Race and Attraction, 2009–2014." OkCupid blog. September 10, 2014.   137

Figure 4.3. "Every Single Person" campaign announcement. OkCupid blog. July 29, 2021.   146

Figure 4.4. "Every Single Pansexual" campaign advertisement. OkCupid blog. July 29, 2021.   148

Figure 4.5. "Every Single Non-Monogamist" campaign advertisement, OkCupid. *AdWeek*. 2021.   150

Figure 5.1. "Root for Your Roots." 23andMe advertisement.
May 2018.   166

Figure 5.2. "Our Services—Ancestry." 23andMe Website.
May 9, 2019.   168

Figure 5.3. Example of a chart explaining common lineage.
23andMe Website. October 31, 2024.   172

Introduction

Technology, Race, and Kinship

In March 2022, independent film company A24 released the cerebral science fiction drama *After Yang*. The film, written and directed by South Korean American filmmaker Kogonada, narrates the story of a multiracial adoptive family and their malfunctioning humanoid robot, and offers a pensive reflection on themes of kinship, robotic technologies, and what it means to be human. Jake and Kyra are an interracial couple who adopted their daughter Mika from China, and, before the events of the film, purchased a "cultural robot" named Yang to teach Mika about her Chinese heritage. *After Yang* begins when Mika is six years old, and the family discovers something is wrong with Yang. The film then chronicles Jake's pursuit to fix Yang and follows the family's complicated grief in the absence of such a central member.

Interspersed with memories and flashbacks of Yang's participation in the family, the film contemplates Yang's ontology and familial role. His status as nonhuman calls into question what constitutes kinship and how it is produced by the racial and multicultural circumstances that bring individuals together. Mika calls Yang "gege" (older brother in Chinese) and he calls her "meimei" (little sister). And the film leaves open questions including: if Yang is Mika's older brother, does that mean he is Jake and Kyra's child? Is he *really* part of the family or just programmed to act like it? At times he is talked about as if he is a broken computer: a technician discusses "replacing parts," while another calls the issue an "interior core problem." At other times, he is an integral part of who they are as kin: in one flashback scene, after Mika's classmates ask about her "real parents" (a common microaggression for adoptees), to comfort her, Yang teaches Mika about grafting branches onto a tree as a metaphor for adoption. He tells her, "You're a part of the family tree. For real." And she responds, "Then so are you."

Throughout *After Yang*, fraught ideologies about race and culture also underlie the relationships within the family. The first few scenes of the film show an array of hybridized East Asian aesthetics. Jake, played by Colin Farrell with an American accent, owns what appears to be a struggling traditional Chinese tea shop, with rows of jars lining the shelves and discs of compressed tea on the counter. The family's clothes and home reflect the aesthetics of popular Japanese brands like Muji and Uniqlo: practical, minimalist, elegant, and full of light-colored wood, natural fabrics, and mood lighting. At dinner, Mika asks her father if he liked the gochujang (Korean chili paste) sauce she made. After dinner, Mika practices violin, and later, the whole family convenes in the living room for their monthly virtual dance competition. Wearing matching outfits, the four of them begin an elaborate dance routine in unison, evoking the trance music vibe of Japanese arcade game Dance Dance Revolution.

Like many science fiction films that mark futurism through the visuality of multiculturalism, *After Yang* never explicitly mentions race. And yet race is purposefully made visible through embodiment. Yang has taken the form of a young Asian man, is racialized as Chinese (though the actor Justin Hong-Kee Min is Korean American), and was designed to teach about Chinese "culture" which mostly consists of offering fun facts about China and teaching some simple Chinese words. Mika, with a distinctly Japanese name, is the adopted Chinese diasporic girl living in this unnamed multicultural yet Asianized future in which, if nothing else, China still exists as a coherent location of her origins and of her otherness. Kyra, played by Jodie Turner-Smith, is the Black mother whose race is unmeaningful in the world of the film other than in its function of visibility. And Jake is the White father/owner of Mika and Yang with an almost fetishistic admiration for Asian tea. While the film is, indeed, a beautiful reflection on the nature of humanity and our relationship to robotic technologies, *After Yang* feels all too familiar in its use of Asian racial typing as a prism for the tensions between these issues.

These tensions that arise around Yang's hybrid human-robot ontology literalize the broadest contention of this book: that all family and kinship are formed through technologies that have been shaped by the racial and gendered ideologies of contemporary culture. And as such, family and kinship function as sites of technologized racialization. In the film, Yang *is* the technology that has facilitated the formation and enactment of kinship bonds. In this book, these metaphorized threads of family formation, technological development, and racialization manifest in what I call technologies of kinship—such as government bureaucracy, photography, and genetic ancestry tests—that, I argue, actively participate in the formation of kinship in racialized and gendered ways. As this book demonstrates, throughout the twentieth and twenty-first centuries, family itself has been constructed and reconstructed through these technologies that do material, affective, and ideological work. Technologies of kinship are constituted by the things that people interact with and utilize on a material level, and they reify the varied meanings of race, gender, sexuality, and power. Characteristically, they are thus involved in the processes of emergence and construction that not only create new social relationships between individuals but also transform the very terms through which intimacy and encounter are made possible.

Like the world of *After Yang*, systems of racial and gendered meaning both predicate and inform individual formations of family, simultaneously existing independently from the real or fictional family's awareness of them and actively shaping the possible embodiments of that kinship. For example, although Yang's physical form as a young Chinese man does not require Jake and Kyra to consciously grapple with his race or gender, each of their racialized identities creates the basis for his brotherly relationship with Mika and his authority as a cultural resource. It isn't a coincidence that his technologized form and the identities used to make that form meaningful thus prescribe the very relations of kinship enacted by them. This book asks, how has kinship itself been produced and shaped within American culture by the structures of race and racialization that define those that participate in it? How has race been literally and figuratively reproduced by the fantasy and embodied relation of the family?

As long-standing metaphors for the nation, notions of family and kinship have been imbricated in the shifting hierarchies and formations of race in the United States. And these processes of racial formation (as conceived by Michael Omi and Howard Winant) have been distinctly relational, comparative, and heterogenous across racial and ethnic groups.[1] This book offers technologies of kinship as a framework for critically interrogating how race and kinship have been co-constituted in historically, socially, and politically specific ways. And I use the phrase technologies of kinship to highlight the intersectional forms of power that shape and produce the varied meanings and forms of kinship.

While this book is specifically occupied by the triangulation of kinship, Asian racialization, and the technological systems that constitute them both, all kinship in the North American context has been shaped by the history of race and racialization, and as such, technologies of kinship offers an analytic for critiquing power that is not exclusive to a particular racial group. That said, in this book, I focus on how Asian American family formation is a site in which technologies of kinship reveal the specificities of Asian diasporic racialization and kinship. In the broader historical and cultural context, Asians have long been associated with technology, techno-Orientalism, and the cyborg, so much so throughout twentieth and twenty-first century popular culture that this association has become a major facet of Asian racialization and the tropes that define it.[2] Mechanized outsourced labor, robotic model minority students, and cyborg Asian sex dolls reflect the echoes of technology as racialized dehumanization. As Leslie Bow has described, "At the millennium, the racialized templates of the Yellow Peril and techno-Orientalist panic converge in the specter of a machine-like, unending, self-replicating alien labor force."[3] The Asian body itself has been imagined to possess these technological qualities: unfeeling, mechanical, and computing. And racialized Asian inscrutability, originating from the imagined mysticism of the East in nineteenth and twentieth century Orientalism, has now metamorphosed into an inscrutability metaphorized as the black box of computing within the concept of the Asian cyborg.[4]

Paradoxically, despite the persistent image of Asian as cyborg, robot, and nonhuman, Asian and Asian diasporic family and kinship have been narrated in mainstream Euro-North American popular cultures as almost completely natural and uninfluenced by technology or reproductive innovation. In model minority discourse, the trope of the Asian "tiger parents" defines model minority kinship and presumes the naturalized reproduction of the Asian nuclear family. These stereotypically strict Asian parents are most frequently imagined as the same ethnicity, heterosexual, and legally married. And it is true that many Asian immigrant families do embody heterosexual reproductive normativity, a phenomenon explicitly explored in the second chapter of this book. However, as erin Khuê Ninh posits in her argument that the concept of the model minority serves as an active mode of racialization rather than merely as myth, "an identity's materiality is perhaps more appropriately gauged by its fictions and active identifications (what its discourses aim *to* fabricate) than merely by its present circumstances."[5] Indeed, how we represent and imagine the Asian American family speaks to its social construction as much as (if not more than) its demographic realities.

This assumed naturalness of Asian family and kinship is further exemplified by the lack of visibility or representation in American popular culture of encounters between Asians and reproductive technologies. In contrast to the marketing of in vitro fertilization or surrogacy that celebrates the reproduction of the White or even multicultural nuclear family—and despite their actual use by Asians—Asian families are rarely seen or represented as the intended consumers of assistive reproductive technologies.[6] In these industries, Asians are often viewed as the scientists and doctors administering these technological innovations, not the ones using or in need of them. Perhaps this imaginative absence is also due in part to broader globalized concerns and narratives about overpopulation, however unfounded, alongside popular images of crowded and overflowing Asian cities like Shanghai, Tokyo, Hong Kong, and New Delhi.

While seemingly contradictory, the fine-drawn but distinct division between the Asian body as technologized and the Asian family as naturalized evidences the complex processes through which racialization functions in the United States. The naturalization of the Asian nuclear family and its reproduction obfuscates the cultural, technological, and political structures that have historically and contemporarily produced Asian diasporic families. And *Technologies of Kinship* demonstrates the ways in which technology can function not only as a racializing and often racist discourse of Asian representation but also as a theoretical hermeneutic with which to understand how Asian American family and kinship *are* socially and historically constructed, embodied, and represented. In other words, identifying technologies of kinship that participate in these processes reimagines technology, not only as an inherent or immutable quality of Asian racial typing, but also rather as an apparatus with which to highlight the social construction and racialization of family formation itself.

Indeed, while the use of government bureaucracy or photography in family formation is certainly not isolated to the Asian diaspora, identifying and theorizing their historical and cultural mobilizations show the unique and emergent encounters that have been born within Asian American history and cultural formation. Each of the chapters of this book thus provides a case study that highlights a different technology of kinship and reveals how the co-constitution of Asian racialization and kin formation has changed over time. Together, they trace a genealogy of Asian American racialization through the twentieth century to the present. Beginning in the early twentieth century, *Technologies of Kinship* commences with an examination of the Chinese family as a site of racial anxieties and the role of family in regimes of racialized exclusion. By the mid-twentieth century, racial discourse about Asians changed from a focus on maintaining exclusion to promoting inclusion and multiculturalism. Nevertheless, the distinctiveness of Asian as racial category (and as other) has been maintained through the model minority as a racial trope, defined by cultural anxieties about the overpowering collectivism of family that led to seemingly threatening forms of success and achievement. And since the end of the twentieth century, Asian racial categorization as a process of meaning-making has shifted to coincide with the rise of neoliberalism and neoliberal political rationality.

Across these historical shifts, the material and ideological construction of the Asian American family has been continually entangled with the changing meanings of Asian as racial category. And the different technologies used to construct these literal and ideological kin formations have thus also produced new forms of racialized intimacy and fantasies of national, racial, and collective belonging. Even as the family has served as a site of access to the nation, and modeled forms of multicultural and neoliberal inclusion, it has continued to participate in the articulation and regulation of racial boundaries. *Technologies of Kinship* reveals how these processes, ideologies, and embodiments of family formation have played a role in the shifting meanings of race that have defined and characterized the Asian diaspora.

Technologies of Kinship

The story of technology and kinship in this book uses technology in two distinct ways. The first highlights the shared use of technology as a framework from feminist science and technology studies and media studies: a categorical description that refers to the material construction of specific systems and applications of knowledge. This includes the characterization of systems as various categories of "technologies": scientific technology, medical technology, media technology, photographic technology, digital technology, etc. In these fields, modifiers such as "scientific" or "digital" specify a particular discipline and associated materiality through which technology is developed or takes shape. Technologies, in this context, can be touched or held or used as material instruments of embodied processes and procedures: a microscope magnifies organisms, a printing press prints newspapers or texts, a digital camera captures images, a computer processes data. The second use of technology, in contrast, is drawn from cultural studies and employs technology as a hermeneutic framework for thinking about the systemization of racial, gendered, and sexual power. More specifically, I draw on Michel Foucault's description of power and the use of technology to articulate the "organization of knowledge with respect to both domination and the self."[7] To be a *technology of* something is to identify a site in which power, discipline, or regulation function.

The relationship between these two conceptualizations of technology also follows a semiotic pattern for which technologies of kinship serves as a sign. Drawing from a Saussurean tradition of dyadic signs consisting of signifier and signified, the first conceptualization of technology (to material objects and embodied processes) thus functions as signifier. Saussure describes the signifier as the "sound-image," "not the material sound, a purely physical thing, but the psychological imprint of the sound, the impression that it makes on our senses."[8] In other words, it is not the sound of the word "computer" or "photograph" that is the signifier but rather the sensorial or material thing that is articulated by such words. The categorical reference to a set of things variously referred to as technologies thus encapsulates this set of signifiers.

In this simple semiotic model, the broader concept of technology (for which those signifiers/examples represent) could then be named the signified, or the abstract meaning referred to by the signifier. And indeed, from a linguistic perspective, the computer, photograph, and microscope don't have much in common other than that they are all signifiers of technology (which, in semiotic terms, is in turn signified by them). However, in this book, technologies of kinship as a sign system is more specific than technology as a broader sign. And thus, what is signified is more specific to the processes and locations of power that shape family and kinship, articulated by the second use of technology as hermeneutic. Together, technologies of kinship (the sign) are constituted through the physical systems (the signifiers) that participate in the workings of racial and gendered power through the family (the signified). And indeed, this configuration applies to each of the five technologies of kinship identified in this book. Each refers to a physical technology (such as photography or genetic ancestry testing) that characteristically functions as a site of racialization that operates through and on the construction of Asian American kinship.

Technology as Material Signifier

In some ways, the hegemony of biological reproduction in scholarship on the topics of family formation and technology has served as a red herring for the use of technology as a lens to examine race and kinship's co-constitution. Since 1978, when Louise Brown became the first child conceived through in vitro fertilization, assistive reproductive technologies (ARTs) have become almost metonymic with the role of technology in the formation of family. When referenced at all in studies of kinship, technology is usually a categorical term to refer to medicalized processes in industries such as in vitro fertilization, surrogacy, or egg and sperm donation. Scholars conducting ethnographic research in these industries have shown how the politics and social meanings of ARTs have been shaped by cultural understandings of kinship, biology, and biology's relationship to technology.[9] Furthermore, access to these services and stratification along racial, sexual, and class lines continue to shape the politics of reproductive technologies in contemporary global cultures.[10] For example, Dorothy Roberts observes how "the expansion of race-based biotechnology, including genetic selection, fits within the neoliberal trend toward privatization and punitive governance and requires adjusting feminist reproductive dystopias."[11]

This rise in research on the politics and technologies of reproduction demonstrates the rich opportunities to understand how technological developments within biomedicine actively participate in new and old processes of family formation. However, this book very intentionally attends to the multiplicity of other technological systems that participate in kinship formation practices. This is not only to situate reproduction within a much wider array of kinship practices shaped by technology, but also to specifically place these more conventional manifestations of technology within a larger genealogy of racialization through family formation.

For example, media and digital technologies actively participate in the racialized and gendered processes of family formation through their ability to facilitate, represent, and transform individuals' encounters with one another. Scholars including Lisa Nakamura and Wendy Hui Kyong Chun have shown how digital technology has never been neutral or free from the racialized and gendered discourses of its producers or users.[12] And now that the internet and social media facilitate intimacy, sexual expression, and community building in digital worlds on ever-growing scales, kinship formation has taken on new racial digital forms as well. As I discuss in Chapters 4 and 5 of this book, family formation economies like dating, egg and sperm donation, and genetic ancestry testing utilize digital platforms to market kinship in ways that frame racial identification as a consumer choice. We can now "filter" for Asian women to date or White sperm donors with which to reproduce. And medicalized consumer technologies like genetic ancestry tests deliver results to customers on a social media interface with brightly colored maps and racialized percentage breakdowns telling you who you are.

While digital technologies have become a new site for mediating our understanding of these scientific and medical services, this instrumentalization of popular technologies in racializing regimes of power is not specific to the digital age. Raymond Williams helpfully articulates the distinction between "technique as a particular construction or method, and technology as a system of such means and methods."[13] And this systemization and mechanization define and bridge different types of technology, in which photography, images, paper documents, and digital platforms are all organized and moved through the world by intentional structures of management and procedure.

In particular, photography encompasses not only a physical mechanical system (the camera with all of its material and affective accoutrements) and the image that system produces, but also the production of new events, potential encounters, and forms of intimacy, in what Ariella Azoulay calls the "event of photography."[14] As such, photography as technology is a recurring theme throughout this book, precisely because of its racializing phenomenology as technical mechanism, representational practice, and interpersonal encounter.[15] Within Asian American studies, as Thy Phu argues, photography and visual culture have been crucial sites in the articulation of Asian American racial subjecthood shaped by social constructions of civility and citizenship. Phu's discussion of picture brides, for example, highlights how photography functioned as a technology of kinship (without naming it as such) that not only created visual representations of individuals but actively participated in the production of new kinship relations. Practiced primarily between 1908 and 1920, following the Gentlemen's Agreement that restricted immigration from Japan and Korea (which was occupied by Japan at the time), picture brides immigrated to the United States by exchanging photographs and engaging in a proxy marriage before meeting their husbands. As Phu describes, "These portraits were the chief means of introducing men and women who had not yet met, and for this reason the quality of 'likeness' was an important feature."[16] They were exchanged, looked at, shown to others, and used to compare. And thus, the photograph functioned as a material item born from technology that played an active role in these journeys of family formation.

Whether the photograph of a picture bride or the online profile of a sperm donor, these material things and systems constitute physical signifiers of technologies of kinship. They demonstrate the application and development of knowledge and systemization, and they actively participate in practices of family formation. However, as theorized in what follows, these technologies also function in the organization and workings of power when considered in their specific social and historical contexts.

Technology as Power Signified

In addition to its force as a categorical signifier, technology also serves as a hermeneutic framework alongside uses of the term in cultural studies to describe the systemization of power. This often comes in the construction of a *technology of* some form in which power takes. For example, Lisa Lowe briefly asserts that "the administration of citizenship was simultaneously a 'technology' of racialization and gendering" in the history of Asian American racial formation.[17] Elsewhere, Jian Neo Chen refers to "technologies of racial gendering" to analyze the aesthetic practices of contemporary trans of color embodiments.[18] Without explicit historicization of this particular linguistic use of technological phrasing, both scholars gesture towards a Foucauldian approach to the concept.

In Volume I of *The History of Sexuality*, Foucault uses the term "technology" to illustrate a particular set of mechanisms, directly naming both "technologies of power" and "technologies of sex." These *technologies of*, as Foucault constructs them, function as a reference to the specific processes and systems through which power has been constructed, mobilized, embodied, and felt. Foucault describes,

> The analysis, made in terms of power, must not assume that the sovereignty of the state, the form of the law, or the overall unity of domination are given at the outset; rather, these are only the terminal forms power takes. It seems to me that power must be understood in the first instance as *the multiplicity* of force relations immanent in the sphere in which they operate and which constitute their own organization; as *the process* which, through ceaseless struggles and confrontations, transforms, strengthens, or reverses them; as *the support* which these force relations find in one another, thus forming a chain or a system, or on the contrary, the disjunctions and contradictions which isolate them from one another; and lastly, as *the strategies* in which they take effect, whose general design or institutional crystallization is embodied in the state apparatus, in the formulation of the law, in the various social hegemonies [emphasis added].[19]

Indeed, power is not only pointed (what Foucault calls "terminal forms" of power) but also dispersed; it is intentional and inadvertent, material and affective, profound and mundane. But *how* does it operate and *how* is it constructed? Foucault suggests it is through technologies of power: "the multiplicity of force relations," "the process which . . . transforms, strengthens, or reverses," "the support which these force relations find in one another," and "the strategies in which they take effect." Foucault names sexuality as "the set of effects produced in bodies, behaviors, and social relations by a certain deployment deriving from a complex political technology."[20] As such, sexuality is an embodied and ideological construction produced by power, and technology is the complex system through which that power has been reified. In this context, the term "technology" functions not only as a fixed category of physical apparatuses or set of organized techniques (as previously discussed) but also as a framework for illustrating and interpreting the material and ideological constitution of formations such as sex, power, and as later analyzed by Teresa de Lauretis in conversation with Foucault, gender.[21]

To be clear, these technologies of sex or power (or as I argue, of kinship) are never mutually exclusive from one another, neither materially nor ideologically, nor can they be examined in isolation from one another.[22] And the naming of a system, apparatus, technique, or method as a *technology of* is less a declarative categorization and more an interpretive offering in service of disentangling axes of power. In the later "Technologies of the Self," Foucault further articulates this use of technology as a framework for examining the "specific techniques that human beings use to understand themselves," which include four named matrices: technologies of production, technologies of sign systems, technologies of power, and technologies of the self.[23] Technology again invokes the socially constructed qualities of our embodied world that are shaped by the material world, sign systems, power, and our own sense of self. And the term focuses our attention on an interrogation of power and invites attention to the agency and ability of people, systems, and knowledge to shape the world in which they exist. Furthermore, Foucault's conception of power is not merely an abstract or theoretical concept, but rather a way to name the unequal access and distribution of resources, the violences inflicted upon communities and bodies, and the myriad ways that individuals survive and live.

This book brings together these approaches (technology as a categorization of material systems and technology as a description of systemization) precisely to reveal the dynamism of the material, institutional, affective, and ideological systems that construct both race and kinship. The technologies described here are characterized by their active participation in the creation of new forms of kinship in ways that bring individuals, material items, institutional structures, and ideologies into new encounter. They operate rhizomatically, to borrow from Gilles Deleuze and Félix Guattari, and each "ceaselessly establishes connections between semiotic chains, organizations of power, and circumstances relative to the arts, sciences, and social struggles."[24] By attending to the negotiation of individuals, systems, and interactions that constitute the formation of Asian American family and kinship, *Technologies of Kinship* aims to refocus our attention to the "stuff" that make up kinship encounters: the papers or photographs or user profiles that are often overlooked as mere prostheses of human action. As Bill Brown theorizes, "The story of objects asserting themselves as things, then, is the story of a changed relation to the human subject and thus the story of how the thing really names less an object than a particular subject-object relation."[25] In the production of kinship, this subject-object relation is rarely singular. Objects act as things in their shifting relations with people negotiating the landscapes of family formation. A bureaucratic document acts as evidence that a Chinese immigrant is related to an American citizen. A photograph is placed in the crib by an adoptive parent-to-be to help them imagine the child they will travel to meet. A brightly colored map shows someone where their "ancestors" came from.

As these systems become more complex and applied in the world, they take on an unruly quality: people, things, built environments, structures, infrastructures, ideologies, affects are bound to collide and produce unexpected results. Objects change hands and move from one place to another. They are read or seen or touched. They take on a life of their own: a bureaucracy unable to distinguish between families on paper and families in person, a photograph misidentified, a genetic test used to find new family members—this dynamic quality of interaction is what shapes the landscape for encounter, negotiation, resistance, and survival. Indeed, all technologies of kinship offer the potential to oppress, maintain, and also subvert systems of power that shape people's lives. Even a system that is designed to oppress or represent the hegemonic also produces the very opportunities for its subversion. This multiplicity underscores the assertion that even as the family has served as a site of social and cultural "inclusion" in the United States, it has continued to be produced by racialized and gendered forms of border making. Always already a site of ideology, Asian American family formation includes both the reinforcement and reification of racial power as well as alternatives forms of belonging and kinship.

Kinship and the Fantasy of Racial Belonging

Historically and contemporarily, the meanings of family and racial categorization have been triangulated through ideologies of inheritance. Both have a fraught relationship with inheritance that encompasses, and occasionally conflates, social and biological realms. While we may agree that race is not a biological or genetic phenomenon, we live in a world where the articulation of racial meaning is deceptively reliant on genetic, social, and kin-based forms of inheritance. In other words, inheritance serves as the primary logic through which racial categorization is established. On the one hand, determination of one's race is almost solely based on one's biogenetic parentage. This has been evidenced by the outrage and dismissal of White public figures that have fraudulently claimed marginalized racial identities, such as in the cases of Rachel Dolezal or Jessica Krug. Dolezal in particular was publicly rebuffed in her attempts to use the term "transracial" as analogy to "transgender" to claim identification with a race different than her biological parents, thus demonstrating the social and cultural determination that racial identity is not simply a matter of individual choice.[26] And even in more established uses of the term within the context of transracial adoption, in which parents adopt children of a different race than them, the idea that one's race is decided based on one's biological ancestry is widely accepted. In this context, transracial adoptees further exemplify how contemporary culture understands race to be determined by the race of biological parents regardless of cultural identity or affiliation with the family in which they were raised.

On the other hand, we have all also agreed and actively teach that race is a product of social formation and a set of political identities that have been variously mobilized. Even popular culture has caught on to the general (albeit sometimes misinterpreted) idea that race is a social construction, as exemplified by popular educational documentaries like the three-part series *Race: The Power of an Illusion* or the Radiolab episode titled "Race Doesn't Exist. Or Does it?"[27] Of course, within ethnic studies, these nuanced facets of racial meaning are not contradictory. However, they do demonstrate how the articulation, identification, embodiment, and experience of racial categorization is part of a larger complex of social, historical, biological, and intergenerational meanings in our culture.

Similarly, within Euro-North American cultures, ideologies of kinship are rooted in ideas of inherited bodily and social relations. In both genetic and nongenetic relationships, inheritance is used as an act of and shorthand for the forms of care that constitute and articulate kinship. Phrases like "You get that from your mother!" can refer to physical characteristics (eye color or hair texture), behavioral patterns (enjoying romance novels or a propensity for quilting), or intentional actions (the passing down of property or titles). And while the language of inheritance can be used to reference this variety of genetic, phenotypical, social, and behavioral traits, the nature of such inheritances is often undifferentiated from one another. Kinship has been defined by heteronormative biological reproduction, and genetic relatedness carries immense cultural, legal, and affective power from legal inheritance to parental rights to self-conceptions of identity.[28] In the contemporary world, we are all impacted by the hegemony of biological relation as the primary organizer of normative kinship.

Furthermore, and conversely, the very language of biological relation and inheritance has been articulated through discourses of kinship. In scientific research, cultural narratives, and grade-school textbooks alike, terms like "biological" and "genetic" do an immense amount of semantic work to modify and qualify kinship when placed alongside terms like "parents," "siblings," and "cousins." As many are intimately familiar, "parent" and "biological parent" can be completely different people: the first carrying the weight of social and interpersonal kinship and the second seemingly referring to a qualified genetic relation potentially void of social bond. The discourse used to articulate biological relations is thus also inherently defined by the meaning of kinship and, once again, captures the tension between biologized notions of identity and the social and affective forms of belonging they take. As David Schneider suggested in his original *American Kinship: A Cultural Account*, American kinship is a "system of symbols," and as such its invocation by scientific discourse through the language of family, inheritance, and race continue to entangle these symbolic and affective meanings with material and embodied ones.[29]

Indeed, kinship has never been conceived solely through biological relations given that it has included other forms of interpersonal and communal relations including marriage, other forms of romantic and sexual partnerships, queer kinships, and friendships. As scholars in gender and sexuality studies have demonstrated, family and kinship do not necessarily require any forms of genetic relation or biological reproduction. This book's theorization and mobilization of the socially constructed nature of kinship, and the forms of power embedded within it, builds from queer studies approaches to and scholarly reimaginings of "nonnormative" kinship.[30] As Tyler Bradway and Elizabeth Freeman reflect,

> Of course, queer theory frequently eschews the idiom of "kinship." More often, theorists prefer terms such as *relationality, belonging, intimacy*, and *sodality*. . . . To be sure, queer scholarship, including our own, has found great promise in such diffuse and poststructural grammars of sociability. Yet the expansiveness of "queer belonging" may also risk evacuating the historical specificity of kinship as an idiom of state power, white supremacy, and Western modernity.[31]

Technologies of Kinship builds from this articulation of kinship, one that not only critiques those forms of power for which kinship functions as idiom, but also sees the very notion of kinship as inseparable from the social formations and historical specificities that have produced it. It foregrounds what Bradway and Freeman later call "kincoherence," a play on (kin)coherence and (k)incoherence, that "fuses the mutually constituting and complicating forces, desires, practices, relations, institutions, and forms that render kinship a horizon of violence and possibility."[32] And I am also mindful of the distinction between queer kinship and queer approaches to kinship: not all forms of non-normative kinship are necessarily queer, and queer people's experiences of kinship is distinct from a queer or queer-influenced critique of kinship. In this context, *Technologies of Kinship* shares its foundation with queer studies in situating these ideas of relationality, belonging, and intimacy in relation to the fields of power through which kinship has been constructed and made meaningful. To be sure, though the people and case studies of this book would not necessarily be identified as queer themselves and many of them, in contrast, benefit from structures of heteronormativity, this book is indebted to scholarship in queer studies for helping untangle the fields of power within which the various meanings of kinship persist.

How, then, can both kinship and race be theorized and critiqued together as formations of material, affective, and structural power? The technologies of kinship in this book function through what Ellen Samuels has described as "fantasies of identification" that "seek to definitively identify bodies, to place them in categories delineated by race, gender, or ability status, and then to validate that placement through a verifiable, biological mark of identity."[33] Race and kinship are bound not only by their co-constitution but also by this shared articulation of belonging and identification of the self. As Samuels continues, "fantasies of identification are driven by a desire for incontrovertible physical identification so intense that it produces its own realization at the same time that it reinterprets that realization as natural and inevitable."[34] Kinship is a site of this process: individual bodies are identified through their belonging within (or exclusion from) a family, categorized racially based on that belonging, and validated through the biologized discourses that give meaning to both race and family. All the while, the embodied experiences of those (family and racial) identities are "reinterpreted" as "natural and inevitable."

Within Asian American studies, this naturalization of the self has been interrogated through the theorization of the body as a site of racialization. For example, Ju Yon Kim reflects on Asian American racial formation's "vacillations between the extremes of the 'yellow peril' and the 'model minority'" that "constitute an enduring paradox."[35] Kim further argues that this paradox "is sustained through the mundane's ambiguous relationship to the body: it is enacted *by* the body, but may or may not be *of* the body."[36] While Kim's study focuses on the role of the mundane and the individual racial forms and performances that racialization can take, this distinction between racial formation being "enacted *by* the body" rather than merely being "*of* the body" is especially generative for thinking about the formational relationships between race and kinship. How might we think of the Asian American family (variously imagined but also called upon, in this book and within contemporary culture, as the "Asian immigrant family" or "Asian diasporic family") as enacted *by* the bodies within it, rather than merely being an inherent fact *of* the bodies that constitute it? And how has the Asian American family's ontology been constructed through a desire for racial and communal identification and belonging?

In this context, the Asian American family functions as a site in which individuals "seek to definitively identify" their own bodies and sense of self. To be a member of an Asian American family is to identify with Asianness. Belonging itself thus manifests through the workings of individual and collective identification within an imagined, racially coherent family. And this sense of belonging through the fantasy of identification is further complicated within multiracial families. Is a White family with an adopted Asian child an "Asian American family"? Exactly how many family members must be Asian to constitute an "Asian American family"? It is precisely the inability to answer these types of questions definitively that exposes the fantasies of racial coherence—of either the individual or the family. This is not to say these fantasies are immaterial or even unattainable. There are many for whom clear and embodied racial categorization and belonging within a normative family is a material reality. However, this literalization—that we can point to someone and say "Look! But they *are* Asian" or "Look! But they do *have* an Asian family"—coexists with and often belies the racialized and gendered expectations, investments, desires, and affects that structure those material relations.

This book further contends that technologies of kinship participate in the enactment of these gendered and racialized fantasies within American culture that imagine belonging both within a coherent racial identity and within a literal and national family. In her study of reproductive technologies, Charis Thompson refers to this complex of material and ideological factors that shape family formation as an "ontological choreography," or "the dynamic coordination of the technical, scientific, kinship, gender, emotional, legal, political, and financial aspects" of family formation. And, as Thompson suggests, "What might appear to be an undifferentiated hybrid mess is actually a deftly balanced coming together of things that are generally considered parts of different ontological orders (part of nature, part of the self, part of society)."[37] Indeed, these different ontological orders help us organize an understanding of the interactions between the material and embodied world, the meanings that are made from it, and the structures within which they exist.

Fantasy and identity are thus not just possessions, experiences, or desires of the liberal individual. Rather, they make up the collective substance of race within families and locate the affective power of family as an institutional *and* interpersonal unit. Revealing the racial fantasies of identification underlying technologies of kinship thus contributes to the disruption and critique of the multicultural story often told throughout contemporary popular culture about family: that the love and care that connects our individual kin relations are and can be free from the politics, injustices, and forms of oppression of the world around us. David Eng describes this as the "racialization of intimacy," the process that "marks the collective ways by which race becomes occluded within the private domain of private family and kinship."[38] And technologies of kinship further name and reveal how the dichotomy of private and public life have obfuscated the entanglement of love and kinship within structures of power. To examine how these technologies have participated in Asian American family formation is thus not merely to understand the experience of people within those families: it is to recognize how Asian American racialization has occurred through the ideological, affective, and material construction of family itself.

The fantasies of identification embodied by the construction of the Asian American family include both the fantasy that race (even as a social construction) can be identifiable, coherent, and located on the inherited physical reproduction of family *and* that the racially coherent and historically heteronormative idea of family offers recognition, belonging, and identity for those that adhere to its expectations. And I argue that it is not only the Asian immigrant family but also transnationally adoptive, multiracial, and contemporary multicultural families that have been recruited into these articulations of Asian racial categorization. Technologies of kinship thus produce and enable these racial fantasies of belonging (within a racial category and within a family). As each are animated by the people, desires, and behaviors within them, they offer possibilities to both reproduce the normative and challenge it.

Family as a Shifting Site of Asian American Racialization

Together, the chapters of this book follow Asian American family and kinship as a site for new forms of intimacy, racialization, and sociality across the shifting racial history of the Asian diaspora in the United States. As the racialization of this diaspora has changed throughout the twentieth and twenty-first centuries, from narratives of exclusion to inclusion and liberalism to neoliberalism, so too have the ideological and material formations of "Asian American" family and kinship. In *Compositional Subjects: Enfiguring Asian/American Women*, Laura Hyun Yi Kang reflects on this history through the construction of the "Asian/American woman" as material, cultural, and ideological figure. Kang briefly connects this gendered genealogy to the Asian American family, posing,

> If... the family figures so crucially in positioning the nation within some organic trajectory of reproduction and succession, what would it mean to insist that the 'Asian American family' can *not* be vacated of its historical contingency through some invocation of an unbroken lineage? The convoluted delineations of different Asian women as/not American citizens could unsettle, rather than corroborate, the naturalizing and unifying trope of the nation as family.[39]

Technologies of Kinship is occupied with amplifying and locating this historical contingency of the Asian American family as both racial symbol within the nation and material reality for the diaspora, and it is focused on the systems that produce those meanings and experiences. Together the chapters trace how Asian American racial formation has changed over time through changing formations of kinship. As Kang invites, this book aims to "unsettle" the "naturalizing and unifying trope of the nation as family," as well as the trope of the family as a multicultural, microcosmic representation of the nation.

As early as the 1875 Page Act, which effectively prevented the immigration of Chinese women to the United States and contributed to the emergence of "bachelor societies" of Chinese male laborers, Asian immigration exclusion as a process of racialization has directly impacted the formation of Asian American families in gendered and heteronormative ways.[40] The passage of the 1882 Chinese Exclusion Act further restricted immigration by banning all Chinese laborers. It was also the first blanket exclusion of a racial and national group in US immigration history and led to the development of the Immigration and Naturalization Service. However, even within this restrictive regime, stipulations that allowed immigration through family reunification provide an early example of the imbrication of kinship and racial formation. As Catherine Lee argues of this period, "the expression of gendered ideals of marriage, home, and family created a liminal space" for the acceptance of family reunification provisions by policymakers in an otherwise exclusionary system.[41] And underlying the often-invasive and disciplinary processes developed to manage and regulate this form of immigration were racialized, heteronormative, and reproductive norms about what constituted legitimate family relations.

This book begins with this early intersection of the exclusionary history of Asian racial formation and family reunification. Well-documented within Asian American immigration history, diasporic Chinese American families materialized through the strategic and illegal practice of "paper families," whereby individuals memorized, performed, and embodied entirely new identities in order to claim entry to the United States as citizens or family of citizens.[42] Chapter 1 begins by asking, how do we interrogate the archive of governmental immigration bureaucracy as both historical record and technology unto itself? It argues that we must consider archival documents as not only containing information about the history of individuals but also as laying bare the very mechanism of bureaucratic recordkeeping that exists as a material trace of a larger power complex, or what Ann Laura Stoler calls "contrapuntal intrusions" (made up of interactions, productions, and omissions).[43]

To do this, the chapter explores the emergence of "paper families" as a demonstration of how the need to navigate immigration bureaucracy actively produced new claims of kinship. The 1960s Confession Program, which incentivized paper family admissions of entrance to the United States, makes visible the ways that paper families were substantiated by the very system used to regulate them. The chapter argues that government bureaucracy served as a fundamental technology of not only racialized immigration regulation but also Chinese American family formation. Even as scholars of this history and the individuals who lived it have not seen these paper families as "real" in the conventional sense of biological relation or interpersonal relationships (though some were biological kin using falsified records), the survival of paper families and their records show the ways in which the immigration bureaucracy made their kinship real in a different way, through the very materials created to eliminate them.

Throughout the first half of the twentieth century, immigration exclusion also characterized the racialization process for other groups within the Asian diaspora. As mentioned previously, the 1908 Gentlemen's Agreement restricted immigration from Japan and Korea. The diaspora of "picture brides," who married and came to the United States based only on the exchange of photographs, also demonstrates the continued entanglement between immigration restriction and Asian diasporic family formation. This period of the twentieth century likewise restricted migration from South Asia to the United States which also led to the emergence of several multiracial communities in California, New York City, and the American South.[44] And the passing of the Immigration Act of 1917 extended even more severe immigration restrictions to the newly articulated "Asiatic Barred Zone." The 1924 Johnson-Reed Act further solidified this racialized exclusion through the implementation of national origin quotas which, as Mae Ngai describes, established "a *global* racial and national hierarchy that favored some immigrants over others."[45]

Even as immigration policy became more inclusive in the second half of the twentieth century, the reliance of family reunification as a primary mode for Asian immigration and racialization continued. The Immigration and Nationality Act of 1965, also known as the Hart-Celler Act, repealed national origins quotas, developed a preference system that prioritized family reunification, and marked the liberalization of immigration policy in the twentieth century. While this was by no means an even process, the postwar 1950s and 1960s marked a cultural shift from dominant discourses of exclusion to narratives of inclusion and multiculturalism, in which the family served an important role. For example, Christina Klein argues that during the Cold War, "the push towards global integration demanded a national identity formulated in less confrontational and more affiliative terms" with the result "that America's global power was often figured in maternal, adoptive, and familial terms."[46] Klein demonstrates how the multiracial transnationally adoptive family became a popular middlebrow cultural image offering "a way to imagine US-Asian integration in terms of voluntary affiliation: they presented international bonds formed by choice (at least on the part of American parents), rather than biology. . . . The family became a framework within which these differences could be both maintained and transcended, and offered an imaginative justification for the permanent extension of US power, figured as responsibility and leadership, beyond the nation's borders."[47] Indeed, with the rise of adoption from Asia, first from Korea following the Korean War and then from Vietnam in the wake of the Vietnam War, the family operated as both cultural metaphor and embodied manifestation of the United States' simultaneous power abroad and embrace of racial liberalism and inclusion at home.

Amid the waning Cold War, the rise of Civil Rights, and the era of reproductive choice, earlier forms of racial liberalism also gave rise to new forms of multiculturalism. Multiculturalism became defined by what Eduardo Bonilla-Silva describes as the "increasingly covert nature of racial discourse" and the family as metaphor for the nation continued to operate as an icon and social landscape for cultural, political, and legislative debates about race, gender, class, sexuality, and reproduction.[48] In 1967, *Loving v. Virginia* officially legalized interracial marriage, and images of multiracial families have continued to be celebrated as paragons of multicultural progress. At the same time, the increasingly visible model minority stereotype positioned the Asian American family in racialized narratives of success that reinforced racial hierarchies and pitted minorities against one another.[49] In 1966, the *New York Times* published "Success Story, Japanese-American Style," which explicitly linked Japanese American social and economic success to family values and compared Japanese Americans to African Americans.[50] Images of the hardworking heteronormative Asian immigrant family served as a cultural foil for stereotypes like the welfare queen or absent father that were leveraged against Black communities. And these tropes were only further reinforced and reproduced with the rapid increase of Asian immigration in the 1970s and 1980s.

Chapter 2 of this book uses this period of the 1960s through the 1990s, in which popular discourses about immigration shifted from exclusion to inclusion, as a launching point for exploring the changing demographics of newly immigrating Asian families and their transformation from "Asian" into "Asian American." It argues that the combined codification of family reunification, professionalized labor, and refugee status within immigration policy actively produced an Asian diasporic population in the United States whose selection upheld racialized narratives of immigrant success and American benevolence. However, liberal narratives of the model minority as an essentialized racial characteristic of Asianness obfuscated the very structural and legislative factors that determined *which* families qualified to become the "Asian American family." In this context, the immigration preference system reinforced and naturalized cultural narratives that located the family as the site of Asian American model minority success and racialization. And as a technology of kinship, it also participated in the shared racialization of seemingly distinct diasporas of East and South Asian immigrants *and* Southeast Asian refugees. Regardless of individuals' actual embodiment or achievement of model minority success, during this period, the trope of the Asian American family benefitting from and thriving under American multicultural exceptionalism functioned as the narrative against which Asian American racial identity became defined and lived.

Expanding on this emergence of liberal constructions of family post-1965, Chapter 3 considers transnational adoption from Asia and the role of referral photography as a visual technology of kinship. Frequently used in adoption processes both domestically and internationally, referral photographs are sent to adoptive parents to offer information about the specific child that has been assigned to them, usually as part of a larger file. This chapter brings together narratives of 1970s and 1980s adoption from Korea with those from early adoptions from China in the 1990s and early 2000s by analyzing the role photography played in producing the imaginative spaces of kinship formation. While narratives of family inclusion during these later years expanded to encompass new forms of adoptive kinship, ideologies of race and gender became even further solidified through this material and affective incorporation of the Asian baby girl into the (usually White) American family. The chapter concludes with a consideration of the unruly potential of photography in transnational adoption to transform existing relationships and to invite new modes of establishing kinship through an examination of Deann Borshay Liem's 2010 film *In the Matter of Cha Jung Hee*. In this context, kinship is not only a bond formed among individuals *within* a family, but also the relational forms of recuperation and encounter that emerge from negotiating the fraught circumstances that have made transnational adoption possible in the first place.

As discourses of individual choice and consumption continued to become integrated into an economy and culture of neoliberalism and colorblindness in the 1980s and 1990s, multiculturalism itself also became subsumed within a larger system of global capitalism. As Jodi Melamed writes of "neoliberal multiculturalism:"

> It sutures official anti-racism to state policy in a manner that hinders the calling into question of global capitalism, it produces new privileged and stigmatized forms of humanity, and it deploys a normative cultural model of race (which now sometimes displaces conventional racial reference altogether) as a discourse to justify inequality for some as fair or natural.[51]

And in the occlusion of race within the sphere of family through Eng's aforementioned "racialization of intimacy," since the end of the twentieth century, race has taken on a split position of being constantly seen and unseen, both in and on the family.[52] Its importance is evident while its meaning has been disavowed.

Paradoxically, though, this is often only made possible precisely through the visuality and instrumentalization of observable difference among kin. Take, for example, the "Love Has No Labels" campaign run by the Ad Council in 2015.[53] In one of their promotional videos, with over 60 million views on YouTube, a crowded plaza hosts a stage with what appears to be a large "X-ray" screen. On the screen, two skeletons embrace, implying there are two unknown people behind the screen. They then walk towards its edges and around the corner to reveal themselves to be two women. They walk up to one another and kiss for the crowd while everyone claps and cheers, and the screen flashes, "love has no gender." Predictably, the next one reveals a multiracial couple and the screen flashes "love has no race." The video continues with "love has no disability," "love has no age," and "love has no religion." Indeed, love may not have any labels. But the people selected to represent that fact have been chosen precisely because of their visible representation of those very same labels they supposedly lack. Ironically, in the logic of colorblindness, difference must be specifically selected and made visible in order to subsequently and demonstratively disavow it. And that disavowal is then performed through the demonstration of love and kinship bonds.

As the final two chapters of this book explore, as the meanings of Asian American racial categorization have shifted under neoliberalism, so too have the technologies that uphold and produce them. This simultaneous utilization, disavowal, and sometimes commodification of racial difference is characteristic of contemporary technologies of kinship. And family formation serves as a foundation for the naturalization of the neoliberal multicultural marketplace. Chapters 4 and 5 turn to the digital to examine these formations of race and kinship under neoliberalism in the twenty-first century. And although earlier images of the Asian model minority family discussed in Chapter 2 persist in contemporary culture, Asian racialization has also been subsumed into consumer culture. Within the marketplaces of online dating, egg and sperm donation, and direct-to-consumer genetic tests, neoliberalism attempts to abstract race from racism and repackage it as a consumer choice. But in these attempts, these technologies of kinship further reveal the family as the often-unspoken site of race's reproduction, both literally and ideologically.

Chapter 4 explores what I call the "digital profile interface," which refers to the social media model of website design constituted by individual profiles created for viewing and interaction with other users. Analyzing both online dating websites and egg and sperm donation websites, the chapter considers how these two examples of the digital profile interface facilitate the formation of family through the framing of race and kinship as exercises in individual consumer choice. In both online markets, users look for profiles featuring qualities or characteristics such as hair color, eye color, height, education, or "ethnicity" that they find desirable. The chapter investigates how race as a sortable variable within the structure of these economies reinforces claims that desire for or rejection of a particular racial identity is simply a manifestation of consumer "preference." And this narrative of neoliberal choice reifies racial boundaries through filtered pull-down categorizations while simultaneously individualizing the meaning of race in these spaces by framing it as a choice of "identity." Asianness thus becomes narrated as just another flavor in a list of flavors, despite its desirability and meaning being intimately situated and produced by its specific racialized history.

The final chapter extends this consideration of race and kinship in digital worlds to the use of genetic testing services like 23andMe to imagine humanity as a kind of global family that offers the discovery of new genetic family relationships. The chapter locates 23andMe within a consumer culture that both relies on and actively produces the desire to conceptualize the self through the racialized language of ancestry and genetic relatives. In contrast to earlier historical discourses of exclusion, racial difference in this context is made meaningful through narratives of inclusion, in which new discoveries of ancestral genetic connections are presented in terms of multi-colored world maps and suggestions for new cultural practices. With an ethos of shared humanity and the "family of man," the language of race is nowhere to be found, instead replaced with discourses of ancestry, geography, identity, and health. And yet concepts and language *already* racialized in contemporary culture are reinscribed into scientific discourse through the language of percentages and carefully summarized descriptions of how genetics and inheritance work.

Mainstream direct-to-consumer genetic testing services thus represent a foundational triangulation between ancestry, race, and kinship already hegemonic in contemporary US culture. The chapter shows how they capitalize on and promote narratives of kinship in order to claim that their consumer products offer insight into genetic identity as fundamental to the self. This genetic identity is defined in terms of genetic relatedness to imagined unknown ancestors and the (racialized) geographies associated with those ancestors. I call these new imaginaries of relatedness "genetic intimacies," that produce new forms of kinship not only with ancestors imagined from the past but also with other users in the present who are identified to varying degrees of relation like third, fourth, or fifth cousins. As such, direct-to-consumer genetic tests use the scientific basis of genetic inheritance to produce what are largely affective forms of kinship but that are *not* based in social or embodied relationships.

While the co-constitution of family and race through technological systems has changed form over time, the affective fantasies and desires for intimacy, belonging, and identification that kinship embodies have continued to manifest in gendered and racialized ways. And the historical racial systems explored in the chapters of this book continue to shape the way Asian American family and kinship are experienced and made meaningful today. *Technologies of Kinship: Asian American Racialization and the Making of Family* thus theorizes how the systems we use to conceive, and conceive of, kinship continue to shape the changing meanings of race and Asian racial categorization.

1

Paper Families and Family Papers

Government Bureaucracy and Family Formation in the Era of Chinese Exclusion

Housed in the Immigration and Naturalization Service (INS) archives of the New York City National Archives, thousands of folders hold the immigration case files of the Chinese diaspora entering the United States throughout the first half of the twentieth century. Over 2,500 miles away in the Huntington Library collections in San Marino, California, several thousand more immigration records are held in the legal papers of one of the first Chinese American lawyers in California, You Chung Hong. In both archives across the United States, manila folders, stacks of carbon paper, and bureaucratic forms frame the stories and photographs of individuals that arrived on boats, interviewed with immigration officials, and joined family in the United States. Some folders are composed of only a few documents stacked neatly in chronological order, while others are hundreds of pages, folded at the edges and bulging with duplicates and triplicates. These piles of paper constitute the layers of governmental recordkeeping, epistolary communications, and personal family histories that spanned decades and regulated immigration during Chinese exclusion in the nineteenth and twentieth centuries.[1]

One of these piles of papers, composed of approximately sixty-three pages neatly stacked inside of a manila folder, pertains to a woman named Wong Tung Yee.[2] The earliest dated document in the folder is a September 23, 1938 letter from lawyer Albert A. Collins to the District Director of the INS at Ellis Island notifying of Wong Tung Yee's expected arrival and application for admission. Beneath that letter is an affidavit titled, "In the matter of the application of WONG TUNG YEE for admission into the country as the daughter of a native," signed by her father Wong Wing Yick and naming her sister Wong Tung Gee, who had been previously admitted in March 1938, as a witness. Atop these documents are several carbon copies of letters sent between the District Director at Ellis Island and Inspectors in both Montreal and Seattle requesting the case files of Wong Tung Yee's brothers. A convenient reference sheet summarizes the "Records used in connection with this case," and lists the names and case file numbers for her father, sister, four brothers, and nephew. Finally, a letter dated November 9, 1938, from the District Director to Mr. Collins notifies that Wong Tung Yee was assigned a hearing date and directs her "alleged father" and sister to "take the 8:45am Ellis Island Ferry from the Barge Office, New York City" just six days later, on Tuesday, November 15, 1938, at 9:00am.

Memorialized in the archive, the longest file in the document, composed of seventeen pages of tissue-thin carbon paper and included in duplicate, offers us the transcript of what happened that morning of November 15, 1938. After establishing that the Sun Ning dialect interpreter was able to translate, father Wong Wing Yick was interviewed first. In his interview, he described the laundry he owned and operated in the Bronx and answered questions about his previous testimony for his other daughter to come to the United States. He answered questions about Wong Tung Yee such as her birthdate and birthplace, gave descriptions of her appearance including mention of a small scar on her forehead, and shared details about their home village in China. Then, sister Wong Tung Gee was interviewed, answering similar questions about her own life in New York City, changes in her "status" since her admission to the United States (she got married), and details about her sister. Her interview took somewhat longer because she was asked more detailed questions about what she was wearing when she left their home village and during her journey to the United States through Hong Kong.

Finally, Wong Tung Yee herself was interviewed. The transcript describes her as five feet, two inches tall, with several identifying "marks": a pit above her right eyebrow, six faint pits in the center of her forehead, a small scar on her cheek near her left nostril. This was the longest interview of the three. The inspector asked about her immediate and extended family, her siblings' professions, the names of their spouses, and her home in China. Wong Tung Yee talked of her father's work as a laundryman, her mother still residing in China, and her five older brothers and one older sister. Attempting to corroborate their testimonies, the inspector asked her about what her sister was wearing when Wong Tung Gee left their village to compare with her sister's previous answers. After all the questioning was complete, the Chairman's conclusion was recorded on the final page of the transcript deciding that "the record reasonably establishes the claimed relationship" and he moved to admit Wong Tung Yee to enter the United States. Then, dated almost three years later, on September 19, 1941, a Certificate of Identity was issued that included a passport-style photograph showing Wong Tung Yee with her hair cut short, smoothly parted to one side, framing her round face. Overall, more than sixty pages chronicle Wong Tung Yee's lawful arrival and presence in the United States with her father and five siblings.

Twenty years later, just six pages added to the file changed the content of everything. According to an affidavit taken in 1964, one of her brothers, Wong Sik Koey, confessed through the INS Chinese Confession Program that he had come to the United States under false pretenses. He was not the biological son of Wong Wing Yick or the sister of Wong Tung Yee. Rather, he had merely claimed to be in order to enter the United States based on his (purported) father's American citizenship. Records of this confession were distributed to all associated relatives, implicating the entire Wong family as a "paper family," individuals who fraudulently claimed to be related for the purpose of immigration. Indeed, it is likely that Wong Tung Yee, too, had arrived as a "paper" daughter. However, the records stop there, and her bureaucratic existence is left frozen: the embodied truth of her identity is a mystery the archive cannot solve.

Complex family narratives like this one are typical of the files of Chinese immigrants during this period. Following the Page Act of 1875 and the Chinese Exclusion Act of 1882, Chinese immigration to the United States was severely limited and one of the few avenues of entrance was as a relative of a United States citizen by birth or derivative citizenship. As a result, United States governmental recordkeeping regarding Chinese families was both extensive and fundamental to managing Chinese immigration.[3] This necessity to document biological familial ties as part of the immigration regulation process even further bound Chinese immigrants to one another in the history of racialization through exclusion. As historians such as Erika Lee and Estelle Lau have shown, the emergence of "paper families," as a strategy of entrance into the United States based on claims of kinship with a US citizen, demonstrates how individuals navigated such harsh immigration restrictions.⁴ Elaborate systems flourished through which people purchased identities, used coaching books to memorize family details, and claimed kinship to strangers or extended relatives.⁵ These claims were further enabled by the 1906 San Francisco Earthquake in which the Hall of Records burned down, destroying the birth records of most of the city's US-born Chinese Americans. Individuals were subsequently able to claim birth in the United States by citing documentation that had been destroyed in the fire and then sponsor others (their children and "paper" children). The "paper family" system posed a new challenge for immigration authorities in the twentieth century: whose claim to US citizenship was based on biological kinship in the way the law intended, and whose claim was using "paper family" under fraudulent pretenses? As the INS worked to regulate immigration in the first half of the twentieth century, the mobility of all Chinese diasporic families in the United States were not only constituted through the biological, but also through the continual navigation of bureaucratic practices of surveillance, testimony, and official recordkeeping.

Active from 1956 to 1965 as immigration restrictions waned and amid the Cold War, the Chinese Confession Program was implemented by the INS with the goal of not only identifying individual confessions but also eliminating the practice of paper family immigration. While the program sought confessions to expose entire paper families and prevent their further use, it in turn offered Chinese that had entered the US illegally assistance in transitioning to legal status when possible, under existing laws. For example, as historian Mae Ngai describes, "persons who were in the country illegally were eligible for a suspension of deportation and permanent resident status if they had resided in the United States continually for seven years. Aliens who served in the armed forces for ninety days were eligible for naturalized citizenship."⁶ Ngai goes on to describe the routinization of the confession process itself:

> Confession entailed a formal interview with INS officials. After several years, the program became somewhat routinized. Confessors answered questions according to a standardized form, confessing their fraudulent claim to citizenship and listing the names of their true family and paper family members, including their whereabouts.⁷

As the case of Wong Tung Yee demonstrates, the documentation from these confessions were added to the original case files of known relatives within paper families. And as a result, these paper families were both exposed and further made material through these bureaucratic records.

This chapter theorizes these "paper families" as historical formations, in which government bureaucracy was a technology of kinship that both imbricated constructions of family into the practices of immigration exclusion as a racialization process *and* participated in the production of the very forms of kinship that it was attempting to regulate.[8] In this context, constructions of family and racialized bureaucratic immigration regimes were intimately entangled in a continual process of making and remaking Chinese American family and kinship. Conversely, gendered and racialized notions of family were also crucial to the operation of bureaucratic immigration regulation. From the perspective of Chinese immigration history, these piles of paper give indication to what is "real" and what is "fraudulent": identities, names, and kinship bonds were "real" when they were embodied by individuals, and they were "fraudulent" when they did not correspond to the lives of those that claimed them. But what is the role of the governmental recordkeeping itself in making real the kinds of racialized kinship it is tasked with regulating? As Eithne Luibhéid cautions, "immigration scholarship that builds from case files and other official documents needs to critically interrogate the grounds of its own possibility."[9] From a material and new materialist perspective, this chapter examines paper families *not* simply as the fraudulent accounts of potentially "real" families, but as subjects of their own, ones that materialized distinct ideologies of race, gender, kinship, and bureaucratic power. As such, they reveal how government bureaucracy itself and the material traces it produces (case files, testimonies, family trees, photographs, revisions, etc.) have not been mere records or descriptions of family, kinship, race, or identity but rather continue to be active participants in their making.

The common language of "true" and "paper" family can thus be deceptive in its oversimplification of kinship as real or not real. Admittedly, this language is and was extremely functional: it provided a crucial distinction for the purpose of creating order within the structures of immigration regulation. Furthermore, it often reflected the experiences of those that used those terms, especially given that many "paper" family members had never met or were not closely related. Individuals were careful not to confuse identities, and many who confessed or discussed their experiences in paper families used the language of "true" and "paper" themselves. However, as Beth Lew-Williams describes, the embodied experiences of Chinese migrants themselves demonstrate a much more complex negotiation: "In their attempt to navigate the law, many Chinese migrants occupied an in-between space, which afforded them some of the privileges of documentation, but not all."[10] Lew-Williams goes on to suggest, "While government officials, Chinese migrants, and even historians tend to describe these personas as 'true/real' or 'false/fake,' this binary belies the complexity of these identities."[11] Indeed, this seemingly clear divide between true and paper, real and not real, can obfuscate more complex entanglements of power, agency, and "truth" that were continually being negotiated. This chapter further explores this material history of government bureaucracy and its strategies as sites through which not only legality but kinship itself was articulated and contested.

Paper families demonstrate the types of realities that are made possible through the various practices of governmental recordkeeping for the modern nation-state. This is not to endow the state with the sole power to create. However, the state possessed and continues to possess the authority to legitimize certain realities, and also, as this history shows, to inadvertently create new realities that may or may not undercut its very goals for documentation in the first place. As such, the racialized exclusion of Chinese during this period was intimately tied to ideologies of family and kinship that were policed, embodied, and represented on paper. The term "paper family" is thus more than simple shorthand for a subversive practice; it is also a metaphor through which we can theorize how family and kinship have been racialized, produced, and legitimized through the technologies of US government bureaucracy and recordkeeping. As Lau describes, "it was through the *relationship* created within the *interaction* between the Chinese and the INS that the manner and organization of the Chinese family and community were constructed."[12] "Paper" here thus not only functions as metonym for the racialized Chinese family deemed fraudulent by the US government, but also constitutes the very materials in which people (both biologically related and not) claimed, legitimated, and lived kinship with one another.[13]

Paper families thus also help us expand our understanding of how the social organization of family can be used in both regulatory and subversive ways. For example, Luibhéid describes how the management and disclosure of biographical and kin information was used as a technique of power, observing, "if Chinese women refused to provide details of their lives for official scrutiny, they were denied the possibility of immigrating."[14] Following this example, what do we make of an entire system in which Chinese men and women, rather than refused, *created* the very biographical information necessary to survive "official scrutiny"? Not only was the construction of family used as criteria within the immigration bureaucracy to enforce top-down state and authoritative power, but it also became the strategic mechanism through which new modes of kinship were narrated, archived, and lived.

While records of the paper family both documented the "real" strategies for immigration in the first half of the twentieth century and simultaneously revealed "false" claims of identification as demonstrated by the Chinese Confession Program through the 1960s, the physical traces of this history sit deceptively and neatly side-by-side in the archive. The examples that follow in this chapter trace these different genres of bureaucratic production to reveal how paper family kinship was articulated, contested, and produced within this racializing regime. Together, they highlight how the act of producing and conserving these papers within the governmental archive constructs them as a material reality through which we are able to access this history.

Family Trees on and of Paper

Like all family trees, records of family members in the immigration bureaucracy constituted a temporality that spanned decades. This temporality included the recording of family histories and the use of kin relationships as legal evidence, as well as the unfolding of a type of bureaucratic "truth" that eventually documented the exposure of paper families created within that process. Ironically, the embodied process of reviewing these case files that I used to develop this chapter's critique of bureaucratic power and racialization was uncannily similar to the actions taken by the very bureaucratic officials who evaluated claims of kinship to wield that power. To identify verified or suspected paper families, I cross-referenced individual files with those subjects already associated with a paper family. For example, one file might have the confession of an individual naming several paper brothers connected through a paper father. In this file, those individuals might have names and file numbers listed that were also in the archive. Gender also offered an effective filter for finding families in the archive because citizenship and immigration laws required women who were immigrating to prove that they were in some way related by derivative citizenship to a United States male citizen.[15] Using the individual files in conjunction (usually two to four family members), it was then possible to piece together the various family trees that represented these paper and biological families. In a system where paper files represent individuals, paper folders become kin with other paper folders.

The oldest generation of "paper fathers" consisted of those who were in their twenties at the turn of the century and who claimed American birthright citizenship. It is difficult to say how many of these individuals were in fact born in the United States. Many of their files included applications to leave the United States to visit China, with the intention to return, which in fact strengthened their established claims to citizenship because it served as previously accepted documentation from *within* the government bureaucracy that their claims were legitimate.[16] The second generation, which constituted the bulk of the files and family trees suspected to be part of paper families, were the children of this first generation. Their files often reported individuals with six, seven, or eight brothers and one or two sisters. And although most were born in China, they claimed American citizenship as the children of United States-born citizens. Many of the men were married to women in China and also testified to having several sons still there, which provided an opportunity to sponsor another generation of Chinese immigrants. Finally, the children of potential paper sons and daughters consisted of the third generation within the bureaucratic archive. Most individuals in this generation only exist in the case files as a reference made during interrogation due to the end of Chinese Exclusion in the second half of the twentieth century, and many never even existed as anything but a "slot" that was declared in anticipation of continuing a paper family line.

Each generation was entangled with one another, wrapped in narratives on paper that represented, echoed, and made up the reality of physical families. In the archive, we cannot know which families in the original immigration records were or were not "paper families" without the later documentation produced by the Confession Program. While individuals of course knew their own family status regardless of the records kept by the INS, this set of relations *within* the archive helps us understand the uneven relationship between the state's quest to "know" reality and the embodied reality itself. The concept of the "paper family" became meaningful precisely because of its subversive place in the bureaucratic imaginary, which in turn shaped the experience of those living these relations.

Together, the files offer a new type of family tree that reflects the embodied negotiations between technological systems and the people within them. These family trees offer the traces of testimonies given by individuals avowing one another as kin even as they represent a mix of imagined and embodied relationships. One example appears in the case file of Yee On, which contains eighty-two pages.[17] Looking at the documents chronologically, Yee On was first interviewed at the "Chinese Detention Station" in Malone, NY on June 5, 1909.[18] In these documents, he describes being born in American Canyon, Nevada in 1881 where he lived until he was three. With his parents, he then moved to Nom Toon Village in China until he was 22, when he returned to the United States with his brother. In his interview, he disclosed that he was married with one son. According to the second page of the interview, which featured the court's verdict, Yee On was "discharged on the 28th day of May 1903, by reason of the fact that he was found to be lawfully entitled to be and remain in the US."[19] Two duplicate photographs of a man with a neutral expression are stapled to the bottom corner of the page. The next thirty-four pages chronicle his return to China and back to the United States at least twice.

In the middle of the pages is a striking document: a negative copy, its black background and white text are thrown into relief against the pile of white pages. It is a death certificate issued for a "Lee Yee On" stating that he died on November 27, 1930, at the age of forty-nine. The next addition consists of a letter dated May 9, 1936, that indicates the circumstances in which the death certificate was added to the file:

> In connection with the case of his [Yee On's] son, Lee Ock Leung, who was admitted at this port on the 7th instant, as the son of a native, there has been presented death certificate indicating that Yee On (Lee Yee On) died in New York City, November 27, 1930.[20]

In summary, the death certificate not only documented Yee On's passing in 1930 but was also added to the file and used as documentation of kinship for Yee On's son's claim of citizenship.

Then, for almost 30 years, this file sat without addition in the Immigration and Naturalization Service records. On May 25, 1965, forty-six pages were added on the same day. Four matching sets, each titled "Report of Investigation," chronicled the confession of four brothers: Lee Ock Leung, Lee Yin Leung, Lee Fee Leung, and Lee Mon Leung. Together, they confessed that they were the paper sons of Lee Yee On. As the reports reveal, Yee On was a citizen of China originally named Yee Bok On, who had falsely claimed birth in the United States. Using this falsified US-born status, four men had entered as his sons. Two were not biologically related to him at all, while Lee Ock Leung was his nephew and Lee Fee Leung was his "true son." The records named a fifth son named Lee Jung Leung who was described as a "true son, slot never used," indicating that he was a real person who was indeed the son of Yee On but had not claimed citizenship in the United States. And while two of the four individuals were "true" sons of Yee On, the father and five sons were considered a paper family because of the falsified name and claim of citizenship that grounded all their immigration.

Paper families like this one demonstrate how entangled "true" and "paper" kinship were, both in the archive and for each person the archive was attempting to document. Was Lee Fee Leung's identity "true" or "fraudulent"? Indeed, he was Yee On's biological ("true") son and the kinship he claimed that facilitated his migration was embodied in the way the law intended. However, his entrance into the United States used a different legal name than that given at birth and his entry was allowed based on his father's "false" claim as a United States-born citizen. Additionally, within this case, as the biological nephew of Yee On, Lee Ock Leung was indeed his embodied, social, and biological kin. However, norms about the degrees of separation within kinship networks (that son is closer than cousin) had certain values that dictated state-sanctioned mobility. And because uncle and nephew did not fit within the kinship stipulated by the law, the nephew falsely claimed their kinship as father and son. Thus, while the paper family as a construct did not challenge dominant notions of kinship, in practice, individuals capitalized on them by flattening certain biological distinctions.

These varying kinship arrangements were not only a part of the paper family system but reflect the centrality of family and kinship in fully understanding the interactions between the bureaucratic immigration regime and the paper strategies used to subvert it. In other words, family was not just the tool that was used to navigate the system but imbricated within the system itself. And the production of paper families further reflected a deeper understanding by Chinese immigrants of how family was embedded in the principles of immigration restriction. In this sense, it was not only that individuals used family as a strategy for immigration but also that immigration restriction had always rested on understandings of citizenship and belonging that were entwined with notions of family and kinship. Family was not simply a natural reproductive arrangement that the state attempted to track, but rather a social, cultural, and political project facilitated by the state that individuals produced through their navigation of bureaucracy.

Documenting Family, Managing Immigration

As the examples discussed thus far have shown, long before the development of genetic science and DNA tests, Chinese exclusion policy made the verification of kinship fundamental to the functioning of immigration law. For the state, the difference between veracity (true families) and fraudulence (paper families) lay in the presence and legalized confirmation of embodied biological kinship. And the immigration bureaucracy served as the very site upon which racialized and gendered litigation of those constructions shaped people's lives. A technology of regulation and of kinship, that bureaucracy produced a process and an archive that operated like a courtroom: a space where kinship and birthright claims were made, heard, decided upon, and documented. And the results of these decisions formed the grounds for which citizenship and rights were conferred and confirmed. To borrow from feminist science and technology studies scholar Sheila Jasanoff, this relationship between government bureaucracy and paper families exemplifies a kind of "coproduction" that highlights how "the ways in which we know and represent the world . . . are inseparable from the ways in which we choose to live in it." As Jasanoff describes, scientific or objective knowledge "is not a transcendent mirror of reality. It both embeds and is embedded in social practices, identities, norms, conventions, discourses, instruments, and institutions—in short, in all the building blocks of what we term the *social*."[21] Not simply a "transcendent" documentation "of reality" deemed objectively correct or incorrect, these archives of kinship model how the immigration bureaucracy co-produced the very families whose rights they defined and adjudicated. Thus, the bureaucracy functioned as the site upon which racialized and gendered conceptions of family were made real in the context of immigration and citizenship.

Indeed, the ways in which we "know and represent" this bureaucratic technology is inseparable from the ways in which people "choose to live in it." In order to analyze the bureaucracy of Chinese exclusion (and the paper family system within it), we must consider the ways individuals implemented, administered, navigated, embodied, were subjected to, and resisted it. The aim of this research is not to evaluate the efficacy of the bureaucracy, nor is it to try to create a more perfect regulatory system but rather to theorize and understand the ways in which the inevitable encounters of people within structures of power *produce* interactions that ultimately *transform* the workings of the whole system insofar as they are able to change and mold the very strategies of power used against them. For example, in describing cases of Chinese who filed habeas corpus cases after being excluded for lacking documentation, and who then used the oral testimony of those cases as documentation for re-entry, Ngai writes, "The courts' discharge papers in these cases *created* documentation of native-birth citizenship where none had previously existed."[22] Similarly, the documentation produced by the immigration bureaucracy to identify, manage, and exclude paper families also had the unexpected effect of creating the very documentation they used to verify their kinship. Thus, in a type of circular production, family and kinship functioned as a technology of the state to regulate immigration while, at the same time, the state (inadvertently) became a technology of family formation as it created a new type of family and kinship (paper families) that had not previously existed.

Because immigration claims were based on claims to kinship (that then conferred citizenship under the law), it was imperative for the immigration bureaucracy to keep track of the organization of immigrating Chinese families. In what Luibhéid describes as a "vast, meticulous documentary apparatus," standardized bureaucratic forms and photographs were common tools for differentiating individuals while also making them legible within the mechanized system.[23] Michel Foucault, who describes the case file system as an apparatus of disciplinary society, describes the genre as an opening up of "two correlative possibilities: firstly, the constitution of the individual as a describable, analysable object . . . under the gaze of a permanent corpus of knowledge" and secondly, "the constitution of a comparative system that made possible the measurement of overall phenomena, the description of groups, the characterization of collective facts, the calculation of the gaps between individuals, their distribution in a given 'population.'"[24] Their representational power lay in their simultaneous belonging to a recognizable category of purpose and their ability to distinguish individuals from one another.[25] And within this framework, the family itself existed as a unit for which "collective facts" and "the calculation of the gaps between individuals" could be measured.

One of the simplest ways that family was recorded and made material within case files was through the aforementioned reference sheet (Figure 1.1).[26] A single reference sheet was provided in a file, featuring the individual's name and case number listed at the top, followed by a list of "records used in connection with the above case." Utilizing the visual clarity and aura of quantification that tables convey, this list was comprised of approximately fifteen rows divided into three columns for listing the case file numbers, names, and relationship of other individuals within the bureaucratic system that were related to the subject of that reference sheet. One glance at the reference sheet and it is easy to tell if a person had several family members in the United States, only a few, or none.

Reference sheets were an important part of identifying and articulating families because of the organizational work they did in simplifying and making legible networks of family members that could be connected to individual incoming immigrants. To be listed, family members had to have a pre-existing INS case file, and case numbers were registered

```
                    REFERENCE SHEET

Immigration and Naturalization Service,
Ellis Island, N. Y. H., N. Y.

                        No.  125/68

            Name                              Date
        MOY SUE.                          MAY 24 1935
===================================================================
            Records used in connection with above case.
===================================================================
      No.      :      Name           :    Relationship
    ---------------------------------------------------
     125/68    :   Moy Sue            :   Self
     61/737    :   Moy Ham            :   Father
    165/823    :   Gong Shee          :   Mother
    125/118    :   Moy Look           :   Bro.
    125/151    :   Moy Fook           :   "
    167/398    :   Moy Shu            :   "
    167/399    :   Moy Mee            :   Sister
      6/1172   :   Moy Shue Koon      :   Witness re:
    149/102    :   Liu Dock Sing      :   "
    134/112    :   Mui Chun Cheung    :   "
    125/1072   :   Moy Fung Ngee      :   "
```

Figure 1.1. Reference sheet, May 24, 1935. Box 363. Case file 125/68, Moy Sue. Chinese Exclusion Act Case Files. National Archives, New York.

chronologically. Thus, while exact years had to be referenced through individual case files, one could easily see the order in which individuals in a family arrived in the United States. For both the immigration bureaucrat and archival researcher alike, reference sheets became a way to corroborate new claims to kinship entering the system. By connecting these disparate pages across the separate files of individuals, the bureaucracy also created kinship among the papers themselves. Indeed, in tracing the networks outlined by this particular type of form, the form itself became a mechanism by which *all* families (both paper and "true") were constituted.

In addition to specific documents confirming the kinship bonds across immigrants and case files, official questioning by an immigration inspector was standard practice for Chinese entering the United States.[27] Much of the information about the content, form, and detail of these interrogations was derived from official transcripts within individual case files.[28] Because legal entry was contingent on verifying claims of kinship, family organization was a common and standardized subject of interrogation. Describing, recounting, and corroborating kin networks thus provided the information that was then transmuted into the forms and bureaucratic lists like the reference sheet. The ability of official testimonies to record and testify, and the inherent valuation of their ability to endure in the archive, have made them important parts of preserving (and producing) Chinese American and transnational forms of kinship. Testimony thus comprised one of the ways people claimed kinship in a public and official way, and often served as the primary, and sometimes only, medium through which Chinese immigrants actively participated in the production of the archive.

While these bureaucratic contributions to the archive varied in honesty, testimonies and family claims were rarely made without advanced preparation from the subject and their named kin. Paper families often used coaching books and letters with detailed information to memorize the names of family members or the layout of ancestral villages to prepare for their interrogations.[29] In one example in an account from historian Judy Yung of her mother Jew Law Ying's coaching book, Jew Law Ying was truly married to her husband that she was joining in the United States.[30] However, because he had come to the United States as a paper son with the name Yung Hin Sen, Jew Law Ying had to use a coaching book to memorize the mixture of true and false facts that made up their family story within the immigration records. Yung's account of her mother's experience contextualizes the ways in which paper families came to negotiate and redefine the amalgamation of often "true" and "false" family stories that were then delivered in their immigration testimonies. Sharon Luk further theorizes the epistemological tension of these archival items:

> Yet dramatic changes in diasporic knowledge production—manifest in and through coaching letters—were not merely wholesale conscriptions to dominant understandings of subjectivity, identity, history, or geography but rather delimitations of the struggles and negotiations that Chinese migrants had to perform in order to fit their lives into national demands.[31]

Luk uses the word "perform" here to refer to the actions in which Chinese migrants took to navigate these pathways. However, this performance was not only constituted by premeditated conscious actions, but also through the affective embodiment of identity, race, and kinship.

Like the dichotomy of true and paper, it is easy to analogize the coaching book to a fictional script and the interview to a theatrical performance. This would position immigrant as performer and inspector as audience evaluating their performance. However, in the space of the interrogation, *both* inspector and immigrant performed specific roles that each was expected to fulfill. And together they embodied what Erving Goffman calls the "performance" of everyday life that was not metaphorical but rather constitutive of their positions.[32] In this context, to be an inspector was not only to be endowed with the authority, the training, and the material tools necessary to complete the interview, but also to believe in and embody the identity of inspector as a dialectical position in encounter with the migrant. Through their embodied interactions, each person demonstrated what Robin Bernstein has called "performance competence" in which an individual "understands how a book or other thing scripts broad behaviors within her or his historical moment—regardless of whether or how the performer follows that script."[33] In other words, the interview itself was constituted by the performativity of all of those involved.[34]

In one archival example, the case file of Lum Yuet Gay includes three interview transcripts of interrogations conducted by Inspector W. J. Zucker in November 8, 1929, in New York City. That day he interviewed eighteen-year-old Lum Yuet Gay who was processed through Ellis Island, as well as her father Lum Lim Jung and her brother Lum Shu Kwong, who were both already living in the United States and had come to serve as witnesses for her case. During the interview with her father, Inspector Zucker was prompted by a "thing," in this case a photograph, to enact the power of his role as inspector. While the image was not included in the case file, the transcript narrates the performance that this object elicited. With a kind of physiognomic determination, Inspector Zucker questioned father Lum Lim Jung:

> Q: The photograph on the certificate of identity correctly represents the angle at which your ears stand out from your head. The full front photograph on the certificate of discharge referred to show ears to be at a different angle particularly the right ear, and the right ear to be of a different formation from your right ear. The top of the right ear as shown on the photograph attached to the Dudley certificate of discharge is fully rounded, whereas the top of your right ear is somewhat angular. Also, the outer edge of your left ear is irregular, whereas the photograph attached to the Dudley certificate of discharge shows a smooth regular ear edge on both ears. Furthermore, the eyes of the person represented by the photograph attached to the Dudley certificate of discharge, are distinctly of the almond type, whereas yours are decidedly not so. In view of these dissimilarities and the fact that the name of your father, as given by you, does not correspond with that given by your alleged maternal uncle, who testified before Commissioner Dudley in 1901, it is possible that you are not one and the same person who was discharged by Commissioner Dudley on Feb. 6, 1902. What have you to say?[35]

In the transcript, all that Lum Lim Jung replies is, "I was a little younger than I am and sometimes a photograph does not truly represent the person." In addition to the common use of photography as evidence and the poignancy of Lum Lim Jung's answer, which I discuss in the subsequent section, the striking length of the inspector's verbal consideration of the photograph shows how power was performed and reified: his willingness and ability to scrutinize the photograph highlight his role as metaphorical jury, judge, and executioner. His analysis is a performance of power, not yielded out of spite or disdain but out of a sense of bureaucratic civility and responsibility.

In contrast, the role of the Chinese interviewee was to perform their legality. Even for those who were honest about their identities, the interview functioned as a performance of knowledge and an embodied demonstration of identity within the contained platform of the interrogation room. Within this framework, the "truth" of the performance is less revealing than the circumstances of its persuasion. Regardless of paper status, Chinese interviewees often came prepared, and many were deftly able to deliver. Not only did individuals anticipate the literal questions that would be asked and the answers that would yield their desired outcome, but they also understood the social, legal, and material stakes of providing an effective recitation and embodying the kinship that facilitated their inclusion. For example, Lum Yuet Gay was asked extensively about the details of her family:

> Q: With whom do you expect to live in this country?
> A: My father.
> Q: What is your father's name?
> A: LUM LIM JUNG, given name; LUM SOON DOO, marriage name.
> Q: How old is your father?
> A: 46.
> Q: Where was he born?
> A: In the State of MONTANA, US.
> Q: Who told you so?
> A: I heard my mother say that.
> Q: When did you last see your father?
> A: CR 11 (1922).
> Q: How long was he in China on that trip?
> A: About 17 years.
> Q: What are the names of your father's parents?
> A: LUM KAI NGON, he has been dead at least 20 years, and my paternal grandmother was HOM SHEE, she died in the same year as my paternal

grandfather. They were buried in GOW MO CHUN hill, 3 lis south of our village.

Q: Did you ever visit their burial place?

A: No

Q: Name and describe your mother?

A: NG SHE, 48, natural feet, native of TIM YUNG village, now living in GOON OY village.

Q: Has your mother any brothers or sisters?

A: No.

Q: Has your father any brothers or sisters?

A: No.

Q: Name your maternal grandparents?

A: My maternal grandfather was NG FOON BON, and my mother's mother was HUI SHE; they are both dead.

Q: Did you ever see them?

A: No.

Q: How many brothers and sisters have?you? [sic]

A: I have six brothers.

Q: Name and describe them?

A: LUM SHU KWONG, given name; LUM YICK KWONG, marriage name, age 30, born KS 26-8-15 (Oct. 8, 1900); my 2nd brother is LUM CHEE DYE, given name; LUM YICK DYE, marriage name; 24, born KS 32-2-2 (Feb. 24, 1906), my next brother is LUM CHU HOCK, given name, LUM YICK HOCK, marriage name, 22, born KS 34-4-8 (May 7, 1908); LUM CHU LIP, given name; LUM YICK LIP, marriage name, 21, born, SH 1-11-11 (Dec. 23, 1909); LUM CHU TOY, 17, single born CR 8-9-9 (Nov. 1, 1919), that is all.[36]

Rather than read these transcripts only as a stable transmission of information, we can also consider the representational work they did in producing the reality they purportedly documented. The very act of claiming kinship created both evidence and embodied declaration of its reality. For the foreseeable future, regardless of its basis, Lum Lim Jung would legally be considered Lum Yuet Gay's father, Ng She her mother, and the six men named her brothers. And for over thirty-five years, this *was* the legal constitution of the Lum family.

Then, in 1966, sworn testimony from the Chinese Confession Program was added to Lum Yuet Gay's file. Her second oldest brother Lum Chee Dye confessed that his "true name" was Man Wah You, thus implicating the rest of the Lum family. However, from the case files, the details of who was biologically related to whom remains unclear. Transcripts like these and the bureaucratic roles that were lived and enacted within the interrogation room demonstrate the power of government recordkeeping and documentation in constituting kinship. Even in situations without deception, claiming kinship is itself an act and everyday performance of kinship. And the testimonies and existence of paper families provide a foil for which we can understand how even normative kinship can be constituted in part by the legal and institutional acts of documentation and recognition that the government bureaucracy elicits.

Paper Family Photography

Irrespective of the lawfulness of Lum Yuet Gay's case, Inspector Zucker's aforementioned pontification about the photograph of Lum Lim Jung also demonstrates the ways in which photography played an important role in the regulation of immigration and the declaration of kinship. From the extensive analysis of the earlier excerpt, we can see how the continual aspirations of visuality in identifying individuals permeated the bureaucratic process. And in response, Lum Lim Jung also offered a poetic theory on the limits of that visuality as a defense against the skepticism of Inspector Zucker. His claim that "sometimes a photograph does not truly represent the person" may have been an astute response to a challenge by authority, but it also offers a theory of photography that evokes the question Ariella Azoulay theorizes in her essay, "What is photography? What is a photograph?" As Azoulay describes, the "photographed image produced out of an encounter invariably contains both *more* and *less* than that which someone wished to inscribe in it. The photograph is always more and less than what one of the parties to the encounter managed to frame at the moment of photography. The photograph is always in excess of, and always bears a lack in relation to, each of its protagonists."[37] This is true not only for photographer and photographed subject but also for those that wish to use the photograph as what Foucault calls a "documentary technique," or that which "*makes each individual a 'case': a case which at one and the same time constitutes an object for a branch of knowledge and a hold for a branch of power.*"[38]

Within this encounter, Inspector Zucker wished the photograph to reveal a truth that Lum Lim Jung hoped it would not. The angle of an ear or the shape of an eye could only offer "both *more* and *less* than" that which each "wished to inscribe in it." And as such, both aimed to use it as "an object for a branch of knowledge": for Inspector Zucker as representative of the bureaucracy it was also a "hold for a branch of power," and for Lum Lim Jung, it was a hold against that power. Allan Sekula further describes photography's potential to function "both *honorifically* and *repressively*"[39]:

> On the one hand, the photographic portrait extends, accelerates, popularizes, and degrades a traditional function. . . . At the same time, photographic portraiture began to perform a role no painted portrait could have performed in the same thorough and rigorous fashion. This role derived, not from any honorific portrait tradition, but from the imperatives of medical and anatomical illustration. Thus, photography came to establish and delimit the terrain of the *other*, to define both the *generalized look*—the typology—and the *contingent instance* of deviance and social pathology.[40]

This approach to the "bureaucratic handling of visual documents" was a central feature of immigration regulation in the late nineteenth and early twentieth centuries. The earlier exclusion of Chinese women through the Page Act of 1875 was the first time standardized forms of photography were used to regulate immigration in the United States.[41] And this set a precedent for the use of photography in overseeing Chinese exclusion. Photography thus became incorporated into a national project of bureaucratic standardization and immigration regulation.

Through the incorporation of these visual identification practices, the racializing process of Chinese exclusion also further reinforced and reproduced the visuality of race. As Craig Robertson describes in *The Passport in America: The History of a Document*, "The very similarities that allowed an inspector to identify an individual as a 'Chinaman' became the characteristics that prevented the reliable identification of that 'Chinaman' as a distinct individual through a document."[42] As Robertson suggests, the racialized characterizations of Chinese as a grouping led to the circular dynamic in which regulation produced the very means with which to subvert it. Photographs combined with information on forms created what Anna Pegler-Gordon calls the "identity photograph: the visual representation and the written identification of a given individual."[43] And while paper families can be understood as fraudulently capitalizing on this relationship between image and text, these photographs also reflect the desire of the bureaucratic system to achieve a type of perfect categorical identification. Rather than inherently honorific or repressive, identification photography in the era of Chinese exclusion continued a process John Tagg outlines in the second half of the nineteenth century by which "new techniques of surveillance and record harbored by such institutions [of disciplinary power] bore directly on the social body in new ways."[44]

Like the image used by Lum Lim Jung to verify his identity and relationship with Lum Yuet Gay, photography was used as a technology in this way to represent and testify to kinship. And in so doing, the images used, included, and talked about in the case files of paper families did not only represent or illustrate the family, but they also constituted and produced it. In other words, photography was not only a technology in and of itself but also a *technology of* bureaucratic paper family making. It served as an active participant in the construction of new formations of family. And "paper family photography," as I call it, functioned as a subgenre of bureaucratic photography that participated in the processes by which formations of family were continually produced and transformed. The photography of these paper families, thus, constituted both paper "family photography" in the material sense and "paper family" photography in the representational sense.

Conventional forms of family photography were an important part of the immigration process; however, they were often absent in the paper case files. Immigrants used family photographs to testify to their kinship but then kept the family photographs that they showed to inspectors. For example, in *Unbound Feet: A Social History of Chinese Women in San Francisco*, in addition to the previously discussed coaching books, Yung shows the family photographs her mother used as evidence to join her father in the United States using a paper identity.[45] In this case, as with many others, the family photographs were never put into the immigration case file and were only accessible as the possession of the author (passed down from her mother).

The case file of Moy Sue offers a rare example of a group photograph preserved within the immigration archive. The image, almost the full size of a standard piece of paper and printed in black and white that has now yellowed with age, shows three Chinese men seated side-by-side, each with a neutral expression and their hands resting on their laps (see Figure 1.2). They pose in what looks like a studio: gently flowering shrubs and a small footbridge are printed flatly on a backdrop behind them that curls under slightly where it meets a floral rug. On the top left-hand corner, the case file number "NY 125/68" is written along with the date, October 25, 1927, with no other names or text on the front or back. According to several testimony transcripts, Moy Sue's father was an American citizen named Moy Ham, born in 1885 in Renton, Washington. He had returned to China as a child and eventually married and started a family there. He claimed to have had four sons and one daughter, all of whom he brought to the United States and were admitted based on his "status as a US native born citizen." According to an interview transcript in Moy Sue's file regarding his admission to the United States, the following exchange occurred between Inspector P. A. Donahue and Moy Ham about this photograph:

> Q: Did your family ever have a group photograph taken?
> A: Yes, I received a photograph of my three sons about five years ago.
> Q: Have you that photograph with you?
> A: Yes. (Presented photograph showing three Chinese men).
> Q: From whom did you receive this group photograph?
> A: My father sent it to me thru the mail.

Q: (Indicating persons in group photograph counting from left to right) who are these persons?
A: The first on the left is Moy Look, the second is My (Moy) Fook and the third is Moy Sue.
Q: Are you willing that this group photograph be kept on file in this office?
A: I would like to keep that one but I will submit a copy of it. (Group photograph retained temporarily with the understanding that it will be later returned to him and with the further understanding that he is to furnish this office with a copy of same for use of its files)
(By permission of witness, said photograph endorsed with present file, number.)[46]

It is unclear if the photograph included in the case file is the original photograph referenced or the copy that was to be made. The use of family photographs was common in interrogations and references to photographs in testimony transcripts outnumber the actual photographs kept within individual case files. Just looking at the file by itself, we cannot know if the individuals in the photograph were biologically related or not. It is only through Moy Fook's confession added years later that there exists any indication that this was a paper family in some capacity.

In the case of this photograph and others kept in the immigration files, the bureaucracy that gave this photograph new meaning also transformed its materiality. As previously mentioned, on the right-hand corner is written the case file number "NY 125/68" and a number is crossed out underneath the number 125. The photograph is stapled to a blank piece of watermarked INS letterhead. Small rifts litter the photograph as if it has been stapled and detached on multiple occasions. Human hands making errors, attaching, and detaching this photograph have created bureaucratic traces on this family and on this family photograph.

Again, photographs like this one in the archive become both "more and less" than what is framed within it.[47] It is more in its ability to evoke, represent, and testify to kinship. And it is less in its inability to tell a type of truth that those encountering it in the state bureaucracy wish it to tell. Here, the visuality of race further entangles photography in the pro-

Figure 1.2. Photograph submitted with testimony, October 25, 1927. Box 363. Case file 125/68, Moy Sue. Chinese Exclusion Act Case Files. National Archives, New York.

cesses of differentiation. It is precisely because the visuality of familial bonds can be ambiguous and contested that paper families were able to utilize photography to navigate the immigration bureaucracy. Inspectors often struggled to interpret family resemblance while examining these images. Unified by the racial logics that cohered Chinese as an identifiable race, paper families capitalized on the visual *inability* to verify biologically related family members. Therefore, it was precisely because biological relation was not visually verifiable that photography reached a limit in its ability to assist in the process of immigration regulation, and in turn, became a mechanism by which the paper family could come into existence.[48]

As a result, family photography bore an incredible representational burden, and as such, became the very terrain on which paper families were built, regulated, and contested. Furthermore, the role of the Confession Program in disrupting the assumed indexicality of the photograph changes our own encounter with it. For instance, the transcript testimony narrates a simple truth: in the photograph are three brothers in a row, Moy Look on the left, Moy Fook in the middle, and Moy Sue on the right. Their positions match and their expressions are similarly neutral. While there was never any "proof" that these are brothers, their narration as such "made sense." And yet this brief moment of stability throws into relief the confusion of learning that Moy Fook is not necessarily their biological brother. Who are these people "really"? And in what context does that information matter? Like a family photograph that is found among other family photographs but with people we don't know and can't identify, it's hard not to wonder who the people in front of the camera were on the day of this photograph's making. While these photographs cannot answer all of our questions, they can show how the bureaucratic immigration system inadvertently produced the very type of families (Chinese paper families) it sought to regulate and eliminate.

In addition to passport-style and conventional family photography, a new photographic practice also emerged out of the regulatory system, one that we might also consider to be a type of family photography. Here, a kind of family photograph collage was created by the moving, touching, connecting, and pasting of pieces of paper representing individuals that were not biological family but about to become family precisely through what those papers authorized, testified, and meant for the larger government bureaucracy. They were produced in the form of official affidavits that testified to individuals' kinship with one another.[49] The file of Wong Tung Yee demonstrates the typical wording as shown (Figure 1.3):

> I, WONG WING YICK, being first duly sworn depose and say:
> That I am a native-born citizen of the United States as is shown by New York file no. 2525/429.
> That I am executing this affidavit for the purpose of establishing the identity of my daughter, WONG TUNG YEE, and also to assist her in coming to the United States.
> That my prior-landed daughter, WONG TUNG GEE, who was admitted into this country at New York on Mar. 25, 1938, when Certificate of Identity No. 75215 was issued to her—file no. 170/540—will appear as a

witness in behalf of WONG TUNG YEE when she arrives in this country and is an applicant for admission.

That the photographs attached to this affidavit represent myself; the applicant, WONG TUNG YEE, and the witness, WONG TUNG GEE.

At the bottom of this page are three photographs: on the right, a photograph of a man in a suit and tie; in the middle, a young woman in a collared top; and on the left, a woman with a rose in her hair. Handwritten on the photographs themselves and also typed below are their names, Wong Wing Yick, Wong Tung Yee, and Wong Tung Gee. Here, a father testifies to his relationship with his two daughters.

Affidavits like this one were common among the immigration case files and often constituted the only form of photography kept in the file. In Wong Tung Yee's case, we can visually see how family members served as witnesses for one another. Uniquely, Wong Tung Yee's sister served as her witness, though it was more typical for men to testify for one another. According to the file, they had four brothers that had immigrated to the United States using their father's US citizenship status. However, added to the file in September of 1964, almost 30 years after the affidavit was submitted, their brother Wong Sik Koey confessed to have been born Gee Bon Chu, not the biological son of Wong Wing Yick. Despite the exposure of new family secrets, the affidavit and its photographic components remained unaltered in the original case file.

Juxtaposed with conventional notions of family photography, the family photo collage from these types of affidavits offers a different iteration of family photography. By placing individual photographs side-by-side, attaching them in a specific orientation to one another, and endowing this material item with the status of truth, the bureaucracy avowed the existence of these families. What is the purpose of any family photograph but to do exactly that which this affidavit itself attempts to do? Represent a kinship bond, materialize an encounter of relationality, and establish that which Roland Barthes calls the "*noeme 'That-has-been.'*"[50] In this way the family photo collage serves not only as the fabrication of a family to which individuals (both related biologically and through paper kinship) testified, but a process by which family was produced. Here, family was not made physical through biological re-

Figure 1.3. Affidavit, 1938. Box 538. Case file 171/76, Wong Tung Yee. Chinese Exclusion Act Case Files. National Archives, New York.

production but through the materiality of individualized photographs literally glued together into a new corpus.

This affidavit as family photograph collage also parallels the practice of many Chinese families in the twentieth century and their use of collaging to craft family portraits. A common practice during Chinese exclusion, when many families were physically kept apart by immigration policy, cutting and pasting images of distant family members became a way for kin to be together visually. As Laura Wexler writes about Ruthanne Lum McCunn's *Chinese American Portraits: Personal Histories, 1828–1988*, "For almost one hundred years, the only place this family was together was in the pages of the photographic album. In other words, it is the album itself that constructs the family. But it is also the nation that constructs the album."[51] Like these collages, the affidavit family photo collage serves not only as the fabrication of a family to which individuals attempted to represent, but a process by which family was produced. Because family photography preserved in the case files was relatively rare, considering this practice as a new type of family photography both helps us understand the role of photography in the immigration regime's attempt to regulate Chinese immigration *using* images of family and kinship, and reimagine how kinship was both substantiated *and* created in these circumstances.

The Gendered Effects of Government Bureaucracy

While the examples in this chapter thus far have certainly demonstrated the presence of Chinese women within the immigration system during Chinese exclusion, a stark gender imbalance among Chinese immigrants in the United States persisted as men vastly outnumbered women. Sucheng Chan describes that, while patriarchal cultural values and the "sojourner mentality" did impact the disproportionately high number of Chinese men immigrating to the United States, immigration restrictions that impacted the entrance of Chinese women were a more significant factor during this period.[52] This included the 1875 Page Act that specifically targeted Chinese women for exclusion in what Luibhéid describes as a transformation of "immigration control into a system of sexual regulation, which came to encompass any immigrant who sought entry to the United States."⁵³ And following the emergence of paper families, Erika Lee describes,

> Another official concluded that the number of Chinese claiming citizenship was so great in comparison to the number of Chinese women in the country at the time of the applicants' births that there would have had to have been 'at least ten times as many Chinese women in this country ... as actually ever have been in this country since the first Chinaman landed on its shore.'⁵⁴

Indeed, paper families both amplified and made more visible the gender imbalance of Chinese in the United States, which in turn further exposed the practice as incongruent with the construction of kinship envisioned and enforced by immigration restrictions.

This gender imbalance was most prominently reflected in the archive by the frequency with which families (some later identified as paper families and others without designation) claimed to have an extreme disproportion of sons to daughters. By the mid-1920s, families with six to ten sons and one to two daughters became a kind of new family norm documented in the case files. In fact, it was so common that it became a way (for both me as a researcher and the bureaucratic officials at the time) to potentially identify paper families in case files that were not already flagged. Gender was not simply another axis by which legislative exclusion operated but a central form of organization that shaped the constitution of paper families. In this context, the disproportionate number of paper sons was not solely a demographic effect of choices made by individuals but also a new familial *product* of the gendered and racialized immigration system. In other words, the sociolegal constitution of the transnational Chinese American family was being shaped, produced, and molded by the Chinese exclusion regime itself.

The multiple case files that make up the Moy family offer one demonstration of this new gendered norm among paper families.⁵⁵ The file of Moy Hand Fun consists of thirty-two pages, only five of which were created during the era of Chinese exclusion. According to the earliest dated document in this file, from October 4, 1913, Moy Hand Fun was "an American born Chinese person" who had arrived in Vancouver,

British Columbia while returning from a trip to China. The five documents chronicle Moy Hand Fun's entry into Canada and then eventually the United States. However, the remaining twenty-seven pages of Moy Hand Fun's files consist of documents added almost fifty years later through the Chinese Confession Program, and pertain to individuals named Moy Di Wing, Moy Di Yin, and Moy Di Wah. By cross referencing the names mentioned in these documents, multiple case files reveal that between 1935 and 1938, eight sons and one daughter came to the United States as Moy Hand Fun's children.[56] Due to his earlier death in 1928, Moy Hand Fun never testified in any of his claimed children's cases, and the aforementioned documents in his personal case file were primarily referenced only to establish his citizenship in the subsequent cases.

The remaining pages added to Moy Hand Fun and several of his sons' case files consist of documents added between 1962 and 1965 chronicling the confessions of sons Moy Di Wing, Moy Di Yin, and Moy Di Wah. According to Moy Di Wah's testimony in 1961, all seven of the Moy brothers and one sister were paper children that had entered the United States illegally with fraudulent names. However, in 1962, another statement was made and added to all of the Moy family case files: Moy Di Foo made a statement to the INS that he was in fact Moy Hand Fun's biological child. He claimed only him and one other brother, Moy Di Bin, had been the "true sons" of Moy Hand Fun, and that the other six paper sons and one paper daughter had paid a man named Moy Wong Lai $3500 each to be brought to the United States.[57] As the investigation unfolded, documentation was also added to daughter Moy Di Shew's file that showed she had married a man named Carter Moy and had gone by the American name, Dorothy Moy. By the time this information was added to her immigration record, Dorothy Moy had died. She had passed in 1959 from pulmonary tuberculosis, leaving behind her husband and their son. At the time of the investigation, her status as a paper daughter led to an investigative dead end. Her husband and son were both identified as American-born citizens. Regarding Moy Di Shew aka Dorothy Moy, the Confession Program had successfully done its job of exposing her as a paper daughter, and the investigation ensured no individuals would come to the United States illegally claiming to be Moy's child.

Like the Moys, other families chronicled in the Chinese Exclusion Act case files also claimed sons and daughters in disproportionate numbers upon entry into the United States. For example, the Lung family claimed to have nine sons and two daughters.[58] The Louie family had five sons and one daughter.[59] The Chin family had five sons and one daughter.[60] A different Moy family claimed five sons and one daughter.[61] The Wong family headed by Wong Gong had six sons and one daughter.[62] Another Wong family headed by Wong Wing Yick had five sons and two daughters.[63] The Young family had six sons and four daughters.[64] While many of these families were revealed to be paper families through the Chinese Confession Program, it is not possible to assume all families with more sons than daughters were paper families. For example, in a confession given by Eng Kee On (paper name Goon Kin Toy), he confessed that he had three biological sons, all born in New York City, aged sixteen, fourteen, and ten at the time of his confession. However, he himself came to the United States as one of four paper sons of his paper father.[65]

Although the more extreme forms of gender imbalance in so many families are incongruent with normative patterns of human reproduction, the reality of this type of family emerged as a product, not of biology, but of the regimes of racialized governmental regulation. In other words, the seven-son, one-daughter family may not be a biological product of reproduction, but it *is* a social product of a racialized government process. Thus, this particular gendered formation of family was again made real through the bureaucracy of immigration regulation. Like the paper family photographs and the legal testimonies claiming kinship, new gendered norms within Chinese paper families were produced by the very bureaucratic system created to eliminate them.

Despite its prevalence, this significant demographic imbalance in the gender makeup of the Chinese diasporic community was relatively short-lived as the era of Chinese exclusion came to an end in the 1940s. As cultural and political hostility toward Chinese waned during World War II, amplified by Japan's invasion of China and the growing bigotry against Japanese and Japanese Americans in the United States, the politics of immigration exclusion also shifted. While the Magnuson Act of 1943 officially repealed the Chinese Exclusion Act of 1882, immigration continued to be restricted until 1965.

During this period, the Chinese Confession Program effectively saw the end of the practice of paper families and stopped the further amplification of the imbalance of gender by eliminating "slots," individuals that had been named as the children of citizens that could then be used to bring over more people in the future. The Chinese Confession Program ended the same year as the passage of the Immigration and Nationality Act of 1965, also known as the Hart-Celler Act, marking a legislative shift away from immigration exclusion. In 1966, Chinese immigration tripled from the previous year and continued to grow rapidly.[66] In contrast to the previous restrictive period of Asian exclusion, immigration no longer primarily relied on citizenship status, either by birth or as the child of a citizen. However, as certain preferences for entry to the United States continued to depend on familial relationships, as the following chapter highlights, the later liberalization of immigration continued to reinforce specific definitions of family and kinship characterized by heteronormative marriage and biological reproduction.

The paper family may have been an iteration of family formation historically bounded by the periods of Chinese exclusion and Chinese confession. However, its presence in the archive continues to show how the meaning of family shapes and is shaped by structures of state power in racialized and gendered ways. The bureaucracy often failed to detect paper families, but it succeeded in further embedding ideologies of family and kinship, like birthright citizenship and the primacy of family in immigration law, into understandings of citizenship, belonging, and the nation-state. Born from the production of the archive through recordkeeping of the immigration bureaucracy, lived through that record by the power of the state, and remembered through the paper of the archive, paper families demonstrate the ways in which kinship can be substantiated, represented, and produced through the very tools (testimony, affidavits, photography) used to regulate it. In a society that has continued to develop new and increasingly advanced ways of verifying documents and identity through bureaucratic regimentation, aren't all families made from or through paper in some way?

While this chapter has focused specifically on ethnically Chinese paper families, this history of the bureaucratic structure of immigration regulation and the power of the Immigration and Naturalization Service is foundational to racial formation across the Asian diaspora, as well as the emergence of categories like "documented" and "undocumented," that directly impact the distribution of rights and resources in the present. The ongoing entanglement of immigration regulation and the formation of kinship have continued to shape immigration from Asia and the racialization of Asian Americans throughout the twentieth century and into the twenty-first.

2

The Making of the Model Minority Family

*Immigration Policy, Cultural Narrative, and
Asian American Racialization*

In the second half of the twentieth century, alongside rapid economic, social, and cultural shifts of the postwar period, images of Asian Americans in United States culture quickly transformed from immigrant threat to model minority. Model minority narratives marked a shift from nineteenth- and early-twentieth-century popular images in which Chinese, Japanese, and other "Oriental" minorities were depicted as uncivilized and sexually deviant, and then later as wartime enemies.[1] Instead, the vision of the model minority newly painted the narrative of Asians as upwardly mobile, educated, and successful.

In Asian American studies, we know these tales well: in 1966, William Petersen published his now-infamous "Success Story, Japanese-American Style" in the *New York Times* coining the phrase "model minority." In 1986, *Fortune* published a special report titled "America's Super Minority," asserting "Asian Americans have wasted no time laying claim to the American dream. They are smarter and better educated and make more money than everyone else."[2] And in 1987, a *Time* cover showed six secondary school children, adorned in Day-Glo, posed in front of a chalkboard amidst textbooks and a computer, beside the headline "Those Asian-American Whiz Kids." The article marveled over young Asian Americans excelling in school, especially in math and science, and attempted to explain the rapid rise in achievement by Asian Americans at the end of the twentieth century. In each of these narratives, Asian American achievements were supposedly rooted in the enduring otherness, assumed racial coherence, and perceived kinship structures of these Asian "cultures."

This is the model minority "myth": a narrative that has followed Asian Americans around since the 1960s telling us there is something inherent to Asian American achievement. It is not only marked by stories of educational and socioeconomic success but also the presumed coherence of "Asian" as racial community, characterized by an emphasis on and essentialization of the family. But how has the model minority endured for more than half a century now, defining Asian American identity and the formations of kinship that embody it? As erin Khuê Ninh argues, the model minority is not simply a "myth" that can be corrected or debunked but is rather a form of racialization by which individuals make sense of, identify with, and embody racial identity in themselves and through others. Ninh writes, "an identity's materiality is perhaps more appropriately gauged by its fictions and active identifications (and what its discourses aim *to* fabricate) than merely by its present circumstances."³ The model minority as racialization encompasses both the material forms of achievement that appear to substantiate it as "real" *and also* the discursive, affective, and ideological forms of attachment and identification that so powerfully (and painfully) suture it to Asian American identity.

This chapter places the historical emergence of the model minority in dialogue with the ontological cultural narratives of it, as a form of racialization, to reveal the construction of the Asian American family as a conflation of *both* racialized ideological figuration *and* material sociodemographic phenomenon in the second half of the twentieth century. In other words, the model minority has existed as an ideology of culturally specific notions about race, gender, and difference while also being used as a social unit to describe people's embodied experiences of their own families. I argue that, in this context, the construct of the Asian American immigrant family has been hypervisible in some ways and rendered invisible in others, and that has led to the misleading portrayal of Asian racial categorization as a phenomenon defined by cultural essentialism, rather than social formations of power and racial hierarchy. What forms of power have been obscured (and naturalized in their obscuration) when the heteronormative, nuclear family is assumed to be inherent to Asian "culture" in the process of racial typing?

In addition to highlighting the ideology of family within the familiar cultural history of the model minority, this chapter also shows how the immigration preference system established in 1965 has functioned as a technology of kinship that has produced new material and ideological iterations of the Asian American family, even as it has simultaneously been obscured by the hegemony of the model minority as cultural narrative. Still in effect today, the immigration preference system was introduced in the 1965 Immigration and Nationality Act, also known as the Hart-Celler Act, and replaced the previous numerical quota system for immigration with a preference system that prioritized professional skills and family reunification. However, its impact on Asian racialization and kin formation has often been obscured within mainstream model minority narratives. Instead, within these mainstream narratives, the hypervisible heteronormative Asian nuclear family is presumed to be the inherent source of racialized success. In contrast, this chapter explores how the normalized and institutionalized conscription of family within immigration policy has situated Asian Americans within those normative cultural narratives that place them in a relation of debt and gratitude to nation and to family (often as a metaphor for nation). In this context, the cultural characterizations of the model minority (as the thing that seemingly makes the Asian American family racially distinct) is precisely that which obfuscates the role of the preference system in materially producing Asian *American* families that then fit those cultural explanations and narratives in the first place. Thus, theorizing immigration policy as a technology of kinship reveals how the family has been instrumentalized and naturalized in the continuation of the model minority as a process of racialization.

Indeed, while the history of the model minority is well documented, this chapter traces the ideological instrumentalization and figuration of the family through racialized historical narratives to reveal the role of immigration policy in producing the model minority family. I begin by excavating the familiar story of the model minority to show how the family has been framed as a cultural marker of racialized difference. Despite this otherness presumed inherent to the "Asian immigrant family," the model minority family is thus a distinctly *American* cultural and sociological product. In other words, the Asian model minority family is in fact a distinctly American figuration despite its racial association with Asianness. And while American contemporary culture has specifically used the model minority to categorize the Asian American family as racially and culturally distinct, what that has obscured is the role of immigration policy itself in self-selecting and producing the very Asian American families that are congruent with the image of the model minority. And that congruence is marked by the reproduction of and adherence to heterosexuality, legal marriage, biological reproduction, and affirmation of liberal (and later neoliberal) fantasies of the American dream.

The Family as Model Minority Figuration

Within Asian American studies, the hypervisibility of the Asian American family is part and parcel of critiques of both the model minority and the dominance of intergenerational narratives in Asian American and Asian diasporic cultural production. For example, now over twenty-five years old, in *Immigrant Acts: On Asian American Cultural Politics*, Lisa Lowe asserts,

> The reduction of the cultural politics of racialized ethnic groups, like Asian Americans, to first-generation/second-generation struggles displaces social differences into a privatized familial opposition. Such reductions contribute to the aestheticizing commodification of Asian American *cultural* differences, while denying . . . immigrant histories of material exclusion and differentiation . . ."[4]

Indeed, the hypervisibility of the Asian American family marks a historically specific process of racialization in the twentieth century by which racial categorization has been framed through cultural difference. Simultaneously, the naturalization of the Asian American family as an essentialized component of this Asian racial characterization belies those larger structures of "immigrant histories of material exclusion and differentiation" to which Lowe alludes.

In addition to the hegemony of intergenerational struggle as a central form of Asian diasporic cultural representation, cultural and political images have also often incorporated both the family as metaphor and the family as social structure into the racial characterization of both Asians and Asian Americans. For example, Naoko Shibusawa describes how racialized, gendered, and heteronormative discourses became incorporated into the shifting views of Japan following World War II. Shibusawa writes, "The post-war public discourse assumed two 'natural' or universally recognized hierarchical relationships—man over woman and adult over child—and compared them to the relationship between the United States, a 'white' nation, and Japan, a 'non-white' nation."[5] This use of the family as metaphor for international politics became central to postwar discourses of racial order. At the same time, other historical accounts of multiculturalism during the Cold War demonstrate how the nuclear family and familial discourse became integrated into these ideologies of inclusion, multiculturalism, and international relations.[6]

Social scientific explanations and observations about Chinese and Japanese American communities in the United States in the first half of the twentieth century lay the foundations for those later formations of the model minority.[7] For example, Henry Yu shows how social scientists actively participated in the changing meanings of race in the early twentieth century, describing how the "concept of 'culture' was a way of getting away from biological theories of race that had served a similar function of categorizing similarities and differences between humans."[8] Within mainstream politics and knowledge production, these social scientific explanations about race also shifted from claims about racial difference that justified outright segregation and discrimination to claims that explicitly promoted equality while simultaneously attributing inequity to inherent "cultural" differences.

These twentieth century social scientific ideas about race not only reflected but also produced dominant discourses about race and Asian Americans. In charting the model minority as a process of "race making" and the rise of racial liberalism in the 1940s through the 1960s, Ellen Wu argues,

> . . . the racial logic that politicians, scholars, and journalists deployed to invent the model minority generated new modes of exclusion. Their reliance on culture to explain post-war Asian American socioeconomic mobility re-marked ethnic Japanese and Chinese as not-white, indelibly foreign others, compromising their improvements in social standing.[9]

Thus, by the time the term "model minority" appeared in the 1960s, it was emerging from an existing racial logic in the process of defining Asianness through the construction of a coherent and essentialized "culture" of Asian achievement and success, one that many (both

Asians and non-Asians) participated and believed in. Cindy I-Fen Cheng also describes this period between 1946 and 1965 as one in which "popular perceptions of Asian Americans as the foreigners-within cast them at once as 'loyal citizens' to be integrated into dominant society and as 'alien subversives' to be deported." As Cheng argues, these narratives were also generated and reproduced by the state and "were important not only for promoting the nation's Cold War agenda but also for influencing the efforts by Asian Americans to secure their social and political legitimacy in Cold War America and the stories they told about race in the United States."[10] In this context, the nuclear family was a central facet of not only mainstream images of Cold War America but also ideas about the assimilation of the Asian diaspora in the United States.

Sociological ideologies of cultural difference as racial difference did not only apply to Asian Americans but also shaped broader liberal discourses of racial difference and comparative categorization. For example, Wu describes early comparisons between Japanese Americans and African Americans in the 1950s and 1960s, highlighting the infamous 1965 Moynihan Report and its author, Secretary of Labor Daniel Patrick Moynihan. While the report itself did not explicitly mention Japanese or any other Asian Americans, Wu describes a private memorandum from Moynihan to President Johnson that explicitly calls on Japanese Americans as an example of the kind of racial uplift he believed African Americans should use as a model.[11] Within these comparisons, the family served as the explicit, repeated, and essentialized site through which racialized characterization functioned. The Moynihan Report, formally titled *The Negro Family: The Case for National Action*, suggested that upwards mobility for African Americans could only be achieved through the adherence to White heterosexual reproductive middleclass norms, and it explicitly conflated households "headed by females" with "family disorganization."[12] Such claims further evidence Roderick Ferguson's observation that "American sociology ... has proffered heteronormativity as the scene of order and rationality and nonheteronormativity as the scene of abandonment and dysfunction."[13] In relation to the Moynihan Report, Ferguson also describes this underlying implication of the imbrication of family and racialization,

Basing the problems of African American social structure on the troubles of the African American family, the Moynihan Report renders African American intimate arrangements into the obstacle to equality of outcome. As the family was imagined as that institution that prevented many African Americans from "moving ahead," family became that institution that determined the direction of mobility, socializing its members to competitive ideals and practices and granting them equality of results only as the family yielded to heteropatriarchal dictates.[14]

In this way, the Moynihan Report sutured the success of African Americans to adherence to heteropatriarchal norms (embodied by the dominant nuclear family structure), and as such, the family itself functioned as an ideological apparatus of gendered and sexual power embedded into contemporary meanings of race. The concept of "family structure" and the values implied within it were thus purposely and explicitly enlisted into contemporary discourses of race that essentialized these qualities as ones that define racial difference.

Of course, Moynihan was not alone in comparing Asian Americans and African Americans. Just one year after Moynihan published his report, in 1966, two mainstream media articles that established the contemporary iteration of the model minority narrative were published: William Petersen's "Success Story, Japanese-American Style" printed in the *New York Times* and "Success Story of One Minority Group," which focused on Chinese Americans, printed in *U.S. News & World Report*. Both pieces focused on family structure and explicitly compared Asian American success to African American failure. In contrast to the pathologization of the African American family, the racialization of the Asian American family in the 1960s was defined through its heteronormativity and assimilation to those "heteropatriarchal dictates" (to borrow from Ferguson). Petersen used family to frame Japanese American success in cultural terms, writing,

> The two vehicles that transmitted such values [that have led to success] from one generation to the next, the family and religion, have been so intimately linked as to reinforce each other. By Japanese tradition, the wishes of any individual counted far less than the good reputation of his family name, which was worshipped through his ancestors.[15]

Similarly, "Success Story of One Minority Group" quoted Victor Wong, president of the Chinese Consolidated Benevolent Association in Los Angeles saying, "Basically the Chinese are good citizens. The parents always watch out for the children, train them, send them to school and make them stay home after school to study. When they go visiting it is as a family group . . ."[16] The article then went on to quote a "high-ranking police official in Los Angeles" saying, "Our problems with the Chinese are at a minimum. This probably is due to strict parental supervision. There is still a tradition of respect for parents."[17] For both commenters, the family and cultural values about family were framed as responsible for producing Chinese as "good citizens."

These tropes of filial piety and collectivist culture have become all too familiar in model minority narratives from the 1960s through to the present. Many early Asian American activists and scholars were quick to challenge and critique the model minority narrative. For example, in the introduction of the 1971 *Roots: An Asian American Reader*, editor Amy Tachiki wrote,

> Basic to the success story are the means by which Asian Americans have assimilated. They have often adhered to this society's prescribed mode of behavior for minority assimilation: through hard work, education, quietly remaining in the background, inaction in the face of injustice, and blind faith to the American dream of equality and opportunity for all. The danger in upholding this success myth is that it reinforces the underlying value structure that created it. The Asian success story functions to validate the fundamental soundness of this system to support the "truth" that all deserving people of color can and should earn a middle-class position and life style within this society.[18]

In describing how the model minority "reinforces the underlying value structure that created it" and affirms the bootstraps narrative of the American dream, Tachiki presciently points to the reasons for its endurance over time. During this period, both activist communities and mainstream media featured critiques and rejections of the model minority "myth" or "stereotype," contrasting it against the realities of exclusion, racism, and struggle many Asian Americans faced.[19]

Alongside these ongoing cultural debates about the model minority, for many in the 1960s through the 1990s, understanding the problems and successes of minority groups became a question of producing sociological knowledge *about* those groups, rather than looking to the institutional, legal, and economic structures of social and cultural life. As Ferguson points out, citing George Lipsitz, the Moynihan Report demonstrated a broader sociocultural shift in which "the problems facing communities of color no longer stem primarily from discrimination but from the characteristics of these communities themselves."[20] And as Asians (as a demographic racial group in the United States) began to grow in number and in visibility, this focus on the "characteristics of these communities" rather than "discrimination" on a structural level came to dominate conversations about Asian Americans and their presumed "success." It makes sense, then, that later model minority discourses produced by liberal social scientists and mainstream media thus explained the seemingly great success of Asians as a minority group by relying on the language of family and culture: "characteristics" of Asian success were used to further essentialize and criticize African American "failure" in a process that solidified Asian and African American racial difference as defined by inherent cultural difference.

At the same time, mainstream media (including some of the same outlets publishing critiques) and other Asian Americans themselves used the model minority and its attachment to family as the very discourse with which to proudly characterize their own experience. As Viet Thanh Nguyen describes, "Unlike the stereotype of the yellow peril, which is resolutely negative and therefore easily rejected by those who are labeled with it, the stereotype of the model minority is regarded by Asian American intellectuals as insidious precisely because of its ability to be internalized by Asian Americans."[21] For example, in 1987, the *New York Times* published a piece titled "The Drive to Excel," which presented the high-schooler David Kuo as the quintessential example of the model minority. When interviewed for the article, David's father was quoted saying, "Taiwan has different educational form from the United States . . . Now here they do it by themselves. Asians come here to get a better education, so they work hard." His mother is quoted attributing his success to their family, saying, "We are very close in our family life. That is all."[22] These individual testimonies of personal experience certainly align with narratives of immigrant success and family values. However, rather than only existing as evidence of the validity of broader claims about "Asian" work ethic (somehow brought to the United States, preserved, and then applied here), David's father's identification with "Asians" as a racial group and their claims about family also demonstrate the extent to which they themselves had come to narrate their experience through the existing US logics of Asians as a legible racial group that is characterologically successful.

These connections between social scientific claims about the role of family within model minority narratives and narratives of African American pathologization, and the internalization of those embodying them, thus constitutes a cultural genealogy that shows the conscription of family and kinship into contemporary processes of racial characterization. Neither the "African American family" nor the "Asian American family" have ever been simply apolitical demographic categories with inherent traits, but rather have been produced and continue to exist as constructions of racial power used to articulate and define these racial categories. Moynihan, Petersen, and others' critiques of black matriarchy exemplify the heteronormativity and patriarchy entrenched in visions of the family as the site of potential success and mobility. And the flipside of those critiques is precisely the invisible assumption and privileging of heteronormativity and biological reproduction in the assumed success of the Asian American model minority family. Again, this is not to say the family itself is made invisible, since these thinkers and many others have actively called on the Asian American family as a hyper-visible racialized model. However, those invocations of the model minority family only explicitly name familial "habits," "values," and "stability," while the unspoken assumption and privileged status of heteronormativity, patriarchy, and biological reproduction remained the quietly presumed prerequisite for those spoken traits.

Indeed, it is no coincidence that the heteropatriarchal family has become an essential part of the model minority as both narrative and racialization. However, the institutional investment of racial, gendered, and sexual power within the model minority has been historically obscured by this cultural figuration and essentialism. Moreover, that investment, and the family that embodies it, has been reproduced through immigration policy and its role in determining the demographic makeup of the Asian diaspora in the United States from the 1960s to the present.

The Contemporary Preference System as Technology of Kinship

How, then, does immigration policy uphold the model minority family as racial form? The model minority has functioned as a discourse of the post-1965 era of immigration through which specific forms of immigration policy have been rationalized, practiced, and naturalized in ways that become mutually reinforcing. In other words, the model minority as discourse for Asian American racial categorization (as previously discussed) reinforced and naturalized immigration policies that actively selected Asian immigrants that fit its image. As those immigrants arrived, they further embodied the model minority as an effective discourse for understanding their experiences. And the heteronormative, reproductive, and racial family structure that marks Asian American model minority racialization is the glue that binds these configurations together.

Certainly, and as discussed in the previous chapter, the family has been crucial within immigration policy since long before the model minority. Since the mid-nineteenth century, family reunification within immigration policy has been a cornerstone of immigration. As the previous chapter explored, with the passing of the Chinese Exclusion Act in 1882, one of the few ways Chinese could enter the United States was as the wife or child of a United States citizen, and paper families capitalized on those family reunification provisions in ways that actively produced new forms of kinship and circumvented immigration exclusion. Additionally, Japanese and Korean picture brides at the turn of the twentieth century used family reunification provisions to enter the United States, even after Japanese and Korean men were excluded following the 1908 Gentlemen's Agreement. And as Catherine Lee argues, "family reunification is not simply the physical uniting of immigrant family members. Family reunification is an expression of what constitutes a legitimate family, which families should be united, and whether such families should be allowed to join the nation."[23] From a legislative perspective, the construction of this "legitimate family" has always been predicated on normative notions of heterosexuality and biological reproduction.

Despite this historical prevalence of family reunification in immigration policy, the demographics of the Asian diaspora in the United States and the role of family reunification in immigration practice rapidly shifted with the repeal of the Chinese Exclusion Act in 1943 and then the passage of the Immigration and Nationality Act of 1952, which abolished racial restrictions on naturalization and provided a precursor for the later preference system. Importantly, in 1952, the elimination of the racialized category of "aliens ineligible for citizenship" (which had functioned as precedent for the exclusionary racialization of immigrants from Asia in the famous court cases *Ozawa v. United States 1922* and *United States v. Bhagat Singh Thind 1923*) had direct implications for the utilization of family reunification provisions. Even before national origins quotas were eliminated in 1965 (which many mark as the start of the liberalization of immigration), because immigration of immediate relatives of US citizens was not subject to numerical limits, the ability for Asians to naturalize as US citizens also increased the number of potential family that could join them through reunification. Indeed, in 1951, the year before the racial provision was changed, 11,462 immigrants were admitted as immediate relatives of US citizens. After the provisions ended, in 1953, that number jumped to 22,543 immigrants admitted in the same category. The number of immigrants entering in this category continued to grow every year until the quota system was eliminated with the passage of the Immigration and Nationality Act of 1965.[24]

The codification of family reunification within the contemporary preference system introduced by the Immigration and Nationality Act of 1965 marked a shift in some ways away from those earlier policies of exclusion. As Mae Ngai observes, the policy's "abolition of the national origins quota system garnered the most attention and defined the law as a progressive measure."[25] But, while the new preference system ushered in an era of rapidly increasing immigration from Asia and Latin America, it did not unequivocally transform the exclusionary ideologies that the previous decades had established. In fact, it further naturalized the continued use of numerical quotas in limiting immigration. And in reference to this seeming contradiction (between the celebration of eliminating national origins quotas while simultaneously naturalizing numerical quotas), Ngai argues that "the thinking that impelled immigration reform in the decades following World War II developed along a trajectory that combined liberal pluralism and nationalism."[26] As a result, numerical quotas became so naturalized by contemporary discourses of immigration that popular debates in US media assumed their existence and merely questioned the particular quantity and stipulations for which those quotas would include.

The language of the Immigration and Nationality Act of 1965 confirmed existing definitions of "immediate relatives" of US citizens as including "[minor-aged] children, spouses, and parents," all of whom were (and continue to be) considered non-quota immigrants and thus still not subject to numerical restrictions. However, the Act newly established the preference system that ranked the allocation of quota visas as follows:

1. ... unmarried [adult] sons or daughters of citizens of the United States...
2. ... spouses, unmarried sons or unmarried daughters of an alien lawfully admitted for permanent residence...
3. ... members of the professions, or who because of their exceptional ability in the sciences or the arts will substantially benefit prospectively the national economy, cultural interests, or welfare of the United States...
4. ... married sons or the married daughters of citizens of the United States...
5. ... brothers or sisters of citizens of the United States...
6. ... immigrants who are capable of performing specified skilled or unskilled labor, not of a temporary or seasonal nature, for which a shortage of employable and willing persons exists in the United States...
7. ... [refugees] who satisfy an Immigration and Naturalization Service officer at an examination in any non-Communist or non-Communist dominated counter...[27]

Each category included a specific percentage of the total number of allowable visas, out of 170,000 per fiscal year, which increased in 1968 to include a separate numerical cap of 120,000 visas for the admission of immigrants from the western hemisphere. In 1978, separate hemispheric limitations were dropped, and a worldwide quota was established, capping total immigration to 290,000. Following the implementation of the new system, approximately three-quarters of visas were designated for the family members of United States citizens or noncitizen permanent residents.

Media reception to the changes in immigration policy was mixed and included concerns of the rapidly changing demographics of immigration. The significant increase in immigration following the implementation of the policy was often explicitly attributed to the role of non-quota family reunification in the new system. One 1966 article published in the New York Times titled "50,000 Enter US Under New Law" featured the somewhat enigmatic subtitle "Thousands of Parents." The section quoted the State Department which claimed that, under the new policy, "Thousands of parents of adult American citizens were enabled to join their families here without restriction by numerical limitations."[28] Within the preference system, the combination of explicit prioritization of kinship relations with certain forms of professional, skilled, or in-demand labor significantly contributed to the rapid change in immigration patterns from the previous period. In addition to continuing the existing provisions for immigration of immediate relatives of US citizens (which now included naturalized Asian immigrants), the Immigration and Nationality Act of 1965 thus extended family reunification provisions to the family of noncitizen immigrant residents. Like the paper families of the earlier era but on a much larger scale, Asian immigrants quickly built migration chains through professional and kinship ties. Ngai offers the following demonstration:

> For example, a Korean war bride brought as a non-quota immigrant by her US-citizen husband could then become a naturalized citizen in three years and then bring her parents as non-quota immigrants and her siblings under the fifth preference. In turn, their spouses and children as second-preference immigrants. Similarly, a student from Taiwan who entered for postgraduate studies as a non-immigrant could, with labor certification, apply for permanent resident status and, from there, bring over relatives under the second preference.[29]

As the different categories of these examples show, ideologies of kinship and class were imbricated within the very content of immigration legislation and subsequently shaped the diaspora of contemporary Asian immigrants. Notably, circumstances of kinship and class were often *not* separate in immigration practice. Between 1966 and 1990, approximately 15% of immigrants subject to the numerical cap admitted under the preference system arrived through employment-based preferences. This occupational category for professionals accounted for a significant proportion of immigration from Asia across different countries newly including Taiwan, India, South Korea, and the Philippines.[30]

During this period, the articulation and discourse of Asia as a meaningful geographic and cultural unit also shifted in popular media and culture. Although Asia had already been a significant geographic reference within debates and legislation of immigration exclusion in the twentieth century (perhaps most explicitly reflected in the Asiatic Barred Zone Act of 1917), the new preference system and influx of immigration made "immigrants from Asia" a newly coherent and visible category of public scrutiny. For example, in 1973 the *New York Times* published an article titled "Asia Biggest Source of Brain Drain to US" that observed, "The largest single increments of scientific and technical manpower from abroad in recent years have been scientists and engineers from India and physicians from the Philippines. . . . In 1972, however, more physicians immigrated to the United States from India than from the Philippines."[31] In this description, we can see how immigration policy facilitates the convergence of skilled labor that, followed by family reunification, gave rise to an influx of immigration from Asia. What do scientists and engineers immigrating from India have to do with physicians immigrating from the Philippines? The model minority narrative might assume a cultural commonality of success, but as the piece highlights, the Immigration Act of 1965 facilitated their shared migration and the subsequent migration of their families.

Indeed, this was a period in which particular kinds of professional class migration were not only enabled by immigration policy but also incentivized and governmentally supported. For example, as Catherine Ceniza Choy describes in *Empire of Care: Nursing and Migration in Filipino American History*, government-sponsored training programs, professional recruiting, and what Choy calls a "culture of migration," wherein narratives about immigration shaped individuals' motivations to migrate abroad, facilitated the rapid increase of Filipina nurses immigrating to the United States in the second half of the twentieth century. Furthermore, as Choy describes, scholarly narratives that reduce migration during this period solely to individual choice or to the search for upward mobility actively obfuscate more complex histories of colonialism and imperialism in favor of US exceptionalism and benevolence.[32] Similarly, narrating the liberalization of immigration policy as unconnected to the racialization and class figuration of Asian Americans as the model minority during this period also obfuscates the ways that immigration policy and the preference system participated in the creation of the emerging Asian American family as model minority.

By the 1960s and 1970s, the model minority already functioned as a discourse through which newly immigrating Asian diasporic families were expected to fit. Within this narrative, the transformation of the "Asian" family into the "Asian *American*" family was ideologically predicated on its expected successful assimilation, educational and professional achievement, and upward socioeconomic mobility. In other words, the very racialization process by which Asian immigrants were made legible (as Asian American) within a US racial schema was defined and measured against the fulfillment of the model minority. And as demonstrated by the organization of the preference system, Asian immigrant families entered the United States from an often-predetermined location in relation to heteronormativity, labor, and class, that facilitated the reproduction of that upwardly mobile class composition.

In this way, the preference system as a technology of kinship actively and materially participated in the production of the contemporary Asian American family through the standards of the model minority: a heteronormative reproductive family provided the opportunity for socioeconomic success and inclusion into the nation by way of American exceptionalism, under the condition of assimilation and adherence to that liberal (and later neoliberal) multiculturalism. This hegemonic racial narrative of a coherent "Asian family" and of "Asian family values" was then projected onto subsequent families of immigrants and refugees entering through the preference system, and served as an explanation for the policy's perceived success. As I discuss in the following section, these model minority narratives of Asian American family and kinship continued to be projected onto the preference system and subsequent immigration from Asia.

Family Reunification, Refugee Migration, and the Model Minority

While the preference system helps account for observable trends in Asian American educational achievement and socioeconomic success beyond essentialist narratives of culture and family values, it also contributed to what Lisa Lowe describes as the contradictions of capitalism, Asian American immigration, and racialization. Lowe highlights the predominance of immigration after 1965 from countries like South Korea, the Philippines, South Vietnam, and Cambodia and argues immigration from these countries "differs from that of the earlier migrations from China and Japan, for it embodies the displacement from Asian societies in the aftermath of war and colonialism to a United States with whose sense of national identity the immigrants are in contradiction precisely because of that history."[33] Indeed, the preference system and subsequent legislation facilitating refugee immigration offered opportunities to emphasize the benevolence of American exceptionalism in the face of displacements for which it had caused.

As the family reunification and labor provisions of the preference system produced a professional-class demographic of Asian Americans, the family reunification provisions combined with established and emerging refugee provisions also contributed to a bifurcation in the class composition of Asian diasporic families in the United States. Lowe characterizes this division as "a heterogeneous Asian immigrant population made up of both low-wage, service-sector and manufacturing laborers and ... 'middle-class professionals,'" and further theorizes what she calls the "white-collar proletariat," "which describes US capital's demotion and manipulation of skilled labor in the period of transition from entrepreneurial to corporate capitalism after the 1960s."[34] This particular form of proletarianization under US capitalism (and eventually neoliberalism) thus also marked Asian American racialization, whereby, regardless of socioeconomic mobility or wealth, Asian Americans were othered from the professionalized status defined by the White middleclass norm.

Because of the specific convergence of family and refugee migration within immigration policy, the preference categories during this period also actively shaped this process of racialized proletarianization. Lowe further emphasizes the role of the state in this co-constitutive process, arguing that ". . . legal institutions *reproduce* the capitalist relations of production as *racialized gendered relations* and are therefore symptomatic *and* determining of the relations of production themselves"[35] In this context, legal institutions such as the combination of preference system categories, reproduced "the capitalist relations of production as *racialized gendered relations*," or in this case, the proletarianization of Asian American labor in ways that were and continue to be implicitly conceived as heteronormative and racially other from White American labor. Materially, this manifested in the diverse Asian immigrant workforce of low-wage, professional-class, and refugee workers arriving in the United States, not as the itinerant single bachelors of the nineteenth and early twentieth centuries, but as laboring *families* whose unification and maintenance had been actively selected and produced by the preference system. And thus, this legal codification of the heteronormative and biological family was also "symptomatic *and* determining" of the "relations of production themselves."

In other words, the existing structure of liberal capitalism, already contingent on the labors of nuclear, heteronormative, biological family, both underpinned and was perpetuated by the preference system that further naturalized the Asian immigrant and refugee family as nuclear, heteronormative, and biological. Furthermore, the result of the preference system's implementation under liberal capitalism was precisely the class bifurcation observed by Lowe and others, wherein middleclass professional immigrant families embodied the model minority (both intentionally and inadvertently perpetuating it) while there continued to be a significant number of Asian immigrant and refugee families that were low-wage, service-sector, and manufacturing laborers frequently from countries directly impacted by American colonialism and imperialism abroad.

In this context, not only did immigration policy predicate refugee subject formation but it also functioned as a site for constructing the refugee family through the existing logics of Asian American model minority racialization. Amid the ongoing wars in Southeast Asia in the

1970s, efforts to increase aid to refugees culminated in the passing of the Refugee Act of 1980, which redefined the category "refugee," increased the admissions of refugees from Southeast Asia, and sought to establish procedures and federal support for refugee resettlement programs in the United States. The 1980 Act relied, in part, on the hegemony of family reunification in immigration policy that had been codified by the preference system. While the 1965 Act included the relatively small seventh preference category in reference to refugees (allowing 6% of the 170,000 cap) it offered precedent for the subsequent legislation regarding the migration of refugees in the 1970s and 1980s. The Refugee Act of 1980 explicitly amended the Migration and Refugee Assistance Act of 1962 and the Immigration and Nationality Act of 1965 in its objective to "provide a permanent and systematic procedure for the admission . . . of refugees of special humanitarian concern[.]"[36] Quickly, by 1982, refugee immigration from Asia peaked with over 130,000 refugees and asylees from Asia admitted and granted permanent resident status, comprising 84% of all refugee immigrations that year.[37] Between 1980 and 1993, the total immigration from Southeast Asia exceeded that of immigration from the Philippines, China, Korea, or India individually, which were each the subsequent successive top countries for immigration from Asia to the United States during this period.[38]

As Yến Lê Espiritu argues, US refugee policy constituted "a key site for the production of Vietnamese refugees as grief-stricken objects marked for rescue and the United States as the ideal refuge for the 'persecuted and uprooted' refugees."[39] Even the term "refugee" situated the subjectivity of Southeast Asian diasporic individuals and families within a relationship of US militarism and liberal imagination. And within this ideological production of the refugee subject, family "unity" and reunification represented a crucial aspect of this "rescue" as well as the language through which the United States could further enact its identity as "refuge." This occurred in both the language of the legislation as well as media narratives about refugee migration.

In the language of the Refugee Act of 1980, the spouse or children of a refugee who qualified for admission were also "entitled to the same admission status as such refugee if accompanying, or following to join, such refugee."[40] Congruent with the previously established preference system, the 1980 act gave the Attorney General the ability to waive various provisions at their discretion "for humanitarian purposes, to assure family unity, or when it is otherwise in the public interest."[41] Family reunification thus also became imbricated into the legislative structure of the refugee diaspora and contributed to the discursive figuration of refugees *as* Asian immigrant families. Southeast Asian refugees arriving in the 1970s through the 1990s were thus thrust into the existing racial landscape of the model minority as Asian American racialization.

Amid cultural debates about the validity and racism of the model minority "myth," the newly arriving refugee diaspora became the site of both anxiety around the model minority's constructedness and efforts to reaffirm its reality. As Linh Thủy Nguyễn argues, family served as "a site of cultural capital and value" that shaped "the racialization of Vietnamese as yet to be Asian Americans consistent with 'positive' model minority racialization."[42] Nguyễn examines sociological knowledge production as a site for "naturalizing refugees as immigrants."[43] And the same instrumentalization of the family as a mode for refugee racialization occurred in popular media narratives as well. However, this process of narrating Vietnamese and other Southeast Asian refugees through the model minority was uneven, reflecting these anxieties about the model minority's effectiveness in racially categorizing the new Asian diaspora. Exemplified by headlines like "Asian Poor Neglected" in the *Los Angeles Times*, news media expressed concern that Southeast Asian refugees did not exhibit the same kinds of socioeconomic and educational achievement that East and South Asian immigrants had.[44]

In another example, *Fortune* published an article in 1986 titled "America's Super Minority," in which Southeast Asian refugees were referred to as "The Super Minority's Poor Cousins." The sidebar claimed, "experts worry that second-wave refugees may remain mired in poverty and unemployment." The section quotes a social work professor comparing Hmong refugees to "Appalachian whites" and a Berkeley research scientist claiming "it doesn't pay for refugees with families to work," followed by the suggestion that Southeast Asian refugees might rely on welfare instead of getting jobs.[45] In this context, Southeast Asian refugees represented the existing anxieties about race and class suggesting the underlying *instability* of racial categorization based on previously essentialized cultural traits. By comparing them to poor Appalachian Whites who had failed to achieve the class normativity of Whiteness, and evoking the already racialized fear of welfare exploitation that had been sutured to the Black matriarch in that very Reagan era, this anxiety was embodied precisely in the perceived potential for Southeast Asian refugees to fail to live up to the standards set by their racial categorization. In other words, the possibility that they might not live up to the model minority as the marker of Asian American racial categorization posed a potential problem to their belonging in US society.

As previously discussed, the actual disparities in socioeconomic success were in large part a result of the differing immigration preference provisions that prioritized the immigration of professional class labor in some cases and refugee migration in others. However, as a structural circumstance that betrayed the geopolitics of American liberal ideology and imperialism, immigration policy as a cause of disparity was markedly minimal in discussions by news media about Southeast Asian upwards mobility and lack thereof. Despite this anxiety about the existing racial order, the premise of family reunification, set by the earlier preference system and that continued in the context of refugee immigration, offered liberal ideology the potential for continuity between the professional class diaspora that embodied the model minority and the poor and refugee diasporas that had the potential to undercut it. By framing refugees on a teleological track towards model minority achievement, both liberal ideologies of American exceptionalism and the legitimacy of the model minority could be affirmed.

By this logic, newly arriving Southeast Asian refugees might *begin* by relying on government assistance and struggling to rise above the poverty line, but one must start somewhere to pull oneself up by their bootstraps, and as they continued to assimilate and learn English, they too, would achieve success. For example, a 1979 *New York Times* article titled "Boat People' Find a Haven in the State: Haven for Refugees" tells the story of Ai-Linh Huynh along these very threads of family migration and upward achievement. Beginning with her journey "after five days on a small crowded and leaking boat and nine months in a refugee camp," Mrs. Huynh was able to come to New Jersey with her mother and three sons under "the aegis of a United States Government family reunification program." However, according to the piece, "before they can integrate themselves into American life, Indochinese refugees need financial aid and other guidance." Mrs. Huynh is then quoted emphasizing her eagerness for her children to go to school and describing schools in communist Vietnam as "teaching politics, not knowledge."[46] While narratives like this one highlighted the lived experience of some of those who migrated as refugees, they also often eschewed structural critiques of American militarism abroad in favor of more optimistic human interest pieces that produced refugee families as (potentially) appropriate subjects for model minority racialization. In another example, published in 1985 by the *Wall Street Journal* titled, "Indochinese Refugees Adapt Quickly in US, Using Survival Skills," the author explained, "The values they came with—a dedication to family, education and thrift—are cited as a main reason [for their quick integration into American society] by people who have observed refugees."[47] Again, the language of "values" and the family situate the refugee diaspora within broader discourses of model minority racialization. And even for the more concerned *Fortune* piece about "The Super Minority's Poor Cousins," the sidebar concludes, "Indochinese refugees may eventually solve their problem themselves by becoming assimilated.... Moreover, following a classic pattern of Asian American adaption, the Vietnamese are forming mutual aid societies to help themselves launch their own small businesses."[48]

Reflecting what Mimi Thi Nguyen calls the "gift of freedom" (which I will further discuss in the next section), this kind of liberal ideology rooted the integration of new immigrants into Asian American racial narrative as the key to Southeast Asian refugee success. Because family reunification provisions in immigration policy influenced who arrived, the heteronormative reproductive family thus became the stronghold in which to shore up their place within the model minority. Circularly, refugee families as immigrant families thus reinforced model minority racialization as rooted in normative family structure. And the naturalization of that normative family structure (through the prioritization of family reunification) kept refugee families within the bounds of that process of racialization.

Racial Debts to Family and Nation

The combination of family reunification preferences with other categories and provisions for immigration from Asia produced the heteronormative reproductive Asian American family as an emblem of model minority racialization. Materially, the preference system and the precedent it set dictated who and in what kinship organization Asian immigrants would be admitted and thus transformed from "Asian" to "Asian American." Ideologically, that transformation was contingent upon the integration of those subjects into a racial category in part defined by measurement and (potential) fulfillment of the model minority. As a technology that structured the organization of power and resources, the preference system not only produced a specifically Asian American formation of family but also engendered that family with the racial debts of liberal and emerging neoliberal ideologies. Invoking these debts to family and nation, as theorized by Nguyen through the "gift of freedom," and by Ninh through the "debt-bound daughter," I conclude this chapter by highlighting the reliance of those debts on the embodied and ideological figure of the model minority family.

The history of Asian American racialization has long been burdened with expectations and debts of gratitude that have been, first, foundational to the national self-conception of the United States as a "land of opportunity," second, deftly integrated into early formulations of the model minority, and third, further amplified in the positioning of the United States as a site of refuge. This is quite concretely and dramatically demonstrated in an interview with controversial figure S. I. Hayakawa, published in the 1971 *Roots: An Asian American Reader*. Born in Canada to Japanese immigrant parents, Hayakawa established his career as an academic in the United States, most notably at San Francisco State College (now San Francisco State University), where he was named acting President in November 1968 during the student strike to which he was very publicly opposed. During this time, he was quoted frequently in Asian American publications representing pro-US military, assimilationist, and anti-activist views. In 1973, he changed his political affiliation from Democratic to Republican, and like Patrick Moynihan, later went on to be elected as a senator.

While Hayakawa did not necessarily identify as liberal, his public conflicts with Asian American radicals in the 1960s and 1970s represented the tension between challenging the racial structures of the United States at the time and the discourses of liberalism that aimed to justify them. In the interview published in *Roots*, Hayakawa was asked

"Do you believe that the Vietnam War has any impact on the image of the Asian American community now?" He responded:

> No, but here is something that bothers me . . . Why should Asian Americans say the same things about the Vietnam War that White people do? Because if you talk to a Korean from Korea or a Filipino from the Philippines, they are damn grateful for the American intervention in Vietnam. South Koreans like the South Vietnamese, are deeply, deeply grateful for the American intervention in South Vietnam and so are all the Filipinos I know. Now, you guys are Asian Americans. You say the same things as the SDS [Students for a Democratic Society] and the White radicals. That makes me so damn sick. Why don't you have your own eyes? You are not white, you are not Jewish intellectuals from New York. But you are aping the same things that Jewish intellectuals are saying.[49]

Hayakawa's impassioned insistence that Asian Americans are "not White" and "not Jewish intellectuals" as a stance against involvement in radical politics exemplifies the racial expectation previously discussed for Asian Americans that was emerging during this period. The implication here is that Asian Americans must shore up the model minority as representative of their racial categorization. According to this logic, then, to act outside of the model minority (through radical politics or a lack of gratitude) meant to act outside of Asian American racial characterization and thus meant to act like a different race.

Hayakawa's invocation of gratitude relied on the assumption of benevolence in US colonialism and military involvement in South Korea, the Philippines, and Vietnam. And that benevolence has been sutured to the gratitude that is then owed by Asian Americans in the United States. This geopolitical and potentially intergenerational assumption (that Asians in Asia are properly grateful, and Asian Americans are led astray by their ingratitude) also implicitly reinforces ideologies that the views and experiences of first-generation immigrants and Asians in Asia are both politically separate from *and* simultaneously more authoritative or authentic than the views of second- and third-generation, or self-identified, Asian Americans. While many Asian American publications and individuals actively used Hayakawa as an example of the precise political positions they were combatting, Hayakawa's intertwining of gratitude, racial identity judged through political involvement, and the meanings of racial difference reflect the broader entanglement of Asian American racialization with the debt of the model minority.[50] In this context, the expected success and gratitude of the model minority can be used to both other Asian Americans from the racial marginalization of other communities of color while simultaneously maintaining their otherness from Whites.[51]

Hayakawa's expectation of gratitude as an appropriate and prescribed racialized affect for Asian Americans again demonstrates an example of Nguyen's "gift of freedom and the debt that follows."[52] Nguyen specifically situates the gift of freedom as it defines refugee subjectivity by expanding on Derrida's articulation of the gift as "impossible" because "the gift as the transfer of a possession from one to another shapes a relation between giver and recipient that engenders a debt, which is to say that the gift belongs to an economy that voids its openhanded nature."[53] The gift of freedom defines the terms of refugee subjectivity within a dialectical and indebted relationship with their "refuge," and characterizes this relationship as one of power: "the gift as a *power over*, and its duration *over time*."[54] The freedom that has been gifted, too, is fraught by liberal empire. Nguyen reminds us, "Indeed, an attachment to freedom is foundational to liberalism's heightened attention to its presence or lapse, an attention that thereby continually commits free peoples to sustain or manufacture it in all directions, across the globe."[55] Rather than attempt to concretize or abstract its conceptualization, Nguyen understands freedom as that which needs to be continually reaffirmed, rearticulated, and reproduced by liberal empire in order to rationalize its own actions.

It is precisely through subjectification of the Southeast Asian, *as* refugee subject defined by the gift of freedom, that the ethnically distinct Vietnamese, Hmong, Cambodian, or Laotian subject is reconstructed by the racial meaning of US liberal empire: first as "Asian" othered by and subject to US military violence (rationalized by liberal notions of freedom), and then as "Asian American" supposedly gifted freedom (and thus access to the success associated with the model minority) through that same US liberalism and militarism. Thus, the gift of freedom as a participant in the subject formation of the Southeast Asian refugee participates in their racialization as Asian *American* subject, a transformation that does not escape the debt inherent to the gift of freedom but rather sutures it to the debts of the model minority.

As mentioned at the start of this chapter, these model minority debts are also experienced by Asian Americans in embodied familial terms. Ninh configures the model minority within the "debt-bound" relations of familial discourse, often evoked by the language of "filial obligation" and its relation to the Asian immigrant family. Here, the family functions as a crucial site in which the fantasy of belonging and racial coherence are embodied through the model minority. Or, as Ninh asserts, "An effective understanding of the Asian American subject's relation to the nation must therefore come to terms with the immigrant family as that nation's intermediary and agent."[56] In this context, the second-generation Asian American daughter becomes brought into earlier models of "child-as-capital-investment" previously applied to sons, in which children are seen as owing a debt to their parents and expected to produce profit both literally and figuratively.

This is also a familiar discourse: filial obligation, immigrant parent sacrifice, making the family proud. And it fits neatly into contemporary neoliberalism as, what Wendy Brown calls, "a form of governmentality" and its involvement in "extending and disseminating market values to all institutions and social action."[57] In this context, as Ninh contends, individual Asian American children of immigrants are configured as market actors in debt to their parents. And this debt can only be fulfilled through the individual achievement of the model minority, for which parents and children each play their roles. Furthermore, this governmentality of neoliberalism, that configures the model minority family as the site of neoliberal embodiment and economic participation for both parent and child is, importantly, racialized in their material and discursive application to what it means to be "Asian" in the first place.

On a national ideological scale, the family is thus a crucial site upon which Asian Americans owe this debt to the nation economically, reproductively, and culturally. Whether arrived at through immigration via the original preference system or through refugee status, the United States has produced itself as the source from which the gift of freedom, inclusion, and opportunity are bestowed. Economically, the professional preference category *and* the anxieties around the refugee family relying on welfare for too long reveal the debt the model minority family is expected to repay through their literal economic labor. Immigrant families are both implicitly and explicitly admitted with the expectations that they participate in the United States capitalist economy as laborers. Reproductively, because the family itself has been historically and contemporaneously used as a metaphor for the nation, and configured as heterosexual, able-bodied, and biologically reproductive, the Asian American family is also indebted to uphold and affirm these norms through its literal reproduction. For example, the common tropes and suspicions around "green card" marriages demonstrate the ways in which family and kinship are very specifically policed for immigrants to the United States to uphold the presumed sanctity and authenticity of normative legal marriage and heteronormative reproduction. Finally, culturally, for Asian American families, this debt to nation is also expected to be fulfilled through a collective reinforcement of the model minority. We are expected to materially embody and outwardly attest that: indeed, we are not threatening the heteroreproductive norm of nuclear family; indeed, we are racially distinct in our success; indeed, the United States has provided us with opportunity.

As Ninh reminds us, the actualizations of this debt-fulfillment are less important than the structures of feeling that situate the Asian diasporic family in a racialized relationship by which being "Asian American" is measured. How many of us have felt like "bad Asians" when we failed to embody the model minority in one way or another? Indeed, the model minority as debt-bound racialization operates as a kind of affective governmentality that conscripts the family in collecting on those debts. And it is within this affective register, of what is both materially achievable or aspirational and what is felt in the experience of that aspiration (or failure to aspire), that both the gift of freedom and the model minority have such power to define the embodied experience of our racial categorization. Congruously, the family as the literal and figurative originary site of both love and self-conception brings together these conflicting affects within which we desire and are attached to the very prescriptions that police our behavior and dictate our identities in the first place.

Contrary to popular belief that such images can be dispelled with the debunking of stereotype or myth, the investment in the Asian American heterosexual, reproductive, successful immigrant family runs through the very immigration policy and preference system that has facilitated its construction. The contemporary preference system and its effects on family reunification have functioned as a technology that has produced the model minority family as an embodiment of Asian American racialization and its heteronormative expectations. And, as the following chapters explore, as the meaning of race has rapidly shifted in the United States and we find ourselves in a culture invested in neoliberal colorblindness and multiculturalism, the racialization of kinship, too, has taken new forms. Nonetheless, efforts to dislodge the model minority at its roots are crucial to the rearticulation of Asian American racial identity from one of debt to one of solidarity.

3

Photographic Conceptions

Kinship Formation in Transnational Adoption from Asia

In the 2004 series finale of the popular television show *Sex and the City*, now newly relevant by the franchise's 2021 series revival *And Just Like That*, preppy protagonist Charlotte York finally discovers she and her husband Harry Goldenblatt are going to adopt a baby after struggling to conceive. In the heartfelt scene, she is unpacking a dinner of Chinese takeout when he walks in the door of their Park Avenue apartment. Jokingly, Charlotte calls from the dining room, "Hi honey, I'm a bad wife! I ordered Chinese!" Opening a manila envelope as he walks into the room, Harry says in disbelief, "I got something from China too . . . They're giving us a baby." In response to her shocked reaction, he continues, "I guess God remembered our address. We get her in six months." Harry then pulls out a photograph showing a Chinese baby leaning against a soft white background wearing a red shirt and pink pants. Charlotte takes the image in her hand and looks at Harry with tears in her eyes. Nodding and full of emotion, she says, "That's our baby. I know it. That's really our baby!" Together these new expecting parents embrace, cheeks pressed together, looking at the photograph of *their* daughter.

The mid-2000s marked a contemporary zenith in the visibility and celebration of the multiracial family in American culture, characterized by the popularization of transnational adoption both in practice and in media narratives like this one. In 2005, adoption from China reached its peak, comprising approximately thirty-five percent of all transnational adoptions to the United States that year.[1] And this growing trend was reflected in television, film, and advertisements like the John Hancock ad of a lesbian couple at the airport with their newly adopted daughter, as analyzed by David Eng in *The Feeling of Kinship: Queer Liberalism and the Racialization of Intimacy*.[2] While Charlotte's experience offered a fictionalized narrative, it also reflected a normative adoption practice: the introduction of the adopted child into the family through an encounter with a photograph. Still common today, expecting adoptive parents receive a "referral" for a specific child, which includes a photograph and additional information. In both real-life practices of adoptive families and fictional representations of them, these referral photographs serve as important memories of the early days of family formation.

At the same time, the incorporation of the Asian child into the (usually) White family is also a site upon which racialization occurs, in what Catherine Ceniza Choy calls "global family making" or the process "involving the decisions made and actions taken by people who create and sustain a family by consciously crossing national and often racial borders."[3] While adoption from mainland China is a relatively recent phenomenon that began in the 1990s, transnational adoption from Asia has long been a part of twentieth-century American and Asian American history.[4] In the second half of the twentieth century, Americans adopted Japanese, Korean, and Vietnamese "war orphans," many of mixed racial parentage and some that did have biological kin in their countries of birth.[5] And adoption from Korea and Vietnam continued through the 1970s and 1980s, even after US military occupation in these nations officially ended. Throughout this long Cold War period, American families with adopted Asian children came to visually represent a form of US humanitarianism that simultaneously reified forms of racialized, sexualized, and gendered global power. Transnational adoption from Asia marked and enacted a shift of American imperialism *from* military occupation and explicit violence *to* the exertion of "soft power" or influence through cultural diplomacy and international relations.[6] This shift has extended into the contemporary moment and throughout global circuits that include transnational and transracial adoption from countries in Africa, South and Southeast Asia, and Central and South America.

Adoption from mainland China officially began in 1992 when the People's Republic of China enacted the Adoption Law of the People's Republic of China, which opened the doors for international adoption and was a response to the increased availability of orphaned infants as a result of China's one-child policy. As Kay Johnson writes about abandonment of infant Chinese girls in the 1990s and early 2000s, despite common stereotypes about ancient Chinese traditions, "son preference," and the figure of the "unwanted Chinese girl," many of the infants that were eventually adopted internationally were relinquished "under conditions of strong external pressure to limit births under threats of severe punishments . . ." and were actively wanted by their birth families, who made what Johnson characterizes oxymoronically as a "coerced choice."[7] Furthermore, Johnson shows how "adoption regulations and laws that sought to suppress customary domestic adoption . . . contributed significantly to the conditions that gave rise to international adoption by channeling a large pool of adoptable healthy infants into the hands of the government rather than allowing them to find homes with local families that wanted to adopt them."[8] And this shift towards transnational rather than local adoption fit with the shifting geopolitical landscape of the period, in which China was seen as globalizing and modernizing following the reform and "opening-up" of the post-Cultural Revolution era.

The years between 1992 and the peak of transnational adoptions from China in 2005 also reflect a distinct period of American multiculturalism and transnational adoption in which racial difference was not only embraced but also spoken about openly and valued as a global project of mobility in what Jodi Melamed has coined "neoliberal multiculturalism."[9] Not only was this era marked by the economic restructuring of global capitalism but also the emergence of neoliberalism as what Wendy Brown has described as a "political rationality" and form of governmentality in the Foucauldian sense.[10] Of this entangled cultural context, Thuy Linh Nguyen Tu also writes that during this period, "At a time when America's economic losses were being tied to Asia's economic gains, Americans were continually reminded not of their distance from the East but their connections to it."[11] Tu describes this tension as a kind of "inescapable intimacy" that becomes even further reified in the context of transnational adoption from China.[12] And the integration of Chinese infants into White American families served as another emblem of the continued "opening up" of China in the post-Cultural Revolution era, the globalization of the United States as an economic world power, and the continuation of transnational and transracial adoption which has long been entangled with the stratification of race and gender.

Historical and cultural analyses like that of Eng, Choy, and Jodi Kim have shown how transnational adoption as a practice encompasses not only the development of US military, imperialist, and neoliberal engagement with Asia but also a contemporary diaspora of racialized immigration to the United States and other Euro-North American countries.¹³ Complementing these critiques, ethnographic accounts like those of Eleana J. Kim, Sara K. Dorow, and Andrea Louie demonstrate how ideologies of race and gender are incorporated into the material practices of adoptive parents and adoptees in uneven and often unconscious ways.¹⁴ And although scholarship produced by adoptees critically theorizing transnational adoption has grown, primarily from the Korean adoptee diaspora in the work of Kim Park Nelson, Kimberly D. McKee, SooJin Pate, and others, many in the adoption community outside of academia do not see themselves through the terms of social and cultural analysis.¹⁵ It is within these varied theorizations and embodiments of adoption that this chapter asks, what are the material and affective practices by which racial and gendered subjectification through incorporation into the adoptive family occur? In other words, how is it that race and gender are made meaningful within the experiences of adoptive families regardless of individuals' awareness of them?

To explore these questions, a theorization of referral photography refocuses our attention on the materials and narratives that make up the "stuff" of transnational and transracial adoptive kinship. Charlotte's narrative provides a culturally familiar image of adoption that highlights the particular affective agency that objects like a photograph carry within the family formation process. And, as the accounts that follow demonstrate, photography operates as a technology of kinship to create emergent modes of relation shaped by the racialized and gendered conditions of transnational and transracial adoption from Asia. In this context, photography not only records or represents family and kinship but actively participates in its construction in ways that reflect the organization of power within and beyond the adoption process. Furthermore, as a technology of kinship, photography contributes to and demonstrates the process of racialization and racial subjectification that, like in the previous chapter, transforms *Asian* into *Asian American*. Once again, the family and its formation function as the sites of this racial categorization and legibility in the United States context.

Photography also specifically operates as a technology of kinship insofar as it acts on and through individuals in ways that produce and reproduce the very meaning of kinship, race, and nation. Theorizing photography and memory, Marianne Hirsch suggests that despite the historical specificities of photographic practices, one constant throughout the twentieth century "is the existence of a familial mythology, . . . an image shaping the desire of the individual living in a social group. . . . It survives by means of its narrative and imaginary power, a power that photographs have a particular capacity to tap." As Hirsch notes, photographs mediate the "space of contradiction between the myth of the ideal family and the lived reality of family life."[16] This contradiction is not only a tension between an imagined and embodied intimacy but also between the myth of family as a positive symbol of the nation and the reality of the family as imbricated in global histories of trauma, injustice, and exclusion. By moving things like adoption referral photographs out of the category of passive tools for human agency and considering how they can actively create new forms of interaction and encounter, we can more clearly see family and kinship as a contested site of racial and gendered meaning.[17]

Because referral photography is used across domestic and transnational adoption practices, adoption from Asia also offers a case study through which to understand how systems like photography can function as a technology of kinship more broadly. Crucial within the family formation process, I argue that referral photography participates in the specific shared racialization of Asian (American) adoptees, wherein, despite their individual national and ethnic origins, adoptees become subsumed under their racial categorization as Asian American. This is not to say that adoptees themselves all consider themselves to be Asian American. In fact, some even identify as White due to their cultural understanding of race and affiliation with their White adoptive families. However, they become racialized as Asian in the dominant schema of racial categorization in the United States. The narratives of this chapter thus bring together engagements with referral photography in adoption from both South Korea and China, two of the most visible and demographically significant diasporas of US adoption from Asia. And together, they show how referral photography participates in the racialization of the Asian adoptee as a subjectivity through the formation of adoptive kinship.

This chapter begins with archival accounts of how adoptive families engaged with referral photography as adoption from China was beginning to increase in the 1990s and early 2000s using the archives of the community organization Families with Children from China of Greater New York, Connecticut, and New Jersey (FCCNY).[18] Founded in 1993 by a small group of newly adoptive parents, FCCNY was one of the first community organizations promoting adoption from China and supporting families adopting in the wake of China's one-child policy. In January 1994, FCCNY began a regular newsletter published four times a year that featured the stories and testimonies of adoptive parents as well as pieces written by or excerpted from adoption professionals. For many at the time, the 1990s newsletters actively participated in the family formation process by advising prospective parents and offering ways of interpreting affective, logistical, and bureaucratic experiences. Referral photographs were a recurring theme in the newsletters, one that gestured towards the complexity of transnational and transracial adoption as a mode of family formation. To supplement these early narratives written solely by adoptive parents and other adult professionals, I also conducted oral history interviews with the adopted daughter of one of the group's founders, as well as four other adoptees who were adopted during this period and were members of FCCNY.[19] These interviews provided additional narrative interpretations that contextualized the newsletters as an archive, the close reading of the film included subsequently in this chapter, and observations I have made as a member and researcher in the adoption community over the last ten years.

To further explore the role of narrative and the expansive ways in which kinship can be conceived and crafted through referral photography, I conclude with an analysis of the journey of adoptee and filmmaker Deann Borshay Liem in her 2010 second autoethnographic film *In the Matter of Cha Jung Hee*. Following her first film *First Person Plural* which was released in 2000, *In the Matter of Cha Jung Hee* offers one meditation on the use of what could be considered referral photography to search, not for her birth family (which she found in her first film), but rather for the stranger whose identity she was given as a child in order to be adopted to the United States. As she searches for Cha Jung Hee, she discovers another form of kinship that might be possible, produced by photography and the global circuits of transnational adoption.

Together, these texts and narratives demonstrate how material and affective encounters with referral photographs produce new forms of kinship shaped by ideologies and institutions of race, gender, and nation.

And rather than make ethnographic claims, I aim to show the ways in which the very act of telling and retelling stories about encounters with photography in newsletters, personal accounts, and film can expand the social and affective possibilities of adoptive kinship formation in racialized and gendered ways. A single referral photograph has the agency to affect and effect kinship, to reproduce relations of power, and to provoke new questions.

Photographic Conceptions

Without an embodied experience of conception or birth, adoptive parents have had to make sense of their family's beginnings in ways that are different from those with biological children. In addition to serving as a rich narrative archive of individuals' experiences, the FCCNY newsletters also participated in the family formation process for many.[20] As one adoptive parent wrote in the April 1995 issue, "Maybe that's the big adoption difference. We have each other. Since family is about what is familiar, I feel an affinity with you parents who are on a journey so much like my own. We not only have each other, we need each other." As this author articulates, the community itself formed a kind of tertiary kinship based on a shared experience. She describes family as "about what is familiar" and understands the similarities of adoptive parenting "journeys" as a form of affinity.

First published in January 1994, the FCCNY newsletter was one of the first ways that members of the community connected with one another. While there were a few general online message board communities about adoption (some of which were later referenced in newsletters), the centrality of Internet forums had yet to become mainstream. Only four pages, the first newsletter exclaimed on the front cover, "China is Open!" quoting the sign above the organization's table at a national adoption conference held in November 1993.[21] This short issue outlined the basic framework for newsletters to come, featuring information for "those who are preparing to adopt," legal advice, and "cultural" events and resources for families. The newsletters proceeded with four issues per year and, in their early iteration, capture something unique about the growth of this community: they offer an honest and often unflinching look at adoptive parents, made by and for each other, in the process of creating a community and trying to make sense of their own family beginnings. One mother that adopted from China described,

> Dealing with our kids sleeping and feeding routines and learning how to balance parenting in our busy lives is ... pretty ordinary stuff. On the other hand, conceiving through apostiles and photocopying, getting on a plane to fly 10,000 miles to a place where we don't speak the language and then to join our lives with children about whom we know next to nothing makes us daring.

The author refers to her own family formation as a type of "conception," however, rather than biological reproduction, this conception is one constituted by the embodied social, logistical, and bureaucratic practices that make adoption possible. And thus, before the moment of physical encounter with their children-to-be, the referral photograph became another object through which individuals embody and actualize parental identity.

As ethnographer Jon Telfer describes, the referral photograph in both domestic and transnational adoption practices "signals the imminence of shared history."[22] Telfer elaborates from his interviews with adoptive parents, "... upon confrontation with a photograph of the allocated child, a number of participants felt transformed into the realms of parenthood, loving, wanting and feeling strangely connected to the photograph of a child or baby who was to become their permanent parental responsibility."[23] Situating this practice specifically in the context of transnational adoption from China, Sara Dorow builds on Telfer's account, describing how the referral photograph "marks the possibility of the child becoming real to her parent(s) across the layers of geography that separate them."[24] Neither Telfer nor Dorow discuss the role of the photograph in the racialization of the transnationally adopted child. However, both describe what Dorow calls "rituals of using images to call kinship into being," including activities such as carrying the photograph around, making multiple copies, or enlarging it.[25]

I similarly found these practices described in the FCCNY newsletters and accounts and extend this theorization to bring together the different roles that photography plays in both producing new forms of kinship *and* racializing and gendering the adopted child. In one example, Leah described to me how her referral photograph became embedded in a collective family memory:

> I had really spikey hair in the photo. My mom blew it up really big and she put it in my crib. And then she gave one to my dad, so he showed everyone at his work. And she had it in various places around the house. But it was really big in my crib, so it was like the baby was there. And she'd go in at night and look at it! . . . It was like my parents were nesting or preparing a nest, getting ready.[26]

Like the scene of Charlotte looking at the image of her baby-to-be, stories like this one ask us to reconcile the entrance of the photograph into the family album even before the entrance of the child into the family. The materiality of the image was made meaningful to Leah's parents as it was magnified and reproduced, positioned in "various places around the house" and shown to people at work. And while in the present the photograph continued to represent an important memory in the family album (what Dorow calls "a piece of identity narrative"), in the moments before Leah physically arrived in her family, it functioned quite differently. Rather than a memento suturing past and present, it functioned as an inception creating the affective conditions upon which she could be brought into the family.

In this context, referral photographs were not only doing representational work to identify the child, but they also became material objects with agency in the process of family formation. In another example, Kelly, who was adopted in 1995, similarly recalled a family memory,

> The home videos that my dad made leading up to their trip, were just so ridiculous! . . . My dad photocopied [the referral photograph] like eight times and put them in different frames around the house and then filmed the photograph with dramatic Chinese music in the background and just panned to each one in different rooms.

I will return to the striking detail about Chinese music in the following section. However, specifically in relation to the role of the image in material practice, Kelly's father's act of replicating and filming the referral photograph further demonstrates the ways in which family formation can be constituted through a multitude of photographic, affective, and imaginative practices. Rather than functioning simply as a surrogate for the child, the referral photograph does a particular kind of work that highlights the performativity of photography relative to embodied reality. It's purpose is not to substitute or stand in for the child, but rather to anticipate and imagine the child within the family. And thus, kinship in this context is embodied through a relationship to a photograph before it is embodied through a relationship to a physical person. In lieu of biological reproduction, the reproduction of the referral photograph becomes a way of (re)producing and imagining kinship itself.

In *Camera Lucida*, Roland Barthes grapples with the *in*ability of photography to fully represent or capture an embodied past. He describes looking at photographs of his late mother,

> Photography thereby compelled me to perform a painful labor; straining toward the essence of her identity, I was struggling among images partially true, and therefore totally false. To say, confronted with a certain photograph, 'That's *almost* the way she was!' was more distressing than to say, confronted with another, 'That's not the way she was at all.'"[27]

Barthes's pain comes directly from the disjunction of the photograph as a physical object separate from the subject it represents. In the absence of that subject, all who view it must contend with this ontological distinction. However, in the Barthesian inverse, what then does it mean for a parent to look at the photograph of a child that has yet to become physical reality for them and "strain towards" the "essence of identity"? In this sense, Barthes mournful "almost" becomes the adoptive parent's anticipatory "maybe": "confronting" the photograph and imagining "This is how it *might* be!" rather than "That's *almost* the way she was!" In this sense, the photograph in the crib reproduced all around the house, does not attempt to *be* a baby (in the same way that Barthes realizes his mother's photographs will never *be* her). Rather, it produces the very encounter necessary to feel the formation of kinship, or to use Leah's phrase, "to feel like you're carrying a child," a child yet to arrive but whose imminence has been solidified by its very photographic existence.

What might it mean then to be the parent of a photograph before being the parent of a child? In one FCCNY newsletter, a single father talked about the role of the referral photograph in initiating the relationship between him and his four-year-old daughter-to-be: "A one-inch photocopy arrived from the other side of the earth, a puffy pouty face. For weeks I studied it, propped it up on the dinner table and over my speedometer, talked to it, and pretended I loved this girl." Like the other stories, the child enters his consciousness through the tactile interactions with the photograph as material object. Here, the term "pretend" reveals the distance that the photograph seeks to conjoin that is thrown into relief by the tenuousness of anticipation. Ariella Azoulay's notion of the "event of photography" further helps distinguish this relationship between photography and the reality it ostensibly represents, suggesting that ". . . at a time in which nearly everyone possesses photographic tools—photography has become a potential event even when there is no camera visible."[28] Here, the physical production of a photograph yielded from an event is distinct from both the event itself and the *potentiality* of photography to represent it. Again, inverting this photographic logic, referral photography and adoptive kinship suggest there could be a photograph even when there is no "event" yet. In other words, rather than an event of kinship formation suggesting the potentiality for photography, the photograph produces the potentiality of the event.

These encounters between embodiment and imagination also mirror normative narratives of pregnancy where ultrasound technology and fetal imagery, which have become ubiquitous in United States pregnancy culture. In her study of fetal images and visual culture, Rosalind Petchesky, observes the affective power of visual representation:

> . . . [Pregnant women] frequently express a sense of elation and direct participation in the imaging process, claiming it "makes the baby more real," "more our baby"; that visualizing the fetus creates a feeling of intimacy and belonging. . . . Some women even talk about themselves as having "bonded" with the fetus through viewing its image on the screen.[29]

Dorow also compares the referral photograph to ultrasound images and uses the same language, describing that "the referral photo makes the child *real.*"[30] Like the description in Kelly's story of her father taking a video of her photograph, technologies of movement such as the ultrasound or home video become ways of representing a child that has yet to physically arrive in the family.

This is not to suggest that adoptive parents are mimicking or appropriating discourses of pregnancy but in fact to emphasize how *both* adoptive and biological parents are socially imbricated within the embodied photographic practices of family formation. As Tina Campt describes in the context of family photography and the African diaspora, the reproduction of images that articulate these relations of kinship function as "repetitions with a difference—a difference inflected and infused with racialized, gendered, class-specific, and diasporic meanings."[31] Indeed, I also want to emphasize here *for whom* the referral photograph makes the child real (the parents), and how this reflects specific relations of power and agency. A child does not need a photograph to be real to themselves nor are they necessarily able to comprehend the contents of an image. And thus, the description of a photograph that makes a child "real" is not only a discourse of embodied experience but also a process in which parents have the agency to accept or deny their future child both literally and emotionally. Theorizing photography as a technology of kinship formation highlights not only these affective and material encounters that constitute the experience of family but also, as I discuss in the following section, how photography participates in situating those it represents within the structures and histories of race and gender.

Racialized Interchangeability

This agency of photography to actively participate in the production of kinship also connects adoption from China (and Asia more broadly, as I will discuss) to the longer history of Asian American family formation. Not the first time the technology of photography has been used to facilitate the formation of new kinship bonds, it was similarly used in the diaspora of picture brides in the early twentieth century. Following the 1908 Gentlemen's Agreement that restricted immigration from Japan and Korea, picture brides served as a means of circumventing exclusion and forming Asian families in the United States. As the name suggests, photographs were sent between prospective husbands in the United States and prospective wives in Japan or Korea, and after agreement from both parties, couples participated in a proxy marriage, often without having met in person.³² It is estimated that between 1908 and 1920, approximately twenty thousand women immigrated as picture brides.³³ In *Picturing Model Citizens: Civility in Asian American Visual Culture*, Thy Phu theorizes the use of photographic technology specifically in this practice, writing, "With the advent of photography's mechanized process of imitation and its vaunted naturalism, the concern with likeness, and the accompanying belief that the portrait could disclose an authentic truth about the person it represented, was energetically renewed."³⁴ This mechanized process of imitation, concern with likeness, and ideas of authentic truth imbued photography with the power of technological representation. And these qualities also offer a framework for interpreting referral photography in transnational adoption. Like the picture bride and husband-to-be, the referral photograph of the adoptee-to-be acquires meaning through its likeness to someone that has yet to arrive.

Both picture brides and transnational adoption also exemplify a particular triangulation of photography, kinship, and Asian American racialization in which photography plays a crucial role in the construction and embodiment of kinship. Whereas picture brides had to navigate a system of restrictive immigration already suspicious of Asian women established by the 1875 Page Law (which effectively barred the entrance of Chinese women to the United States), transnationally adopted children have not endured such scrutiny. David Eng calls this difference between Asian women of the early twentieth century and Chinese adoptees a "reversal of this gendered history of racialized exclusion."³⁵ And indeed, in this history of immigration regulation, this does constitute a reversal from exclusion to inclusion of Asian female subjects.

Yet, the racialization of these subjects also constitutes a *continuation*, whereby their subject formation as Asian American has always been contingent upon the gendered claims of kinship that made their migration possible. As I described in the previous chapter, family reunification has served as a cornerstone of immigration policy since the nineteenth century and it has directly shaped the constitution of the Asian diaspora in the contemporary United States. And while transnational adoption might not technically constitute a form of *re*unification, the creation and maintenance of the family remains the basis for this form of immigration from Asia (of the newly adopted child). Furthermore, this family formed through adoption is neither free nor separate from the institutions of heteronormativity, the hegemony of consanguineal kinship, and the normative power of the nuclear family.

In this context, adoption has a fraught relationship to queerness, one that is defined by individuals' position in relation to power. On the one hand, as discussed in this book's introduction, queerness challenges the oppressive power of heteronormative constructions of reproductive kinship. And similarly, adoptees are positioned against and challenge those very constructions that assume biological relatedness is the strongest, most legitimate, or most "real" kind of kinship.[36] As Kimberly McKee observes, "There is an expectation for both queers and adoptees that they be grateful for their acceptance within their families, who often do not inhabit their subject positions."[37] And in this context, being queer and being adopted both share positions of marginalization marked by non-normative relations to the normative structures of kinship.

On the other hand, both McKee and Eng critique the broader instrumentalization of adoption to reproduce normative ideologies of family. Although in contemporary popular culture adoption seemingly expands ideas of who can become a parent and how (to include older, single, and queer parents), the transnationally adoptive family has historically served to reinforce and naturalize a particular racial, gender, and sexual order. Early adoption from Korea and Vietnam in the second half of the twentieth century remained accessible only to heterosexual, married couples.[38] And, as Christina Klein and Matthew Guterl have both described, the image of the transracially and transnationally adoptive family in popular culture has historically affirmed and naturalized both the metaphor of White paternalism as well as the growing embrace of liberal multiculturalism.[39] Eng specifically theorizes the use of adoption from Asia by queer couples to access inclusion in reproductive normativity in his analysis of queer liberalism. Furthermore, within contemporary culture, adoption continues to be narrated and affirmed through its comparative similarity to normative biological kinship: adoptive kinship is often affirmed or insisted to be "as-if-biological."[40] In these ways, adoption functions as a continuation of the logics of family reunification and its participation in maintaining a particular racial, gendered, and sexual organization of family and kinship.

In this contemporary context, the gendered migration in adoption from China specifically, which was overwhelmingly comprised of infant girls relinquished in the wake of China's one-child policy, is also not the first diaspora of Asian women integrated into (mostly White) families already in the United States.[41] For example, the migration of almost one hundred thousand Korean military brides to the United States over the second half of the twentieth century constitutes another gendered diaspora based on kinship claims.[42] And while the gendered nature of adoption from China most directly fits within these histories of Asian American women's migration and family formation, adoption from Asia more broadly fits within gendered ideologies about adoption and rescue that originate from US wars in Asia. As scholars including SooJin Pate, Christina Klein, and Susie Woo have shown, Korean women and children were crucial in the formation of American empire throughout the second half of the twentieth century. As Woo describes of the early Cold War, Korean women and children "were subsumed into the private space of the American home under the tutelage of white parents or husbands."[43] These families served as narrative metaphors for the nation, in which White American paternalism was naturalized into celebrations of racial difference and the multicultural family/nation.[44] And even as Korean (and later Vietnamese) adoptees included children of both genders, the infantilization of the Asian orphan, raised by but always "under the tutelage" of White paternalism, maintained this gendered sense of racial order.

It makes sense then that the later adoption of infant girls from China was not only palatable but actively embraced and normalized in United States culture as liberal discourses of multiculturalism were celebrated even further in the 1990s. Already positioned as non-White, the picture bride, military wife, and Asian adoptee are situated as subjects within Asian American history and definitions of racial difference through their incorporation into a heteronormative family existing or imminent *within* the United States. For the picture bride, this incorporation is into a family collectively racialized as Asian (or Asian American), whereas the military wife or adoptee is (most frequently) brought into an existing White family made multicultural by their very presence.

Although on an experiential level adoptive parents have not necessarily seen themselves as part of this broader history, the interpolation of adoptees as Asian into the family has occurred through these discourses of contemporary multiculturalism, acceptance of difference, and the embrace of cultural heritage. Ann Anagnost describes how this "discourse of multiculturalism sets up the paradox of absorbing 'difference' into the intimate space of the familial while also reinscribing it."[45] And in relation to photography's role in this process, this is further exhibited in the example of Kelly's father filming her referral photograph with "dramatic Chinese music" in the background. Before even physically encountering his daughter-to-be, he associates her with his view of "Chineseness," in this case through his choice of "Chinese music" to play in the home video alongside her photograph. Ethnographer Andrea Louie has also observed these types of activities, describing, "In the context of adoptive families who are incorporating aspects of cultural tradition and identity that are not part of their own family traditions, Chinese identities are worked out through the imagination and reinvention of both parent and child identities as they 'triangulate' with Chineseness."[46] This serves as a departure from earlier White American families adopting from Korea, in which many adoptees were raised without exposure or acknowledgement of the national or ethnic communities from which they were born.[47] In fact, many parents adopting from China in the 1990s consulted with or sought advice from adult Korean adoptees to further understand how to raise their children with a sense of racial and ethnic awareness.[48] However, in the United States context, this "imagination" and "reinvention" is deeply entangled with the racialization and commercialization of what "Chinese culture" is and how it is performed.

These infants, still yet to arrive, are already being narrated through their association of racial and ethnic otherness. How do we reconcile the undeniable fondness of memories like Kelly's (of a relationship of genuine love between parent and daughter) with the racializing effects of it? I contend that the answer lies in the uncomfortable tension inherent to transnational and transracial adoption that both serves as a foundation for racialization and for which referral photography operates as a hinge: the interchangeability of the orphan that becomes transformed into the individuality of the adoptee within her family. Adoption scholar Barbara Yngvesson describes these two subjectivities as dialectical, creating the "tension between a generalized child whose canceled past makes her or him adoptable and the racialized child that re-emerges in the adoptive family and nation...."⁴⁹ Yngvesson highlights this precondition in which the "orphan" must be interchangeable insofar as she could potentially belong to *any* willing adoptive family. Or as Jodi Kim writes, "The very production of the adoptee as a legal orphan... renders her the barest of social identities and strips her of her social personhood. This social death is paradoxically produced precisely so that the orphan can legally become an adoptee...."⁵⁰ It is through adoption that this child is bestowed the identity of "adoptee," by which they are not only individuated as belonging to a specific family but also, in the case of transnational and transracial adoption as Yngvesson describes, racialized in their belonging to both a new "adoptive family and nation." Not only is she legally transformed into an American citizen, but she becomes racialized as Asian (American) within the cultural framework of racial difference in the United States. And as I have argued elsewhere about adoption, race, and photography, this racial difference is laid bare by family photography and the role of visuality in its representation of transnational and transracial kinship.⁵¹ Regardless of whether race is seen or acknowledged by the family, photographs of its members make it visible.

Referral photography thus specifically functions as a technology of racialization here precisely in the changing status of the referral photograph itself within the adoption process. While the photograph is a materially consistent object (insofar as the literal image does not change), as an object of racial meaning, it does immense work in altering the modes of relation and subjectivity of individuals. As Lisa Cartwright writes in relation to images of "waiting children" within the transnational adoption market, "children's fates are determined not simply by the fact of displaying their images but by the meanings assigned to them in their intersecting uses...."⁵² While Cartwright demonstrates how photography participates in the classification of children in ways that hierarchize race, identity, and disease (especially in relation to discourses of "special needs" children), I extend this framing to referral photography specifically and its role in racializing the child within the transnational adoption process itself. Tracing the photograph's pathway, it begins as an image of an "orphan," marking this status of "social death" and the child's interchangeability as a foreign national subject. The photograph and the child it represents thus have the potential to belong to any number of adoptive parents. It is then incorporated into the referral file and sent to expecting parents abroad, where it participates in the tentative individuation of the child as (Asian) American adoptee. This is the moment when Charlotte sees the photograph and enacts recognition in her exclamation "That's our baby!" And, if everything goes according to plan, the child physically enters the family already individuated through the precedent of her photograph. She has already been positioned as an (Asian) American racial subject through her photographic incorporation into the American family imaginary.

While the referral photograph offers itself as a generative site to construct kinship, its role in narratives of disjuncture also further reveals the inevitably racialized nature of interchangeability in this adoption process. In one FCCNY newsletter, an adoptive mother demonstrates how fraught this interchangeability can feel and the ways in which the referral photograph impacts its affective realities. After beginning the adoption process, the author recounts receiving in the mail "a video and photographs of the loveliest three-and-a-half month old baby girl" named Ji Tang. She holds a baby shower and is devastated to find out the day before her and her husband's trip to China that Ji Tang is critically ill and has been reclassified as a "special needs baby." Another infant named Di Ling has been chosen for them and awaits their decision: either to continue with the adoption of Ji Tang or accept the newly assigned Di Ling. After an inquiry about adopting both children, which is not possible, they eventually accept the new assignment. She writes,

> It was a long, solemn flight over [to China]. Sleep eluded me and when I was able, I awoke to the soft luminous face of the child we'd never see. I couldn't shake her presence. We were unable to fix our hearts on the new assignment . . . In a scramble against the clock, all we had to go on was a highly distorted image of a fax of a fax.

The author highlights how important the referral photograph becomes in the kinship formation process. Beginning with "a video and photographs," the representational image of the first child becomes the foundation upon which anticipation is built. It initiates a baby shower, itself an anticipatory event, and facilitates the start of a family imaginary.

The importance of the image as a representation is thrown into even further relief by its negation and contrast to the image of the new infant assigned to them, who is represented through "a highly distorted image of a fax of a fax." Whereas the "video and photographs" served as indexical representations of a first child they are able to bond with (in her perspective at the time), this "fax of a fax" becomes a simulacrum too far removed and compounded by the rushed timeframe to fully facilitate that affective bond. However, upon meeting Di Ling for the first time, the new parents are quickly occupied by her own health issues, which eventually resolve following their return to the United States. The author concludes with a reflection on Ji Tang: "I often think about the child we didn't take home. I've called the agency many times asking about Ji Tang. No news yet. I felt compelled to write this saga for those going over who are faced with hard choices, perhaps life and death decisions. I also write this out of sadness and longing for little Ji Tang who has forever touched our lives." This story highlights the imbrication of both adoptee and adoptive parent within systems of commodification and interchangeability built into the adoption process as well as the embodied tension between that commodification and genuine care within adoptive kinship.

Parents and children may be the most visible figures in the adoption process; however, both are situated within what McKee calls the "transnational adoption industrial complex" that perpetuates the neoliberal economic profitability of the practice.[53] Within this system, global legal, administrative, and social work economies rely on the continued availability of adoptable children, an availability that requires this continued racialized interchangeability. The transformation of Di Ling from malnourished orphan to healthy adoptee highlights the successful individuation and incorporation of the adopted child into her American family. And yet it was implicitly contingent upon the interchange that brought her into it.

While adoptive parents may be beneficiaries of this kind of racialized interchangeability, this account also demonstrates the uneven distribution of agency in how it is yielded and reproduced. Indeed, these parents made a choice between two children. However, they did not consent to being forced to choose nor were they allowed to adopt both children. The adoptive parents even asking such a question suggests an individual refusal of interchangeability. Using their individual Chinese names throughout and expressing a continued affective attachment to Ji Tang, the author makes clear that these two children were not interchangeable in her embodied perspective, even as they may have been switched literally. The role of photography mirrors this tension: like the child herself, the photograph fixes their image as visually and materially singular. And yet, this physical individuality becomes moved and narrated within the changing meaning of who the child will become and to what family she belongs.

Narratively, this individuation of the orphan before adoption is a departure from other accounts of adoptive parents who often serve as figures of erasure and commodification in their role as recipients (or "consumers") of adopted children. For example, Jodi Kim discusses the ways in which Korean adoptee Deann Borshay Liem's family inadvertently deploy a discursive "racialized logic of consumption, possession, and ownership" to describe her belonging in their family in her first film *First Person Plural*.[54] Borshay Liem's discovery that her parents were originally going to adopt a different child named Cha Jung Hee (whose place she took) parallels the story of Di Ling and Ji Tang; although unlike the two Chinese infants, Borshay Liem was forced to take on the identity of the child she replaced. Together, these narratives show how racialized interchangeability functions as a system across practices in adoption from both China and Korea that ultimately end in the refiguration of the transnational adoptee as "Asian" within US racial meanings.

Photography's New Kinships

While adoption may not require photography to proceed, referral photography as a technology of kinship also carries the potential to shape the experience of adoptees beyond its initial use. Like the unintended consequences of the immigration bureaucracy in the first chapter of this book, kinship can be formed in unlikely places that connect people and histories that were never intended to meet. Likewise, photographs can be unruly and encounters with them can disrupt long-held truths and propel individuals on unexpected journeys. Turning to Deann Borshay Liem's second autoethnographic film *In the Matter of Cha Jung Hee* offers an opportunity to expand a theorization of photography even beyond conventional narratives of loss and reunion with birth family. In so doing, the film reveals how photography can participate in the formation of new modes of kinship, defined by the gendered and racialized histories that make them possible.

In her first film, *First Person Plural*, released in 2000, Borshay Liem recounts coming to the United States from Korea as a child with memories incongruent with the information on her adoption records. According to her documents, her Korean name was Cha Jung Hee and she was an orphan. However, Borshay Liem finds two photographs: one is a picture of herself as a child and another is an unknown Korean girl of approximately the same age. Both photographs have the name Cha Jung Hee written on the back, but the children are clearly different from one another. Borshay Liem learns that Cha Jung Hee was another girl at the orphanage that was going to be adopted by the Borshays. However, before she was sent to the United States, Cha Jung Hee's father came to the orphanage to retrieve her. In her place and without telling the Borshay family, a girl named Kang Ok Jin was sent to the United States instead, and that is the child that became Deanne Borshay Liem.

Released in 2010, a decade after the first film, *In the Matter of Cha Jung Hee* follows Borshay Liem's journey in search of Cha Jung Hee, the girl she came to replace and now a woman in her fifties. Choy theorizes the film as a reflection on "the loss of adoptees' histories and memories in the context of the transformation of Korean international adoption into a global industry."[55] And Borshay Liem's search for Cha Jung Hee lays bare the ways in which histories and memories have been lost, transformed, and re-narrated over time. In this context, I specifically analyze the role of photography in providing the foundation for new forms of kinship and reconciliation amid the affective longing that characterizes Borshay Liem's search.

Visually and narratively, the film is propelled through an exploration of photography. At the beginning of the film, and in what Choy describes as "a detectivelike ambiance," Borshay Liem stands in a dimly lit, blue-tinged room, taping photographs to a glass wall between herself and the camera.[56] In voiceover, she says, "I would have gone on to live my life happily as Cha Jung Hee. But years later I discovered photos of two different girls, each labeled with the same name." Displaying her evidence, she tapes the image of Cha Jung Hee that her adoptive parents received, enlarged in black and white on clear translucent paper to this glass wall on display for the audience. The photograph shows a Korean child standing outdoors in front of a stone wall with trees in the background, wearing wide-legged pants, sneakers, and a collared,

Figure 3.1. *The two Cha Jung Hees.* Courtesy of Deann Borshay Liem.

buttoned-up jacket. Her hair is cut into a bob with blunt bangs across her forehead, and she looks into the camera calmly but with a tentative expression (Figure 3.1, left). The next image that she tapes to the glass shows a different child, resembling Borshay Liem at a young age, wearing a light, short-sleeved dress. Her expression holds a slight frown, and her hair is cut in a bob (Figure 3.1, right).

Later, when the film shows the original photographs, a pair of hands turns them over in unison to show the backs: both have the same cursive script in pencil with the name "Cha Jung Hee." The hands flip them over and puts the one originally introduced as Cha Jung Hee down. Holding only the photograph of the other child, Borshay Liem narrates, "I recognized one of them as myself and knew instantly that the other girl was Cha Jung Hee and that I wasn't." In this scene, to borrow from Cartwright above, the "meanings assigned" to these images are literalized in the one name written on both photographs, claiming that these are one child. And this insistence actively determined the "fate" of the child that became Borshay Liem. However now, many years later, their incongruence with reality is made visible through the photographs, and this incongruence offers new possibilities to seek reconciliation.

Within the events of the film, the materiality of these photographs is central: they literally facilitate the search process as they are magnified, enlarged, carried around, examined, and discussed. Borshay Liem travels to Korea, to the orphanage where she and Cha Jung Hee lived, then to the town Cha Jung Hee was from, and then to the existing social welfare archive. She brings the two photographs with her to meet with social workers and people she thinks could be Cha Jung Hee. Several times she shows others the images and asks, "Could this be you?" or asks the people accompanying them, "Do you think she looks like the child in the photograph?" Their function as images is clear: they are the visual reference for which all else is compared.

The photographs also do metaphorical work as material representations of identity, interchangeability, and loss. They appear analogous: both are the same size and shape with the subjects standing with the same posture, at approximately the same age, and with similar haircuts. The backgrounds look similar: perhaps they were taken in different parts of the same courtyard, a shared point of origin. The visual comparability of the two images directly references this space, one that subjectifies each as "orphan" available for adoption. Phu also analyzes how photography functions as a site through which civility is mobilized both within and against Asian American racialization and citizenship. In particular, Phu's elucidation on how photography and visual culture participate in the construction of the model minority stereotype as an image of civility allows us to apprehend the stakes of positioning these children as subjects possessing the *potential* to be transformed into "model citizens."[57] Their similar expressions and upright stances suggest at least momentary obedience, positioned carefully by themselves gesturing to the lack of family, and convey the embodied process by which these children have been made into subjects of potential civil life through adoption.

In multiple scenes, Borshay Liem is shown comparing the photographs alongside one another with other people: the orphanage director, the social worker, a woman she believes might be the right Cha Jung Hee. With almost physiognomic specificity, they discuss jawlines, eyebrows, and face shapes. Borshay Liem's awareness of this potentiality of photography to materialize the fraught meanings of interchangeability manifest in her aesthetic narration as the filmmaker. Her own staged scenes trying to piece together this journey present the photographs as malleable and participatory. In one scene, Borshay Liem presents the photographs enlarged to show just the children's faces and cut into horizontal strips: one strip of just eyes or another of a nose or another of a mouth. She shows herself moving and exchanging these strips between the two photographs. Like a forensic collage, Borshay Liem's own childhood facial features become entangled with and sutured to those of Cha Jung Hee. Reappearing throughout the film, this visual display of psychic dissonance further underscores the forms of dislocation layered into the aforementioned, racialized interchangeability of all adoption from Asia. At one point, Borshay Liem narrates in voiceover,

> It scared me how easy it was to replace one girl with another. The first step was to take my picture and write Cha Jung Hee's name on the back. . . . Looking at these documents made me see my relationship to my adoptive family in a new light. Because I wasn't the child my parents had originally fallen in love with, there was a part of me that always questioned whether I belonged. And whether I had a right to accept my family's love and to love them.

The photographs become imbricated within this narrative of racialized struggle precisely in their analogy, their constant switching between one another, and the continual reminder that one took the place of the other. Borshay Liem highlights their power as a technology of her adoptive family's kin formation: to write Cha Jung Hee on the back of a photograph of a childhood Deann is to name her Cha Jung Hee, to replace the "child my parents had originally fallen in love with" with herself. Thus, while Borshay Liem's story is compellingly unique, the central problematic of the film highlights the tension of racialized interchangeability inherent to adoption and the broader fear that the adoptee might not have the "right" to accept her family's love.

This psychic tension becomes interpersonal when Borshay Liem does eventually find the Cha Jung Hee for whom she has been searching, the individual who was originally planned to be adopted by the Borshays. However, this Cha Jung Hee is also *not* the child in the photograph that Deann has been calling Cha Jung Hee. Looking at the photograph together, Cha Jung Hee says in Korean to Deann, "This, especially the eyebrows . . . I don't think it's me." Despite this inconsistency, her experience is congruent with the girl who was originally assigned to be adopted by the Borshays but was later retrieved from the orphanage by her father. There must have been a third child, whose image was placed in Cha Jung Hee's file and sent to the Borshays.

As the film concludes, returning to the photograph Borshay Liem originally thought had been Cha Jung Hee as a child, cut into strips and displayed on a lightboard table, Borshay Liem reflects on the woman she has just met,

> Many of the facts I thought were important don't match her history. But my heart tells me she's the one I've been looking for. I believe she was the original Cha Jung Hee sponsored by my parents. After she went home with her father, I think this girl [in the photograph thought to be Cha Jung Hee for most of the film] was put in her place. It's unclear who this girl was. But her photo was sent to the Borshays. Then something happened to her. And I became the third Cha Jung Hee. Cha Jung Hee became a template, for a perfect orphan. Once the templated existed, any girl could step into it.

Borshay Liem revels in the painful reality of her and these two other children's interchangeability. She is chasing a ghost of herself by fixing her gaze on the photograph and by asking the photographs to answer a bigger question: not just, "Who is Cha Jung Hee?" but "Who have I become in the absence of Cha Jung Hee?"

This is also a racial question, whereby Borshay Liem's identity as an Asian *American* woman is contingent upon the adoption that was only made possible by her and Cha Jung Hee's childhood subjectivities as South Korean girls. In her own narration, finding the real Cha Jung Hee reminds Borshay Liem that she is "connected to a generation of Korean women" and offers an image of a life she imagines she could have had in Korea. Adoption and its negation have made Borshay Liem an American adoptee racialized as Asian and Cha Jung Hee a Korean woman. They exist as two sides of the same coin of United States empire. This gendered figuration, which as Susie Woo highlights "emerged as a result of US geopolitical needs during the Cold War that brought Americans into Korea and Koreans into the United States," haunts the intersections of Borshay Liem and Cha Jung Hee and their childhoods of the 1960s. However, in the present of the 2010s, in which adoption has taken on new forms and meanings, their photographs are evidence that these two subjectivities are bound together, propelling Borshay Liem on the journey of the film and crafting a new kind of kinship that reconnects their separate presents to their shared past. In other words, the relatedness of the photographs in the Borshay family archive, of two orphans composed as one, has produced an emergent kinship many years later between these two women, as mirrors for one another reflecting a future that was never realized for the other.

While the film certainly represents a unique story, it captures the affective racial tension and the negotiation of loss that is inherent to the adoption process. All adoptees must lose their family of birth in order to become adopted, which often includes the transformation of kin identity, nationhood, and racial subjectivity. As this chapter has shown, as a technology of kinship, referral photography participates in this transformation, fraught with the racial hierarchies embodied within multiracial adoptive families. However, it also offers a point of coalescence for seeking new forms of recuperation from severed origins. By expanding the search for recuperation beyond normative narratives of the search for birth parents, Borshay Liem thus also opens up the possibilities for photography to produce other forms of "adoptive" kinship connected to the life experiences of the adoptee and the agency to engage with one's nation of birth as an adult.

Both the narrative accounts within Chinese adoption communities and *In the Matter of Cha Jung Hee* show the potentiality of photography to create new ways of constructing and embodying transracial and transnational adoptive kinship. In the imagined and literal family archives, referral photographs do not only function as memories of a family origin story that has already occurred. They also operate as a mechanism for the racialization of the Asian orphan into Asian American adoptee, and at the same time generate new modes for fashioning kinship. By making visible this connection, photography as a technology of kinship helps us unpack Asian transnational adoption and the forms of kinship that result from it as complex sites of both love and intimacy *as well as* racialized and gendered power.

4

Making Racial Choices

The Digital Profile Interface in Economies of Family Formation

On the California Cryobank public website, as part of the donor search, any visitor can view a grid of more than two hundred individualized and anonymized sperm donors from which customers can choose (Figure 4.1). Rows of boxes side-by-side represent the profiles of each donor with details like "5'10—Brown Eyes—Black Hair" and "6'1—Green Eyes–Brown Hair," with a case number in place of each name. A blank space sits where a photograph would be, and some include cute nicknames like "Trilingual Ambivert" or "Optimistic Audiophile." More information and images can be acquired upon registering for the site. The left-hand side of the webpage offers a list of nineteen filters that customers can also use to help select a donor, including height, eye color, hair color, education level, and religion. Several categories such as hair texture, ethnic origin, or ancestry (self-reported) explicitly reference race or racialized features.

Visually, this and other egg and sperm donation websites look uncannily like the classic format for online dating websites, in which rows of profiles show potential romantic partners from which individual can choose. In both online dating and egg and sperm donation websites, individuals possess a "profile" that represents who they are, and from which others can see and select. Through these profiles, websites provide a platform for people to "browse" for who and what they want. Historically categorized using rolodexes, paper filing systems, and binders, these databases of potential matches in both economies currently offer an online format with which users are already familiar.[1] Options are presented in grid-like matrixes with seemingly endless scrolling. And filtering becomes a precarious tool that flirts with the line between preference and discrimination.

Amid the rise of digital technologies in contemporary culture, this chapter explores the racialization of family formation through this digital

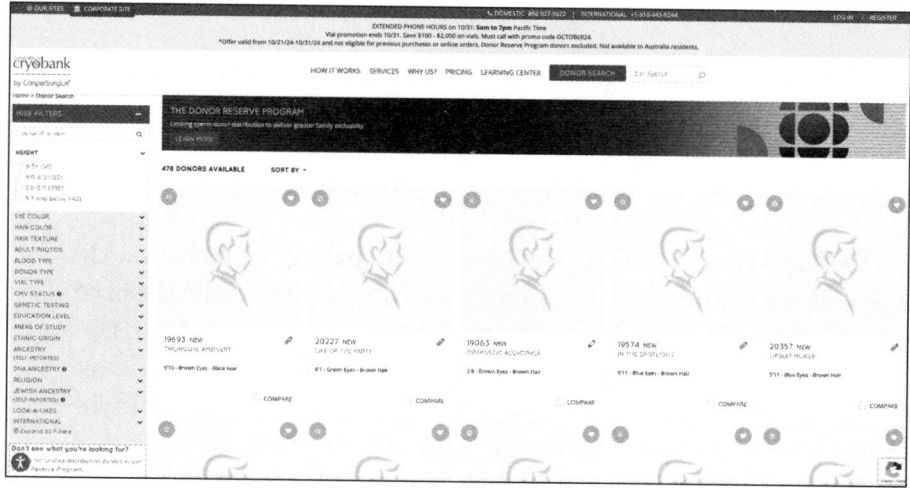

Figure 4.1. Screenshot of the public donor search webpage from California Cryobank. October 2024. https://www.cryobank.com/.

structure of what I refer to as the *profile interface* in the era of neoliberalism. Thus far, *Technologies of Kinship* has traced an arc in the formation of Asian American family and kinship from an era of racialized exclusion to an era of liberalism and multicultural inclusion. In the previous chapter, transracial and transnational adoption from Asia demonstrated the ways in which technology participates in not only the formation of new kinship relations, but also the articulation of racial difference in the contemporary multicultural family. Transracial and transnational adoption in the 1980s and 1990s, and the multicultural ideologies it came to represent, also marked a shift from liberalism into neoliberalism and neoliberal multiculturalism. Whereas transracial adoption has historically represented an outlier in the incorporation of economic logic into the family formation process (characterized by the commodification of the racialized adopted child), under neoliberalism, both race and family formation have been economized in new ways, often through the digital. In this context, neoliberal consumption occurs not only through the continued subsumption of racialized adopted children into the family within adoption practices but also through the consumption of racialized traits in social and biological processes of reproduction.

Despite the somewhat disparate cultural landscapes that online dating and egg and sperm donation occupy, these economies together exemplify the use of the digital profile interface as a technology of kinship that reflects the changing neoliberal landscape of racial consumption through family formation. Indeed, in theorizing the role of race in the market for human gametes, Heath Fogg-Davis argues, "Racial choices made in this arena [of assisted reproduction] publicly reinforce and make explicit the routine use of racial discrimination in the choice of a partner for procreative sexual intercourse."[2] And I further argue that the profile interface is used to represent and categorize individuals in ways that directly suture the marketability and reproduction of race and racial ideologies to the production of kinship. I consider these two types of sites alongside one another precisely because of their uncanny visual similarities and their shared use of profile interfaces as a tool for contemporary family formation.

Less concerned with individuals' experiences of the sites themselves or people's perception of the services, this chapter's analysis reveals the underlying discourses and ideologies about race, kinship, and the digital that are embedded and reproduced in the structuring of these economies. To do so, it examines the interfaces and marketing from several popular companies giving focused attention to *how* information has been structured and presented to users.[3] In contrast to content analysis such as that of Cynthia R. Daniels and Erin Heidt-Forsythe in their study of free market reproductive technologies or sociological research such as that of Celeste Vaughan Curington, Jennifer H. Lundquist, and Ken-Hou Lin on race and desire in the era of online romance, I specifically consider the ways in which the interface itself and the cultural meanings it perpetuates function systematically to organize the racialized and gendered choices individuals are able to make about family formation.[4]

While indeed not all forms of affective, sexual, or intimate connection in either economy necessarily constitute kinship (or even attempts to form kinship in the context of online hookup culture), the normative narratives around family and kinship circulating within them demonstrate some of the new forms of racialized social relation and intimacy generated by the profile interface. In these digital spaces, the articulation and mobilization of "Asian" as a racial identity category also reflects contemporary neoliberal and multicultural logics of race within consumer culture: rather than a historically and politically specific identity of racial solidarity (based in a shared racialization), Asianness has been abstracted into another flavor in a set of consumer choices. Although racialization has always been a relational process, within the logic of these economies, Asian American family and kinship is treated as distinct only insofar as it is articulated within a set of what Lisa Nakamura calls "menu-driven identities." As Nakamura describes, ". . . a menu-driven sense of personal identity . . . works by progressively narrowing the choices of subject positions available to the user, an outcome that seems to fly in the face of claims that the Internet allows for a more fluid, free, unbounded sense of identity than had been available in other media—or, indeed, in the world—before."[5]

The normalization of these menu-driven identities in digital worlds further solidify and reproduce the hegemony of these categories like White, Black or African American, Latinx, Asian, etc. for self-identification, and justify their continued use as demographic organizers of social populations.[6] As Nakamura argues, like the categorization of race in the US census, in this menu-driven framework, non-normative racial categories like "mestiza or other culturally ambiguous identities—such as those belonging to hyphenated Americans—are rendered unintelligible, inexpressible, and invisible, since they can't be (or rather, aren't) given a 'box' of their own."[7] Indeed, these menu-driven categories are not only ways for individuals to be externally measured (by the US government or sociological data collection), they also function as ways and limits for individuals to identify, compare, and make meaning of their own sense of self within these digital worlds. However, the ongoing cultural focus on identity as a form of possessive individualism often severs these identity categories from the very politics (both oppressive and liberatory) that made them meaningful in the first place. And, private companies' attempts to depoliticize race, often while consciously capitalizing on its visuality to promote diversity within the free market, as I will discuss subsequently, merely belie existing racial meanings rather than transform them in any kind of liberatory way.

This tension (between racial categories as consumer categories and racial categories as connected histories of oppression and racialized meaning) also explains the turn in the final chapters of this book towards these contemporary processes of classification, racial categorization under neoliberal multiculturalism, and the specificity of Asian racial forms within these landscapes. As I show in this chapter, despite neoliberal attempts to render Asianness discrete from its political and racialized associations, the uses of Asian as identity category and the representations of Asians within these economies continue to carry those fraught meanings, both in the embodied effects of the profile interface and in the racialized marketing narrated by these companies. Furthermore, they also uniquely demonstrate the relationship between how race in general is imagined in the free market and the inescapable racial meanings and histories by which it is defined.

The Old Is New Again: Neoliberalism and the Digital Marketplace

As discussed in previous chapters, by the start of the twenty-first century, the meaning of race in popular culture had largely shifted from a structural identity shaped by access to certain social and political resources to an individual identity with assumed or essentialized cultural traits. This shift from race-as-political-identity to race-as-consumer-identity coincides with two corresponding transformations in social, political, and economic life at the turn of the twenty-first century. First is the shift from liberalism to neoliberalism. Wendy Brown describes the unique characteristics of this turn to neoliberal political rationality, including,

> the extension of economic rationality to all aspects of thought and activity, the placement of the state in forthright and direct service to the economy, the rendering of the state *tout court* as an enterprise organized by market rationality, the production of the moral subject as an entrepreneurial subject, and the construction of social policy according to these criteria . . ."[8]

Within this system, it then makes sense that family as a metaphor for the nation has been positioned in "direct service to the economy" under neoliberalism and narrated through discourses of market rationality. Furthermore, to return to my earlier discussion, Jodi Melamed describes how neoliberal multiculturalism specifically functions as,

> a central ideology and mode of social organization that seeks to manage racial contradictions on a national and international scale for U.S.-led neoliberalism. It does this through a form of official antiracism, now often reduced to a nonracialism, which hinders thinking about or acting against the biopolitics of global capitalism.[9]

At the intersection of race and the consumer cultures of dating and egg and sperm donation, discourses of individual preference and personal choice demonstrate this ideology. Here, the "racial contradiction" lies precisely in the simultaneous desire to denounce race as a meaningful category of human difference while consuming race as a coherent identity that produces racially categorizable products (like egg or sperm).

The second historical shift across this period is witnessed in the rise of the digital. Early roots of neoliberalism, neoliberal multiculturalism, *and* digitization were laid in the 1970s and 1980s with the rise of deregulation and the expansion of free trade. And they continued to flourish in the 1990s with the passage of NAFTA, burgeoning wars in the

Middle East, and increased spending on national defense including the development of military digital technologies like GPS that have since been incorporated into everyday life.[10] The success and mass consumption of digital technologies and personal devices since the early 2000s have undoubtedly been facilitated by the rise of the free market and the emergence of largescale global supply chains. Furthermore, ideologies of technological innovation themselves have been transformed by this neoliberal political rationality. As Kaushik Sunder Rajan describes in *Lively Capital: Biotechnologies, Ethics, and Governance in Global Markets*,

> Even the ideology of innovation, which gained enormous traction under Ronald Reagan's presidency, in the 1980s, under the influence of neoliberal thinkers such as George Gilder, suggests a value system of capitalism that is in some ways quite distinct from that which Marx traced during the industrial revolution, whereby the magic of capital lies not in the creation of the surplus through the apparent exchange of equivalents, but rather in the creation of what Michael Lewis refers to as 'the new new thing.'[11]

Indeed, computing and digitization have served as the landscape for the ongoing creation (and recreation) of "the new new thing" under neoliberalism throughout the twenty-first century. Anyone who has lived through the COVID-19 pandemic or the advent of ChatGPT recently can attest to the ways in which the digital age has continued to transform the means, economy, and embodied experience of contemporary everyday life.

While digitization has certainly changed the potential scale of human interactions, like these other shifts, the era of the digital has been born out of the economies, politics, and ideologies of the earlier twentieth-century liberalism. And family formation has functioned as a site for these contemporary transformations of neoliberalism, multiculturalism, and digitization precisely through the incorporation and normalization of the new into the old. As Wendy Hui Kyong Chun asserts, "our media matter most when they seem not to matter at all, that is, when they have moved from the new to the habitual."[12] Thus, while the digital profile interface represents the shift from analog to digital (from old to new), its embrace and continued normalization (from novel to habitual) within practices of family and kin formation have occurred through the integration of the new into the previously established kin practices and economies. More concretely, as I discuss in this chapter, the embrace of the digital marketplace for online dating or egg and sperm donation was precedented by existing non-digital economies for these services. Even before the availability of the digital, dating, egg donation, and sperm donation in the United States had been based on the premise of individual choice and consumption mediated by technology.

In contemporary dating culture, choosing a romantic partner for oneself is narrated as an act of liberal personhood and individualism, one that is the subject of countless forms of cultural representation and narrative. And the language of economics has often been invoked in discourses of dating in references to the "dating market" or the "marketability" of certain traits as attractive or unattractive. In the 1970s and 1980s, technological intermediaries flourished in relation to dating and consumer behavior, from print newspaper singles ads to video dating to matchmakers.[13] Thus, by the time the first largescale commercial online dating websites were established in the mid-1990s, the ideologies of searching through profiles, selecting partners with the assistance of computing technology, and spending money on for-profit services to assist with dating had already been established.

In a more defined shift, sperm donation also underwent a transformation from medical practice to commercial economy in the 1980s (during which procedures for egg donation were still being developed). As sociologist Rene Almeling highlights, during this period, the responsibility of choosing a donor shifted from doctors to patients. And, concurrently, more and more information about individual donors was provided to patients to facilitate that choice. As the sperm bank economy shifted from a medical model to a commercial one, more granular information about donors became a crucial part of that consumer model. Almeling quotes a physician describing this transition:

> ... that's the difference between a university program and a commercial program. The university asks very simple questions: eye color, height and weight, perhaps something about ethnicity. So it's going to a socialized store and a capitalist store. [The commercial bank] has much more information, but it's commercial, so they're selling a product. We were providing a medical service."[14]

And while Almeling shows that egg donation has historically and contemporarily been narrated in gendered ways that frame it as a "gift" and form of altruism for which egg donors' internal motivations are important (in contrast to sperm donation which is narrated as a job), she also explains, "The trajectory of egg donation did mimic that of sperm donation in one crucial way: the medical profession eventually had to cede control of egg donor recruitment to commercial agencies, a process driven by rapidly increasing recipient demand."[15] Thus, even before the emergence of digital platforms, both dating and egg and sperm donation were situated within social and cultural ideologies of commercialization and consumer choice. These processes of commercialization reflect what Michelle Murphy calls the "economization of life," by which practices "differentially value and govern life in terms of their ability to foster the macroeconomy of the nation-state, such as life's ability to contribute to the gross domestic product (GDP) of the nation."[16] Not only do these commercial, for-profit companies contribute to national capitalist economies directly, they also participate in the process by which individuals are "differentially valued" based on racialized, economic logics of atomization.

The Digital Profile Interface

With the rapid popularity of digital and social media sites in the twenty-first century, human exchange (both socially and monetarily) has been amplified by the capitalist marketplace model that displays individual profiles as an opportunity to pick and choose others.[17] Interaction itself becomes a form of neoliberal consumption. As Jeana H. Frost, Zoë Chance, Michael I. Norton, and Dan Ariely observe, "Most online dating sites use a 'shopping' interface like that used by other commercial sites, in which people are classified much like any commodity, by different searchable attributes . . . which can be filtered in any way the shopper desires."[18] The authors distinguish between "search goods" and "experience goods" to theorize how people experience the online dating marketplace. Search goods are characterized by variation "along objective, tangible attributes, and choice among options can be construed as an attempt to maximize expected performance along these measurable dimensions." In contrast, experience goods are "judged by the feelings they evoke, rather than the functions they perform." And the authors argue that dating has presented people as "search goods" when it might be more productive to understand people as "experience goods."[19]

Extending this framework to consider race as a "searchable attribute," the digital profile interface categorically presents racial categories as "search goods" with tangible and distinguishing qualities. For example, upon registering for Match.com, users are asked to answer a set of questions regarding what they are looking for on the site as well as basic information about themselves such as height, "body type," and "ethnicity." The question asks, "What ethnicities best describe you?" and the options provided include White/Caucasian, Black/African, Latino/Hispanic, Asian, Native American, Middle Eastern, Pacific Islander, East Indian, or Other. Users can select more than one or skip the question (or any other) altogether. Once registered, users can adjust their search criteria based on gender, age, geography, and a range of other categories. Like the list at the beginning of this chapter, a tab offering filters presents a growing set of choices through which users can search for potential matches. The largest categories include "interests" (including groupings of shared interests like sports, hobbies, and pets, each of which offers several subcategories that users can select and search for), "looks" (including categories for body type, hair color, eye color, and height), "personal" (including family, ethnicity, astrology, education, and languages), and "lifestyle" (including "healthy habits" such as smoking or drinking, faith, occupation, income, and politics). Notably, ethnicity is listed under "personal" characteristics, alongside astrology and education.

Similarly, most egg and sperm donation websites allow the public to view analogous semi-anonymized information about their individual donors. Different pages for egg or sperm donors offer several pull-down menus for users to search for various qualities.[20] For both types of donor searches, users can sort by race, ethnicity, blood type, height, eye color, weight, and hair color. One website boasts that they offer "the industry's largest and most diverse donor selection recruited from world class universities including UCLA, USC, Stanford, Harvard and MIT" and assert that potential donors "are subjected to extensive screening—the end result of which admits less than 1% of all applicants."[21] The logic that a donor's educational achievements are relevant to the genetic material they have contributed and the analogization of all of these individuating details within the profile interface reveals the uneven ideologies of the interface. In this context, "diversity" does not only refer to racial or ethnic diversity but rather the diversity of and within all of these different categories, some of which are directly genetically inherited and others which are not by any means. And the positioning of race and ethnicity buried within these increasingly specific lists of categories demonstrates the production and reproduction of race as an individualized consumer choice in the context of these services, rather than as a social formation or political identity. In other words, as they are in online dating, race and ethnicity are framed as analogous to one's astrological sign or education level: they are matters of individual experience and personal identification.

This kind of racialized, gendered, and sexualized atomization facilitated by the profile interface has become normalized within these digital choice economies. Even as some online dating sites have responded to calls to eliminate filtering by race or ethnicity, the conceptualization of race as an attribute that serves as the basis for evaluating a potential match is characteristic of the profile interface, regardless of whether it is implicit or explicit.[22] Within this digital landscape, the profile interface is defined by its use of an always racialized corpus in order to function. A single profile is meaningless without the broader archive of profiles, and it is only through the relationality of the individual to the community of users that the singular becomes meaningful.[23] Like the bureaucratic immigration archives of the first chapter, the archive itself operates as a technology of categorization in which individual cases take on a relational quality. As Allan Sekula writes of the nineteenth century photographic archive developed in the service of police to categorize criminals using physiognomic methods,

> This archival promise [to categorize individuals on a mass scale] was frustrated, however, both by the messy contingency of the photograph and by the sheer quantity of images.... Clearly, one way of 'taming' photography is by means of this transformation of the circumstantial and idiosyncratic into the typical and emblematic ... Another way is to invent a machine, or rather a clerical apparatus, a filing system, which allows the operator/researcher/editor to retrieve the individual instance from the huge quantity of images contained within the archive."[24]

In this sense, both online dating and egg and sperm donation services extend the ideologies of the photographic archive, giving the profile the power to represent the individual as legible subject within the corpus. Each platform operates as an archive filled with profiles of individuals who desire that "sheer quantity" to choose from while simultaneously seeking out another individual with which to engage (the "archival promise" that Sekula references). Race functions as a basic way to manage this amplified quantitative scale. The profile interface and the filters for various qualities and characteristics operate as the "clerical apparatus" that "retrieve[s] the individual instance from the huge quantity of images contained within the archive." These filters not only offer the user a tool with which to engage with the content of the archive itself but also a way to articulate and individualize the very categories, like race, used to differentiate the individual.

Importantly, this processes of differentiation with which users interact and express desire for others is deeply affective, a literal digital "structure of feeling."[25] As Joanne Garde-Hansen and Kristyn Gorton discuss, "emotion online is encountered when the culture we live is performed on the intersection of the personal and the global through mixed media, one that makes it hard to think compartmentally about specific technologies, audiences, and parts of the world."[26] And while their study examines the role of affect online through the analyses of visual images (a lens through which this book also engages), the profile interface demonstrates how formatting, organization, and presentation can also shape the affective potential of those images.[27] Those that are choosing from these online databases are provided with more than a group of people who check boxes for various desired traits. They are presented with the potential to *feel* connected to other people that will participate in the potential formation of kinship. For example, Almeling quotes an egg bank's assistant director describing the online profiles of egg donors:

> The profile really gives recipients a chance to get to know you on another level. Even though it's anonymous, it feels like it's personal. It feels like they're making a connection with you. They want to feel like it's less clinical than just looking it up on a website, and they want to see which girl best suits their needs. It's about who looks like they could fit into my family and who has the characteristics that I would like in

my offspring? You can never be too conceited or too proud of your accomplishments because they really like to feel like, wow, this is a really special and unique person.[28]

In this description, we can see the way certain notions of intimacy and affect are reflected within the narrative of choosing an egg donor. There is a rhetoric of "feeling" through the acknowledgment and identification of what recipients "want to feel." However, there is also an implicitly assumed entitlement offered to the recipients to be able to choose the donor that "fits into the family" and choose the characteristics they "would like in their offspring." The very question of "who looks like they could fit into my family?" reflects the importance of a constructed sense of familiarity to connect donors to recipients. More systematic than the mere existence or absence of desire for a particular race, this digital structure of feeling produces the very possibilities and boundaries through which race is embodied, imagined, projected, and lived.

Choosing Profiles, Choosing Race

Within digital studies, early critiques about access and the hegemony of straight, White, male users have given way to examinations of the contemporary construction of a multicultural marketplace in which race and consumption are intimately shaped by one another.[29] As Nakamura writes in *Digitizing Race: Visual Cultures of the Internet*,

> Women and people of color are both subjects and objects of interactivity; they participate in digital racial formation via acts of technological appropriation, yet are subjected to it as well. . . . So rather than focusing on the idea that women and minorities need to get online, we might ask: How do they use their digital visual capital? In what ways are their gendered and racialized bodies a form of this new type of capital?[30]

Today, the assumed consumer is *not* exclusively straight, White, heterosexual, or able-bodied; however, stratifications of power like race, gender, and sexuality continue to deeply impact the landscape of digital consumption. Discourses of multiculturalism and colorblindness in the physical world become structured into the organization and obfuscation of race in online ones. For example, Daniel HoSang's theorization of "political whiteness" "in which whiteness functions as an absent referent within a putatively neutral and abstract terms of liberalism" can also be understood as functioning within the digital.[31] Here, and within broader critiques of colorblindness and race-neutral discourse, race does not need to be spoken in order to dictate and shape the social organization of accessible rights, choices, and resources.[32] This orientation becomes embedded into online spaces in which the role of race is less a question of public policy or material rights and rather one embedded in a consumer culture that frames the stratified valuation of different races as a "preference" or individual choice.

The terminology used to reference categories of race and ethnicity in both online dating and egg and sperm donation websites also demonstrate the tension between racial preferences as a filter for profiles and the applied liberal ideologies that race is a social construction and users are not or should not be "racist." For example, both OkCupid and Match.com use the term "ethnicity" to distinguish between common *racial* categories. As described previously, Asian, Black, Latino/Hispanic, Middle Eastern, Native American, Pacific Islander, and White are listed as possible choices of "ethnicity."[33] On OkCupid, this category is listed alongside "religion" under a tab titled "background" with an icon resembling a thumbprint. Similarly, all the cryobank websites that I examined had racial categories listed under terms like "ethnicity," "ancestry," or "heritage." In some instances, "ancestry" was differentiated by countries while "ethnicity" referred to race. Nowhere in any of the websites was "race" offered as a category from which to select. Whereas, within ethnic tudies, ethnicity as "defined in connection to origin, ancestry, parentage, or nationality" is differentiated from race as a formation and product of racialization, in these online spaces, the two are conflated.[34] Furthermore, icons like the thumbprint, which culturally symbolize the aforementioned fantasies of forensic identification, reflect how the situated meaning of race and/or ethnicity here is understood to be a matter of individual identification rather than a political identity of solidarity or structural formation.

Implicitly, race also functions as a corpus (within a corpus of profiles) through which specific racial categories acquire meaning in their relationality. Although users are always able to select more than one "ethnicity," the categories themselves only have meaning in exclusive differentiation from one another. This is further thrown into relief by the history and hegemony of reproducing racial boundaries in both dating culture as well as egg and sperm donation practices. Almeling describes the early-established expectation of maintaining racial congruency in parents and children in the egg and sperm donation industry, quoting a founder of one of the first sperm banks: "In the early days, the physicians we relied on for insight into the marketplace pretty much said any donor will do . . . It just doesn't matter who the donor is, so long as you give a Caucasian donor to a Caucasian woman and a Black donor to a Black woman . . ."[35] Similarly, the long history of anti-miscegenation in the United States has historically maintained the boundaries between racial categories and naturalized the idea that parents and children will share a racial identity.[36] And although transracial adoption certainly demonstrates that shared racial identity has not been necessary for the establishment of kinship in general, its long cultural narration as a liberal (and later neoliberal) act of multiculturalism further evidences its significance as the exception that proves the rule.

As these dating and egg and sperm donation services have gone online, services explicitly catered towards maintaining racial boundaries have also abounded. Sites like EastMeetsEast or BlackPeopleMeet offer self-selected racial categories for dating within a single race. For example, in their own words, EastMeetsEast "is exclusively dedicated to Asian dating. This means our members already have one important thing in common—they're looking for someone with a similar cultural background."[37] Here, the corpus of users from which to meet someone is defined by its racial or "cultural" specificity, referred to as a "similar cultural background." However, even within more diverse online communities, filtering for race serves the same function to include some and exclude others.

While egg and sperm donation has not seen the same rise of racially specific services, the filtering system in both economies serves the same function and assumes the necessity of maintaining the boundaries of legible racial categories. This normalization of racial sorting also further reflects the way race has become a naturalized form of social ordering and provokes important questions about the way race as a biologized phenomenon makes itself visible. In direct reference to the racial sorting of egg and sperm donation materials, anthropologist Kath Weston observes, "Color-coded vials of semen attempt to *re-embody* the anonymous source of a visually homogenous substance, as parents worry about what children might look like as well as inherit."[38] Indeed, these color-coded vials function to maintain the signification of racial difference precisely because the material substances are not visually distinguishable (sperm from a White donor does not look categorically different than sperm from an Asian donor). The discourse of race thus becomes one of many ways to stratify and give meaning to the various "visually homogenous" human reproductive samples. However, in so doing, the meaning of race is further rendered from the embodied experience or politics of the people involved.

In another ethnographic example of the effects of differentiating race in egg and sperm donation in South America, anthropologist Elizabeth Roberts discusses the phenomenon of dark-skinned recipients choosing White donors for the purpose of conceiving lighter-skinned children. Roberts describes,

> In the new practice of anonymous egg donation, both race and kinship are enacted within the specific political and economic history of malleable bodies in the Andes. This history involves the sexual domination of darker women by lighter men, producing lighter illegitimate children.... The history of sexual dominance and lightening persists in the practices of IVF physicians and sperm donors. Female egg donors have become the new actors in this ongoing project, participating in whitening the nation through the bodies of other women.[39]

As Roberts suggests, this example demonstrates the ways in which the role of race within economies of reproductive technologies are directly shaped by geographically specific histories of racial violence and hierarchy. Regardless of individual intention, egg and sperm donation thus serve as forms of race making, and Roberts suggests that "IVF participants who wanted children whiter than themselves are part of a long-standing project of whitening, based on the premise that race can be changed at both the group and individual level."[40]

Within the United States, recent media stories have also further highlighted a phenomenon that stratifies the value of eggs based on race.

Almeling observes an atypical inversion of the valuation of racialized biological materials:

> Due to the difficulty of maintaining a diverse pool of donors, both egg agencies [in the study] often increase the fee for donors of color, especially Asian Americans and African Americans. This results in a situation where they are often more highly valued than white women, which is unexpected, given that the reverse is often true in other contexts, including the labor market and in adoption agencies. But in this market, race is seen as a biologically based characteristic, and sex cells from women of color are perceived as scarce, which contributes to their increased value.[41]

This trend was further reported on by the *LA Times* in 2012 in a piece titled, "Asian women command premium prices for egg donation in US."[42] The story was then picked up by popular website *Jezebel*, in a piece titled, "Want to Sell Your Eggs to Pay for College? Be Asian."[43] In contrast, the popular news stories did not feature similar coverage of the higher valuation of African American egg donors. This is not the case for sperm donors who are generally paid the same across racial groups. As suggested, the economic explanation for the specific higher valuation of Asian and African American egg donors lies in the gendered and racialized supply and demand of egg and sperm as separate economies.

This valuation of the labor and biological products of egg donation along racial categories demonstrates the market need for a "diversity" of products available for consumers, the ethos of free market choice, and supply and demand logics that define these economies. While these cases especially highlight the fraught role of race in economies of reproduction, all these choices about which donor to choose or which race to date embody the ways in which kinship functions not only as a site of biological or social reproduction but also as a site in which race itself is reproduced and reified. As the following section explores, one consequence of this intersection between neoliberal choice and the reproduction of race is the framing of these racially specific choices as the right of "individual preference" rather than a reflection of broader social or political ideologies. And what becomes obfuscated in this preoccupation with individual choice and market logic is precisely the ways in which race continues to be stratified along existing social and political lines.

Preference and the Obfuscation of Racial Power

One of the primary "racial contradictions" (to borrow from Melamed) reflected in the digital profile interface that neoliberal multiculturalism seeks to manage is that individuals can have a specific and explicit desire for or aversion to certain races and simultaneously claim that they are not racist or prejudiced under the rationale of individual choice. Within this logic, a person has "the right" (under the hegemony of liberal individualism) to have racial preferences within the realm of dating or reproduction without "being racist" precisely because of their entitlement to individual choice. However, this "right" to a racial preference obfuscates the biopolitics of global capitalism that essentializes and commercializes racial categories, reproduction, and kinship formation for a consumer market in the first place.

In one such demonstration in 2014, news broke of the story of Jennifer Cramblett and the Ohio sperm bank that mistakenly gave her the sperm of a different donor from whom she and her partner had chosen. Cramblett and her partner are both White and had originally chosen a White donor, however, to their surprise, they found that Cramblett had become pregnant with sperm from an African American donor. Cramblett went on to sue the sperm bank for "wrongful birth," and headlines like "White woman sues sperm bank after she mistakenly gets black donor's sperm" and "White woman who sued sperm bank over black baby says it's not about race" highlighted the racial aspects of this sensational story.[44] Similarly, in September 2019, another story circulated of a White couple in New Jersey who took legal action against a fertility clinic after "they had a daughter of Asian descent due to a sperm mix-up," in which the wife was impregnated by the clinic with sperm from an unknown Asian person instead of her husband.[45] In both cases, the mistake was identified precisely because of the unexpected and visible racial difference that manifested in the resulting child of the reproductive process. Race functioned as the mislabeled product, the marker of merchandise not delivered as advertised.

Cramblett's own narration of her lawsuit admitted to her view that having a multiracial child was not something she desired, a fact that led to calls that she was racist. However, Cramblett's sense of entitlement over the reproductive process reflects a broader cultural tension between the common understanding that individuals have the right to reproductive choice regarding with whom or by what means they want to reproduce and the popular discourse of multicultural inclusion and acceptance. This expectation of reproductive agency coincides with principles of reproductive justice and autonomy; however, it also highlights the ways in which racial privilege and stratified valuation of different racial categories are embedded in normative narratives of family formation.

Indeed, as scholars on race and assistive reproduction have argued, this tension is inherent to the contemporary gamete economy. Fogg-Davis reminds us that "racial stereotyping is an accepted feature of this largely unregulated market."[46] And Daniels and Heidt-Forsythe argue, "the unregulated free market in ARTs [assistive reproductive technologies] has produced a form of gendered eugenics that compromises choice for donors and exacerbates hierarchies of human value based on stratified norms of race, ethnicity, economic class, and gender."[47] Using information from over fifteen hundred egg and sperm donors, they show the ways in which the current free market model for egg and sperm donation "reinforces the belief that inequality is genetically rooted and not socially produced" and "exacerbates and replicates beliefs that those traits that divide us are an inevitable part of our genetic landscape."[48] In other words, these free markets have created economies of choice through which existing hierarchies of race, gender, and class have been reproduced and visualized.

Similarly, the discourse of individual preference has also become hegemonic in narrating the tensions of racial categorization in online dating. For example, launched in 2004 and currently owned by Match Group (which owns and operates Match.com, Tinder, Meetic, Hinge, and PlentyofFish), OkCupid put themselves at the forefront of these conversations when they published a now-deleted blog post in September 2014 based on their user data titled "Race and Attraction, 2009–2014." The post was based on the "QuickMatch Score" across different self-identified racial groups. At the time, QuickMatch was a system through which individuals could "like" another user's profile either with or without further examination of the textual part of the profile, and the recipient could see that person "liked" them. Presented with a tone of accessible sociological interpretation, the blog post featured twelve tables only applicable to heterosexual dating: for each of the six years between 2009 and 2014, there was one table representing categories of "men rating women" and one for "women rating men."

Each table offered data for four racial categories: "Asian," "Black," "Latina/o," and "White." To explain the number values, the blog post described, "The values in these tables are 'preference vs. the average.' Think of them as how likely people are to want to interact with others when it comes to their dating lives."[49] As applied to the table, a 0% would mean that one group's preference for another is the same as the overall average of all users. A negative percentage would mean that one group's "preference" for another is that percentage less than the overall average and positive would mean that percentage more than the overall average. For example (as shown in Figure 4.2), in 2009, Asian men "preferred" White women 7% more than the overall average, while White men "preferred" Black women 18% less than the overall average.

Each combination's percentage rating was filled in with gradated shades of green or red. And it's no coincidence that negative scores were colored in increasingly alarming shades of red while positive scores were shaded in green. The tables functioned as a demonstration of the economization of racial categories, whereby racial identity was quantified and ranked based on marketplace ideologies of supply and demand that were presumed to be stable and applicable to individual social groups.

The report was quickly taken up by online news media, including *Mic.com*, *Huffington Post*, and *NPR*, as discussing some supposed truth about society. The tables of quantified calculations about desire and attraction were copied and pasted as evidence of "our" racial dating preferences as a national culture.[50] And the assignment of percentages was quickly taken up as an overall representation and ranking of the desirability of those races. The language of preference was crucial in these public conversations about race because it both referenced individual behaviors in these digital worlds while simultaneously constituting a cultural discourse that framed the desire (or lack thereof) for a particular racial identity as a right of individual consumer choice. For example, in the very presentation of the data, The OkCupid Blog offered an FAQ-style explanation of "preference":

2014
DateHookup "Let's Meet" Scores

		ASIAN women	BLACK women	LATINA women	WHITE women
men rating women	ASIAN men rating...	11%	-24%	9%	4%
	BLACK men rating...	7%	-9%	9%	-7%
	LATINO men rating...	12%	-27%	10%	6%
	WHITE men rating...	18%	-30%	6%	5%

		ASIAN men	BLACK men	LATINO men	WHITE men
women rating men	ASIAN women rating...	insuff.	-21%	9%	13%
	BLACK women rating...	5%	13%	-6%	-12%
	LATINA women rating...	-11%	-9%	14%	7%
	WHITE women rating...	-8%	-16%	4%	19%

Figure 4.2. One of twelve tables with OkCupid QuickMatch Scores on Racial Preference. "Race and Attraction, 2009–2014." OkCupid blog. September 10, 2014. http://blog.okcupid.com/index.php/race-attraction-2009-2014/.

Q: Are you saying that because I prefer to date [whatever race], I'm a racist?
[A:] "Preference" vs. racial bias is a much larger cultural debate, especially in the dating sphere. While we hope to help daters look beyond appearance and connect on a deeper level, there is an evident trend showing that race is a factor for many individuals, and in a consistent way. This might say more about the cultural biases passed down in our society than individuals within it.[51]

Referencing the discourse of "preference" as a "much larger cultural debate," The OkCupid Blog highlighted a perceived distinction between "preference" and "racial bias." From the perspective of this post and the "larger cultural debate," preference was thus positioned *in contrast* to racial bias and therefore could be framed as nondiscriminatory.

While the blog post was based on the company's own quantitative data collection and there was nothing to suggest the data itself was inaccurate, the report did not discuss the calculations used to generate those percentages or the algorithmic system that provided the basis for users "liking" one another. Information was also not provided regarding which profiles were presented to users in the first place. However, in their recent study *The Dating Divide: Race and Desire in the Era of Online Romance* published in 2020, sociologists Curington, Lundquist, and Lin empirically confirmed much of what was observed by OkCupid in 2014. Supported by their own data set from "one of the largest US dating websites" and contextualized by interviews conducted with users, the study presents many similarly scientific-looking tables that quantify desire, attractiveness, and the "likelihood of messaging" across racial groups. While they do not reference OkCupid's "data," the authors further describe what they call "digital-sexual racism" that "disguises enduring racial discrimination in intimate life as nothing more than idiosyncratic individual preference."[52] Indeed, on one hand, the language of "preference" is used to refer to what people are doing when they make choices on the online interface. On the other hand, this manifestation of individual preference has become the affective economy and cultural discourse through which race is stratified and given meaning, both in popular culture and scholarly contexts.

While digital-sexual racism undoubtedly abounds in online dating, I argue *both* preference discourse and racial discrimination are produced and reproduced by the very solidification of racial categories that emerge from the profile interface as a technology. And, in addition to more explicit forms of racial discrimination, the profile interface as a technology of kinship participates in the racialization process by which race is made meaningful to users and their resulting partnerships and families. This is not to say that either preference for dating certain races or racial discrimination in dating did not exist before online dating, but rather to emphasize the role of the profile interface as an algorithmic format through which the rearticulation and solidification of racial categories is made possible. Nakamura offers a helpful articulation of this "neoliberal discourse of color blindness and nondiscrimination" in the context of the Internet as a "paradigm in which failure to overtly discriminate on the basis of race, and the freedom to compete in the 'open market' despite an uneven playing field in terms of class, education, and cultural orientation constitutes fairness."[53]

The profile interfaces of both online dating and egg and sperm donation offer the materialization of these logics: the structural organization of the markets are viewed as "fair" precisely insofar as they do not "overtly discriminate on the basis of race" and any "preference" by way of users/consumers falls within the "freedom to compete in the 'open market.'" And in accordance with Nakamura's critique, what fails to go recognized in popular culture is precisely this "uneven playing field," or an examination or critique of the underlying racialized, gendered, and sexual systems of power that produce these consumer desires, demands, and interactions. While the profile interface may present these racial choices as an "even playing field" (insofar as users are seemingly just as able to select a person of one race as they are any other), the meaning of race itself and its role in producing these intimate encounters continue to be stratified and obscured.

In this context, the cultural narration of the "White male, Asian female" or "WMAF" multiracial couple is perhaps one of the most visible demonstrations of both this neoliberal racial logic and the racial histories that it aims to disavow. While there is, of course, no one singular WMAF experience, its *iconicity* demonstrates how preference discourse both obfuscates the specificities of racial meaning under neoliberal multiculturalism *and* serves as site of Asian American racialization through multiracial kin formation. Indeed, the ongoing cultural fixation on the WMAF couple as a symbol of racialized desirability, fetishism, and perceived racism reflects its political flexibility.

In its most neoliberal extreme, the WMAF couple serves as a symbol of multiculturalism, racial openness, and diversity without politics. Within this consumer logic of the profile interface, the WMAF couple is simply one racial combination out of many that can be analogized to any other (such as White male, Black female; or Asian male, Latinx female; etc.). In this context, the couple as a racial unit is defined similarly to neoliberal, individualized racial identity, wherein any single racial combination represents a individual choice made from an analogous set of options and variables. And as such, the mere abstracted fact of racial difference (of being a "multiracial couple") is what is significant, not the specific categories or embodied experiences of race that constitute a couple's identities. In other words, both race and gender are abstracted from their social and political identities and serve as coincidences of difference.

This discourse of depoliticizing race while using its visuality of difference as a symbol of multiculturalism, has been characteristic of many personal narratives, marketing campaigns, and institutional stances aimed towards embracing diversity and inclusion. In one example, in October 2023, the *Washington Post* published an op-ed titled, "Online dating is a personal nightmare. But very good for society." The piece argued that online dating increases users' exposure to "people we would not have met otherwise," thus potentially increasing the number of multiracial marriages which, in turn, would be "very good for society as a whole." The author, Youyou Zhou, a graphics reporter at the Opinions desk of the *Washington Post*, is an Asian woman who cites her own romantic relationship with a White man to support her point. She writes, "Online dating took me out of my comfort zone and nudged me to be more open-minded." And indeed, from her perspective, her own participation in a WMAF couple served as evidence towards the idea that multiracial relationships were "good for society." However, she doesn't explain why or how. Perhaps the underlying logic is too obvious to be made explicit: multiracial couples = diversity = good for society. But does it matter which races are together? And under what circumstances? The article reflects a particular kind of colorblind logic that is neither engaged with the specificity of racial meanings or structural racism, nor is it colorblind at all. For if it were truly colorblind, then how would being multiracial mean anything in the first place?

In addition to and in contrast to colorblind interpretations, the WMAF couple has also come to symbolize racial fetishization in contemporary culture in all its forms: its embodiment, its anxieties, and its denunciation. These are familiar images within Asian American studies and for many Asian women on a personal level, ones that evidence the specificity of the WMAF pairing within a longer history of race, gender, and sexuality in American culture. Sexual stereotypes of Asian women in mainstream White film and media have reflected and reinforced individuals' own views and treatment of Asian women. And scholars such as Celine Parreñas-Shimizu and Anne Anlin Cheng have written on the racialized sexualization of Asian women.[54] This affective range of sexualized racialization is quite broad. On one end of the spectrum are the grey-area suspicions of fetishistic desire or situations of plausible deniability: a White man "just happens" to have several Asian ex-girlfriends. Or, for example, in *Racist Love: Asian Abstraction and the Pleasures of Fantasy*, Leslie Bow recounts a White man describing how he met his Chinese wife by saying he attended an orchestra concert in which she was performing and he fell in love with the back of her head.[55] On the other end of the spectrum are the explicit forms of sexualized racism that target Asian women and actively harm them. Historically, sexual violence abounded against Asian women by American servicemen during the wars in Korea and Vietnam, setting the stage for sexual stereotypes about Asian women in the twentieth century.[56] Since then, Asian women have been the targets of individuals who believe those sexualized stereotypes about them; in 2021, a White man targeted Asian women in his shooting spree of two Atlanta spas.[57]

Indeed, many Asian American women reject and are wary of fetishization. Some have published essays in popular media, with titles such as "You Know What I Say About Men Who F—Asian Women?" or "Asian Women's Bodies Are Not Playgrounds For White People."[58] Others have been quoted by scholars evidencing their awareness of their racial positionalities.[59] And Bow also specifically theorizes questions of Asian fetishism in contemporary culture, writing,

> Invoking the fullness of personhood to counter sexual objectification produces an inherent contradiction: it appears to foreclose racial coalition by insisting on uniqueness (I am *not* identical to all those others), at the very moment that the protestation creates shared experience (*Like* all others, I reject being fetishized). The project to restore the objectified Asian female body to personhood against misrecognition exposes the inadequacies of the public text of race centered on equality; resisting fetishism by asserting individuality seems to forgo collectivity in the very form of its protest.[60]

Bow captures a contradiction in the very meaning of race and identity in the neoliberal context, one that is reflected and amplified in online dating and the digital profile interface. And this contradiction also underlies the fraught meaning of race within the profile interface: what does it mean to self-identify as and with a particular race, or seek out a particular race, without conceding to the premise that race itself is a legitimate basis for generalization?

What makes the WMAF couple such a fraught icon of racialized anxiety specifically is precisely these uncertainties that it embodies, uncertainties that have become amplified and laid bare by the marketplace economy of the profile interface. On the embodied level, the profile manifests the struggle of identification and disavowal: Am I one of *those* Asian women that is being fetishized? Am I one of *those* White men that fetishizes? Are we or will we be one of *those* couples in which he fetishizes her? On a cultural level, these anxieties play out in these circular conversations and calculations about individual preference, agency, and choice.

What is often missing from these popular culture conversations about individual identity and agency is precisely the uneven ground upon which the racialization of the Asian woman compared to that of the White man has occurred and how the historical precedents of this coupling shapes their contemporary positioning against one another. Regardless of individuals' experiences or historical knowledge, the normativity of Orientalist associations of Whiteness with masculinity and Asianness with femininity inform the naturalization of the WMAF as icon within contemporary culture. This iconicity is further precedented by the history of transracial adoption (wherein Asian children were under the tutelage of White fathers) and Asian military wives immigrating with their White husbands. Furthermore, in a society where Whiteness is the racial norm and default, the meaning of Whiteness (and the desire for it) is not necessarily comparable to that of Asianness, especially when Asianness in this context is ladened with such specific and explicit gendered stereotypes. As such, while the interpersonal exchange may be equitable (insofar as an Asian woman and a White man might mutually consent to their own relationship), the social and cultural locations of their racial and gendered positioning will never be the same.

Because race is marketed as an inherent and inherited trait, one that users both cannot change in themselves but can choose in others, the choice of potential romantic partner or donor is always already produced as a choice of racial identity. In placing these choices in the hands of consumers, the profile interface exists in a system that assumes and promotes the idea that it is a user's "right" to choose the race of their potential child or partner. Certainly, this is not to suggest that people should not be able to choose whomever they want in a consenting partner or egg or sperm donor. However, the very discourse of consumer choice and the rendering of that choice from the social and political meanings of race is part of a larger neoliberal multiculturalist structuring within contemporary digital worlds.

Within this framing, the question of whether an individual explicitly desires or rejects a racial category, and whether or not either is "racist," is less important than the systems of racial meaning that have become naturalized to the point of being inconspicuous within contemporary processes of intimacy and family formation. As a technology of kinship, the profile interface has produced new iterations of family in which race has become defined, naturalized, and depoliticized by the discourse of neoliberal individual choice and preference. And thus, contemporary multiculturalism is articulated, not through a framework of equity or redistribution of resources to facilitate more expansive forms of kinship, but rather through the (re)production of family formation as another neoliberal site of economic consumption.

Multicultural Visions and the Consumption of Race

As a site of consumption, the profile interface further sutures the modernity of the digital to a teleological narrative of the multicultural family, one in which the family represents the supposedly progressing diversity of the nation. The digital as an icon of futurity and technological innovation bolsters the image of the modern family that has exercised its (neo)liberal freedoms to choose their own mode of family formation. Melamed also describes how under neoliberal multiculturalism "new categories of privilege and stigma determined by ideological, economic, and cultural criteria overlay older, conventional racial categories, so that traditionally recognized racial identities . . . can now occupy both sides of the privilege/stigma opposition."[61] The result of this incorporation of race into free market consumption is the implicit conflation of multiculturalism with consumer choice as a positive good. Following this logic, "anyone can choose anything they want" is the free market platonic ideal, and diversity facilitates its reification.

From a visual perspective, neoliberal multicultural logic thus manifests in the celebration of visible diversity in for-profit marketing through images of multiracial and queer families and couples. Dating websites and social media as well as egg and sperm donation websites often feature images of couples and families of different races and sexualities happily smiling and enjoying their services. For example, in November 2021, Match.com promoted their eleventh annual "Singles in America" study based on a "demographically representative sample" of 5,000 US singles between the ages of 18 and 98.[62] Amid colorful descriptions of their findings (for example, only 11% of singles want to date casually, or 65% of singles would like their dating partners to be vaccinated), the report featured photographs of a multiracial group of stylish, thin, and conventionally attractive "singles." Resembling screenshots taken from a film, one image simply shows a closeup photograph of a dark-skinned hand clasped gently around a light-skinned hand. One couple, the only one featured in the piece in multiple photographs, consists of a light-skinned racially ambiguous woman paired with a dark-skinned Black woman. In one photograph they laugh, leaning their faces together. In another, they smile at each other as if in the middle of a comfortable conversation. The various images demonstrate Match.com's open celebration of same-gender and multiracial intimacy that has come to characterize this kind of consumptive diversity.

Similarly, the testimonials on egg and sperm donation websites actively feature families of different races, genders, and sexualities. On one homepage, a banner shows a White queer couple holding a baby, with the text "We Support All Family Dreams." The negative space of the "D" in dreams is filled in with a rainbow.[63] Another homepage includes stories of a heterosexual White couple, a single White mom, and a Black lesbian couple as testimonies from customers. Whether staged models or real families, visual representations of certain types of multicultural inclusion mark the contemporary neoliberal digital moment and the ways in which companies market their products.

While this kind of visual manifestation of neoliberal multicultural inclusion extends throughout the digital world in these kinds of mundane and normalized examples, OkCupid again amplified and further exaggerated this cultural subtext in one of their marketing campaigns: designed by Italian artist Maurizio Cattelan and photographer Pierpaolo Ferrari, and presented by the independent advertising agency Mekanism, the "For Every Single Person" campaign was introduced in 2021. The campaign was premised on the idea that OkCupid offers dating for anyone and everyone, "embracing a full range of identities, preferences, and desires."⁶⁴ Self-described as a form of "radical inclusivity" and evoking a kind of camp aesthetic in the wake of the (somewhat critically received) 2019 Met Gala theme, the campaign featured over fifteen brightly colored posters each literalizing, and in many cases satirizing, a different somewhat unexpected "identity" for which OkCupid embraces and offers their platform.⁶⁵

A closeup image of a light-skinned foot with a red lighter between each toe reads, "Every single toker." A portrait of a light-skinned androgynous person with slicked-back brown hair, shoulder tattoo, and white tank top says, "Every single nonbinary." A shirtless man with a small tree coming out of his boxers, while a hand from out of frame pours water from a watering can onto it, stands beside the text, "Every single tree hugger." They're supposed to be eye-catching, surrealist, whimsical, and full of innuendo. Chief Marketing Officer of OkCupid Melissa Hobley was quoted calling the campaign "our most important creative to date: our biggest statement of inclusivity."⁶⁶ And on an Instagram post, she wrote, "Proud to work at a dating app that celebrates inclusivity and diversity and wants everyone to find love."⁶⁷ The campaign was called "provocative" and "identity-forward," promoting the company's reputation as "on the forefront of inclusivity in the dating app realm."⁶⁸

While the campaign indeed explicitly espoused inclusion, it also relied on a particular form of diversity for the purpose of promoting their online platform. Here, the visuality of multiculturalism functioned as both a metaphor for and direct reference to racial, gender, and sexual difference. Often posted in sets on billboards and advertising spaces, the images together created a multicolored effect capitalizing on the visual association of the rainbow as a symbol of queer pride as well as metonymizing the multicolored with the concept of diversity (Figure 4.3). With the exception of pansexual, non-monogamist, and nonbinary, the identities used in the campaign were almost exclusively identities associated with particular lifestyle or political choices rather than social identities of marginalization:

146 | MAKING RACIAL CHOICES

Figure 4.3. Screenshot of the OkCupid blog featuring their "Every Single Person" campaign. "Let's celebrate every single person." OkCupid blog. July 29, 2021. https://theblog.okcupid.com/lets-celebrate-every-single-person-bd135a7c7e1d.

- Heavypetter
- Bear
- Vaxxer
- Tree hugger
- Vegetarian
- Feminist
- Cuddler
- Insomniac
- Pansexual
- Romantic
- Non-monogamist

- Nonbinary
- Book worm
- Submissive
- Toker
- Pro-choicer

Seemingly purposeful in their randomness and lack of analogy, the identities chosen for the campaign thus do the work of representing diversity without needing to account for the politics, privilege, marginalization, or social context of any of them. Of course, OkCupid literally welcomes tree huggers or book worms. However, the placement of several recognized political and marginalized identity categories alongside more parodic "identities" analogizes them under the neoliberal ethos of personal preference and choice. And, for example, while individual viewers may or may not understand that nonbinary identity is not merely a "personal" or "lifestyle" choice, placing them in parallel suggests that it is akin to choosing not to eat meat or enjoying cuddling.

This flattening of historically political identities, formed either from structures of racialized, gendered, and/or sexual oppression, and reclaimed or built around a shared politics, demonstrates the power of neoliberal capitalism to transform and incorporate relations of oppression and liberation into relations of consumption. In addition to the subtextual meaning these identities represent, actual physical markers of race and gender expression that have historically and contemporarily served as the basis for discrimination, violence, and exclusion have thus been subsumed by and analogized with the aesthetic. In other words, race, gender, and sexuality exist within the campaign only as aesthetic artistic choices. As mentioned, nonbinary identity, non-monogamy, and pansexuality are the only exceptions to this, perhaps inadvertently revealing their minoritization and misconception in popular culture as niche lifestyle choices rather than marginalized social identities.

While I have argued throughout this chapter that Asian racial difference has been subsumed by neoliberal multicultural choice as a depoliticized preference among many, the ongoing use of the visuality of Asian racial difference in this campaign further demonstrates the continued abstraction of its specific political meaning. In other words, despite claims of colorblindness, the arrangement of racialized bodies is

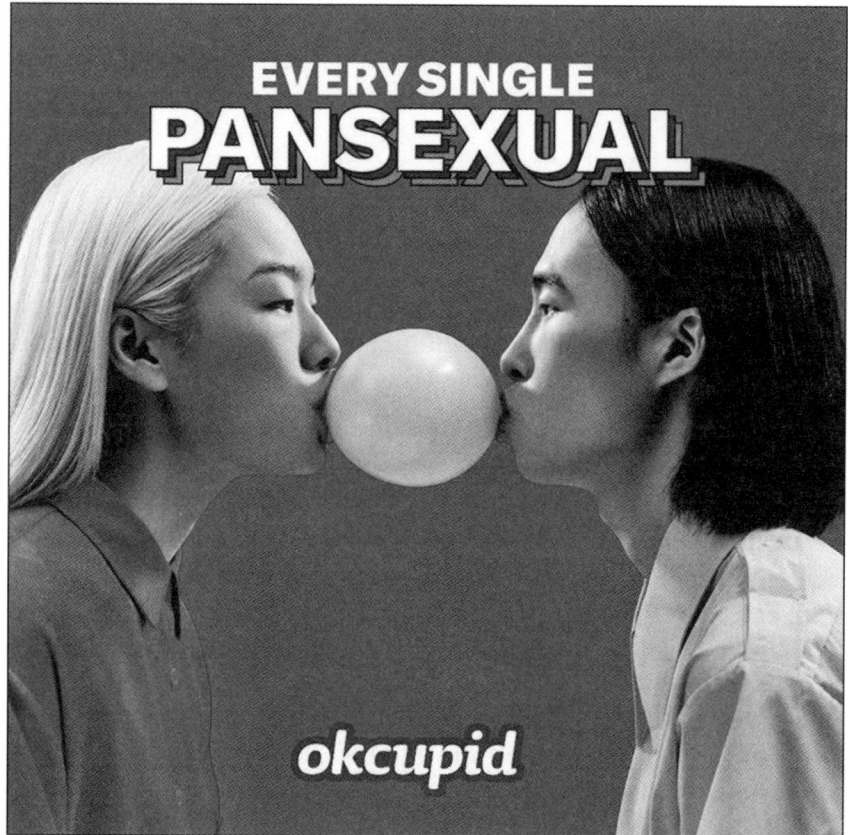

Figure 4.4. "Every Single Pansexual" campaign advertisement. "Let's celebrate every single person." OkCupid blog. July 29, 2021. https://theblog.okcupid.com/lets-celebrate-every-single-person-bd135a7c7e1d.

never random in the neoliberal multicultural vision, thus betraying the continued abstraction and subtextual meaning of racialized difference beyond depoliticized inclusion. The use of Asians in two images of the Every Single Person campaign exemplifies this tension. First, the poster for "Every Single Pansexual" shows a cobalt blue background with two Asians, lips pursed on opposites sides of a bright pink bubblegum bubble, in a style almost reminiscent of *Lady and the Tramp* (Figure 4.4). The scopic message of this particular image is much more gestural than, say, the lighters as a symbol of the toker or the literal tree getting watered in the tree hugger's boxer shorts. Here, pansexual identity itself invokes a question the image intends to answer: how do you represent pansexuality when this identity is defined by attraction regardless of gender?

The couple appears to be a man and a woman, thus seeming heterosexual. So, what makes them pansexual? The campaign uses these two Asian bodies to answer this question. In fact, it is precisely the racialized, gendered, and affective arrangement of these two people in this particular image that reveals the campaign's underlying neoliberal multicultural visualization of this sexual identity. The image presents pansexuality's disregard for gender (as an organizing category of attraction) through the *absence* of gender expression. Both wear simple loose-fitting collared shirts, hers in red and his in the same pink as the bubblegum bubble. Their hairstyles are similarly parted down the middle, gelled flat, sleek and straight. Their faces and style are otherwise bare, without noticeable makeup or accessories. Indeed, androgyny need not be the absence of gender expression, but their racialized bodies and affect further amplify and conflate the alienization of both Asianness *and* pansexuality. Unlike other faces in the campaign such as the submissive's eyes closed in ecstasy under footed heels or the bear looking alluringly right into the camera as he shows his hairy chest with a heart shaved in the middle, both pansexuals look at each other with deadpan expressions. Together, the lack of affect, their Asianness, and their androgyny resembles the techno-Orientalist roboticness that marks contemporary Asian American gendered racialization. This is a racial form born from the inexpressive and emotionally inscrutable stereotype of Asians but also updated to offer inclusion as long as they remain scrutably alien in their engagement with diversity.[69] Thus, the embodiment of race comes to function as a marker of sexuality in the image.

This imbrication of Asian androgyny into a neoliberal multicultural fantasy alongside the evocation of the nonhuman is further amplified in the poster for "Every Single Non-Monogamist," the other image featuring an Asian person (see Figure 4.5). Against a cerulean blue background, a striking and somewhat unsettling pile of limbs and bodies sits on a teal and red bench. A black woman with cornrows in a hot pink jumpsuit sits on a disembodied lap wearing green bell bottoms. A set of disembodied legs in acid-washed denim and bright green socks and sneakers straddle her waist. She leans over an almost corpse-like face-down torso of a brown-haired feminine body to kiss an androgy-

Figure 4.5. "Every Single Non-Monogamist" campaign advertisement, OkCupid. *AdWeek*. 2021. https://www.adweek.com/creativity/okcupid-launches-an-expansive-campaign-for-almost-every-single-kind-of-dater/.

nous Asian man with bleached blond hair. An impossibly-long, dark-skinned, and disembodied arm reaches to caress his head. Again, the bright colors and different races evoke the type of multicultural inclusion the company and most other dating sites explicitly promote. And the provocative extreme of eroticism with anonymous limbs implies that OkCupid is for everyone, even if you are a disembodied set of limbs (or are into that). And yet, given only two people in this image are kissing, non-monogamy as a form of radical polyamorous practice marginalized by heteronormativity is not actually represented here literally. Instead, it is metaphorized by this pile of limbs. Indeed, both posters avoid actually depicting nonheteronormative erotic intimacy, while capitalizing on visual references to racial, gender, and sexual diversity to market them.[70]

While OkCupid may have made them daringly explicit in this particular campaign, making choices using identity-based criteria and espousing inclusion while race and queerness are instrumentalized but never politicized are characteristic of digital profile economies on other platforms. Within egg and sperm donation marketing, this consumer narrative is brought to its reproductive conclusion. Whiteness remains the privileged foundation, but now other races can access the same consumer opportunities Whiteness has historically afforded. For example, one homepage shows an image of a brown-haired White woman leaning gently over a peacefully sleeping infant, kissing the child behind the ear. The heading reads, "Give Life to Your Dream" and then in smaller text, "Complete your family using frozen donor sperm or frozen donor eggs. Or maybe you're interested in fertility preservation? Handpick your future today!"[71] Conveniently avoiding the racialized implications of structures of socioeconomic privilege, anyone of any race who can afford these services is welcome and encouraged. Thus, racial and sexual exclusion and inequality can be obfuscated behind the organization of the free market.

The profile interface continues to endure as a system that facilitates the creation of new forms of kinship in both online and physical worlds. Online dating has become more relevant than ever as world-historical events like the COVID-19 pandemic continue to affect who we are and are not able to interact with in embodied ways. And access to egg and sperm donation relies more and more upon socioeconomic means rather than racial identity. However, as this chapter suggests, egg and sperm donation, online dating, and the websites used to market these services reflect the very changing nature of racial categories that define identities like Asian American. The profile interface frames race as a category in which individuals are entitled to self-identify. And even more significantly, it operates as a means through which individuals express consumer preferences and choose who to bring into their physical, social, and intimate worlds. These profiles provide a site in which racial ideologies, fantasies, and categorization practices are reproduced and normalized.

On a visual level, these websites show the similarities between picking an intimate partner and picking a person whose genetic materials are used to create a child. To choose a race of a person is to choose a race of kinship. And as a result, the family is always already racialized. The construction and representation of race within digital worlds not only reflects cultural meanings about race but also actively participates in the meaning-making process of contemporary racial categories. After almost a century of disentangling race from the body and the examination of race as a "social construction," new technologies have reinscribed race on the body and within kinship in new ways. And rather than disempowering or resisting the power of race to shape United States culture, both the profile interface and the direct-to-consumer genetic tests of the following chapter reaffirm the importance of race in representing the self, the body, and the family.

5

23andMe and the Racialization of Genetic Ancestry Testing

When you purchase the popular health and ancestry genetic test 23andMe, it comes in a smooth white box with a brightly colored design on the front framing the phrase "Welcome to you." The name of the company alongside their minimalist logo, consisting of two rounded lines crossed, one kelly green and the other bright magenta, reminds us of the chromosome pairs taught about in basic biology class and of the clean aesthetic often associated with "scientific" knowledge. The message is clear: we are being "welcomed" into learning something new about ourselves through the power of genetic science. To add to the appeal, underlining the text is a row of ten diploid pairs of chromosome-shaped columns in a rainbow array of other eye-catching colors. Like the OkCupid marketing campaign of the previous chapter, the 23andMe box combines the metaphorical with the representational to convey a clear message about the product: bright colors function as a signifier for human diversity and multiculturalism, while the literal representation of chromosomes connects genetic science to ideas of scientific inquiry, humanity, and the self.

Since it was founded in 2006, media narratives about 23andMe in addition to its own advertising and marketing have presented the direct-to-consumer ancestry test as an innovation of discovery. Not only does it offer the opportunity to discover oneself through the power of modern genetic science ("Welcome to you"), but it also provides the potential to discover other people through the social networking opportunities of its online platform. Users can find and connect with "DNA Relatives" through a tab marked "Family & Friends," where they can send messages, map out family trees, and see where these "relatives" are located on a world map. And with the introduction in 2020 of 23andMe+ Premium, a new annual membership that offers additional individualized genetic reports and access to "advanced filtering of DNA relatives" using categories such "ancestry composition" or "population subregions," the service has leaned into contemporary associations with genetic ancestry testing as, firstly, a private activity related to individual health, sociality, and leisure and, secondly, a personal endeavor connecting consumers to a sense of family, community, and belonging.[1] This ethos of genetic information as entertainment and self-knowledge has emerged in direct contrast to the ways in which medical genetic testing has historically carried, and continues to carry, a much different connotation related to the role of family inheritance in relation to medical pathology and public research.

This chapter examines the entangled narratives of family, race, and genetics within the contemporary consumer culture of genetic ancestry tests, through an analysis of the public marketing and user platform offered by 23andMe. It explores what Alondra Nelson calls "DNA's social power" and considers how 23andMe functions as a technology that produces new racialized and gendered meanings of what constitutes kinship and how it can be formed.[2] And it reveals the ways in which the already existing social relationship between race, inheritance, and kinship has been further solidified and reproduced through popular multicultural narratives around this technology. If we understand and insist in contemporary society that race is a social construction, how does it continue to persist through our ideas and fantasies about genetics and kinship? In this context, geographic locations and relationships are rooted in the imaginary of a global family, one that exists in stark contrast to current social and political realities such as border regulations, resource inequality under capitalism, and racialized violence. Within the 23andMe consumer world, users are able to claim and cross national borders as an activity of leisure and "heritage," even as physical border crossing and racial categories are neither so simple nor loosely regulated. This chapter also argues that 23andMe produces new forms of kinship that essentialize and reinforce neoliberal multicultural categories of racial difference while also offering new opportunities to relate to and encounter others based on the varied meanings of shared genetics.

I specifically focus on 23andMe, not only because they are one of the leading services in this sector of the market, but also because their visual and narrative presentation of what genetic ancestry testing is and how it can be used both demonstrates and amplifies the hegemony of neoliberal multicultural logics of genetics, race, and kinship in contemporary culture. Genetic ancestry tests are not simply comprised of "purely" scientific processes or methods but rather are constantly and continually mediated through the economic, multicultural, and digital ideologies that circulate within the worlds that use and consume them. 23andMe is a for-profit company that became publicly traded in June 2021 and most of their customers are not scientists. Therefore, 23andMe and other for-profit genetic ancestry companies have had to balance making their services (based in advanced scientific techniques) legible to consumers while promoting and prioritizing the profitability of their product. Rather than focus on the scientific environment or genetic knowledge production itself, this analysis reveals these processes of meaning-making for which marketing and digital platforms operate as a mediator, such as in their narration of ancestry through associations with geographic locations or offering kinship connection to "DNA Relatives."[6]

As Dorothy Nelkin and M. Susan Lindee discuss in *The DNA Mystique: The Gene as a Cultural Icon*, in contemporary culture, "Genes, historically invoked to celebrate racial purity, have become symbols of racial diversity and shared human heritage."[3] Their original study, first published in 1995, further theorized the concept of "genetic essentialism" as the reduction of the self "to a molecular entity, equating human beings, in all their social, historical, and moral complexity, with their genes."[4] Still relevant decades later, Nelkin and Lindee also highlight how the underlying metaphors geneticists use to describe work on the human genome "are a characterization of the gene as the essence of identity, a promise that genetic research will enhance prediction of human behavior and health, and an image of the genome as a text that will define a natural order."[5] In a circular relationship, direct-to-consumer genetic tests have both built their appeal upon and further reproduce the social and cultural importance of genetics in defining identity and kinship. Furthermore, genetic testing has capitalized on neoliberal ideologies of consumer freedom and privacy, the digitization of individuals' information and data, and the transformation of scientific and medical data into material for social media-style interactions.[6]

Through technologies like 23andMe, this genetic essentialism also produces new forms of kinship and connection, or what I call "genetic intimacies." These relations are inherently partial, precisely because of their originary reliance on the imagined meanings of genetic connection. However, these intimacies often do become more embodied and experiential forms of kinship as they give rise to forms of interpersonal engagement based on shared experience and embodied interaction. In so doing, they demonstrate the different ways individuals make sense of themselves and others in this era of 23andMe. Rather than aim to reinforce or reject a definition of kinship based on its use in genetic testing narratives or popular culture (often appearing as the logic that family equals genetic relation), this chapter interrogates the racialized foundations upon which the very concept of kinship is built in these contexts. And it further explores, as Keith Wailoo, Alondra Nelson, and Catherine Lee question in their introduction of *Genetics and the Unsettled Past*, ". . . how ancestry testing has transformed our notions of kinship, placing *en famille* those individuals whose association is based on genetic markers and pushing aside notions of family that are based on social norms, interaction, or cultural codes."[7]

Genetic ancestry tests are thus not solely sites of power but rather function as a landscape through which racial meaning and kinship are negotiated in embodied and ideological ways. For example, as Nelson shows, the use of genetic genealogy has offered opportunities for reconciliation and community for African Americans and those of African descent in the United States reckoning with questions of ancestry in the aftermath of slavery. The use of genetic testing by the Asian diaspora also offers new opportunities for further exploration of race and identity on a transnational scale. For example, the fraught relationship between Chineseness as a political nation-state and Chinese ethnic minority populations (to which genetic ancestry tests associate individuals) parallels the entangled relationship between DNA testing and Indigenous claims to land, identity, resources, and sovereignty analyzed by Kim TallBear.[8] Nelson also discusses the use of genetic technologies to investigate and identify individuals in mass "disappearances" in Argentina, a use that has implications for victims of genocide and wide scale trauma within Asia and across the Asian diaspora.[9]

In contrast to the focus on genetic science used for explicit political or reconciliatory projects, this analysis also situates the specificities of Asian American racialization within the broader neoliberal multicultural moment established in the previous chapter, in which Asianness is rendered from its radical, political, and structural contexts (i.e.

as racial formation) and is rather produced as multicultural commodity, which users can then consume by means of identification. In this context, Asian racialization and racial categorization in the European and North American markets of 23andMe takes a specific form that reflects the neoliberal and multicultural shifts of the twenty-first century. Similarly to the online dating platforms and donor banks of the previous chapter, "Asian American" takes on a particular consumer categorization that obfuscates its racialized meaning and political origins. In the world of 23andMe, it becomes attached to images of spatial and geographic diversity that promote images of the metaphorical and literal global family. This is not to say that individuals do not benefit from using 23andMe; as I discuss subsequently, even more commercialized uses of 23andMe can give rise to meaningful kinship formation. However, in the world of genetic ancestry tests, race has become further subsumed by, not only ideologies about ancestry and culture, but also logics of inheritance and genetic relatedness.[10] The narratives and discourses explored here thus show that family and kinship can be constituted in a number of different ways that shape and are shaped by these changing meanings of race, genetics, and relatedness.[11]

23andMe and the Multicultural Consumption of Science

23andMe launched their first product in the United States in November 2007 at the cost of $999 per test. In 2008, *Time* named its saliva-based testing model "Invention of the Year."[12] That year the price was also reduced to $399, and for the next two years the company embarked on specific development projects such as research on Parkinson's disease and a collaboration with NFL players to examine athletes' genetic factors. Promotions like "DNA Day 2010" offered deals at lower prices, and by June 2011, their database had surpassed 100,000 customers. In 2014, 23andMe expanded health reports to Canada and the UK, and in 2015 the company had more than one million genotyped customers. As of 2024, 23andMe boasts of having sold over 12 million kits, representing the sheer amount of information and data they have acquired.[13] In contrast to other direct-to-consumer genetic test services like Ancestry.com or Family Tree DNA, the focus of the name 23andMe highlights the role of genes in the construction of the self.[14]

On their website, 23andMe markets two different "services": an ancestry service for "the most comprehensive ancestry breakdown" and a health service to get "personalized genetic insights that can help you take more informed actions on your health."[15] As of 2024, customers can buy them together as a package for a base price of $229. All purchase options include the one-time fee and the submission of a saliva sample in the collection kit provided. After the sample is processed in a company lab, users then make an account on the online platform to view their resulting reports and interact with other users, much like a social media site. In 2020, the company also released a new subscription-based service called 23andMe+™ for an extra $69 a year that provides additional health reports and "enhanced ancestry features" that include added filters to sort through "DNA relatives," as well as an increased number of those "DNA relatives" to view and with whom to interact. In 2023, 23andMe also announced their new 23andMe+ Total Health™ membership for $99 a month, marketed as a "prevention-based" feature for "individuals who want to augment their current healthcare experience with even more direct access to comprehensive genetic testing, risk assessment in critical health areas, and personalized health plans driven by clinicians with unique knowledge and training in genetics."[16]

The company website and marketing frame the information offered by the analysis of a customer's DNA not only as beneficial to the consumer seeking information about themselves but also as a positive form of knowledge acquisition within a broader scientific project benefitting humankind. Despite controversy around the use of direct-to-consumer genetic test databases by law enforcement (which 23andMe explicitly states they do not share voluntarily), the company offers a public narrative of scientific research and advancement that situates customers as a community positively supporting its endeavors.[17] For example, on their webpage titled "Research," the heading reads, "Becoming part of something bigger." It goes on to claim, "Our genetic research gives everyday people the opportunity to make a difference by participating in a new kind of research—online, from anywhere . . . These contributions help drive scientific discoveries."[18] Indeed, customers have the choice to opt into or out of the use of their data for research. However, the implication of the text is that if you opt out of sharing your data for research you are *not* "becoming part of something bigger" or "making a difference" in contributions that "help drive scientific discoveries." Furthermore, the underlying assumption in this context is that "becoming part of something bigger" and scientific discovery are morally positive activities. Thus, when customers purchase 23andMe, they not only benefit themselves, they are also able to see themselves as benefitting others.

This integration of individual capitalist consumption, scientific innovation, and multiculturalism is part and parcel of the neoliberal economic, political, and cultural landscape. While contributing to "something bigger" may not seem like an individualistic endeavor here, it is only achieved through individual consumption and the making available of one's own personal genetic data. No shared politics, community, empathy, or even interaction with other people required. Contributing to scientific research thus comes in the form of buying a product from a private company and giving them your genetic material. Furthermore, in contrast to research conducted in universities like the Human Genome Diversity Project, or federally funded projects like the Human Genome Project, 23andMe is not beholden to the same standards or regulations regarding scientific research. This is not to imply that the methods or research conducted by the company do not adhere to current scientific standards (they did voluntarily apply and receive institutional review board [IRB] approval from an independent private company in 2010) but rather to highlight the ways in which private, nonprofit, and public institutions differentially structure and serve capitalist aims.[19]

Multiculturalism also serves multiple functions in the public narration of 23andMe. Most visibly, it functions as the discourse through which the company and its employees understand the inclusivity of their mission. For example, 23andMe has devoted a webpage to diversity, equity, and inclusion, focusing on their workforce diversity and linking to their various blog posts on "Genetics, Race, and Research." And the company also uses the visuality of racial difference to market their product and frame diversity in scientific terms rather political ones. Rather than a basis for racism and/or political solidarity, racial difference exists in this 23andMe world as an essentialized quality found in DNA and celebrated as a marker of human genetic diversity.

These deployments of multiculturalism are made more explicit in the website's presentation of some of their employees. Under the subtitle "Meet some of our researchers," there are three figures featured on the website.[20] On the left is a White man named David H., PhD, who is listed as Principal Scientist. Scroll over his image with your cursor and he is quoted saying, "The high quality genetic research we do at 23andMe is possible because of our customers who share their data and want to make a difference." In the middle is a White woman named Joanna M., PhD. She is Senior Director of Research, and says, "I am passionate about genetics because I am fascinated by how humans are different from one another, and what DNA tells us about those differences." On the right is an Asian woman named Joyce T., PhD. As VP of Research, she implores us, "Be curious. Ask questions. The more we understand about our fascinatingly complex selves, the better we can take care of each other and the beautiful world we live in." Together, they not only represent the company narratively, but they also represent the racial makeup of the company wherein a little over one third of the employees at 23andMe are identified as "Asian or Pacific Islander" and 44% are White.[21] David and Joanna both refer to "difference" as an assumed social good: to make a difference and to be different from one another. David credits that social good for the "high quality" of their research and Joanna attributes her fascination with human difference to her "passion" for genetics. Joyce further externalizes this valuation of difference by prescribing that these forms of knowledge will somehow help us "take care of each other."

In addition to the sense of authenticity these ambassadors bring for the company, and regardless of their actual visibility to customers (since they are relatively inconspicuous at the bottom of a page discussing the genetic science of the service), these images demonstrate how 23andMe very intentionally narrates their own image as a company that is innovative, scientific, multicultural, and friendly. They bring passion to the work they do. They see the world as a "beautiful place." And they do this genetic research to "make a [positive] difference" in the world. They also value scientific research as another social and cultural good. However, the very category of "science" as an endeavor of knowledge production here already carries social and cultural meanings that imply its status as objective, trustworthy, and unprejudiced. Or, as Laura Briggs describes of this logic, "Science is not *a* knowledge . . . but *the* knowledge, that which can speak truthfully about the real."[22] Within this fantasy is the idea that science can and should be "objective" and apolitical, and thus it can function for the good of all. Furthermore, the visuality of their racial identities reflects this multicultural ethos and its association with innovation and futurity. Throughout the website and advertising, 23andMe shows people of different races and ethnicities benefitting from the service.

23andMe capitalizes on these teleological fantasies of the morality of science and the futurity of the multicultural world by implicitly proposing that one cannot fully know oneself without knowledge of their genetics *and* posing that such knowledge is simultaneously beneficial to the individual and crucial to scientific progress. However, the belief that the self possesses the power to improve the world through capitalist consumption is a uniquely neoliberal proposal. On an ideological level, it assumes the normalization, acceptance, and even celebration of private companies' determination of the course and implementation of scientific research, research that has already been justified by its valuation as a moral good in its association with science and medicine. And on an individual level, it assumes that agency, participation, and morality in society functions through neoliberal consumption wherein the act of consumption is not only an economic exchange but also a right and freedom. Such a system defines the agency and purpose of the individual through their ability to consume commodities provided and sold by private companies. And one result of this is that the social meanings of race and multiculturalism are also further individualized into discourses of personal identity and consumer choice.

The Global Family and the Depoliticization of Race

23andMe uses the language of shared global heritage to offer a different kind of what Catherine Ceniza Choy calls "global family making."[23] While Choy uses this term to specifically consider the crossing of borders in adoption from Asia to the United States in the twentieth century, 23andMe offers other iterations of the global family that reflect narratives of "humanity as a family" that originated in the Cold War and have been updated through contemporary notions of race and nation rooted in genetic population science. In this context, not only are individuals deconstructed through their genetics to produce and make meaning of genetic connections to global populations, but they are also offered the prospect of actually meeting other individuals with which they share DNA in a kind of kinship formation that has a global reach.

23andMe presents itself as a technology of this kinship that spans nationality, race, and culture, and again assumes this global multiculturalism as a positive good. This fits within the longer history of US multiculturalism and the role of humanitarianism as another continuation of, rather than divestment from, forms of US imperialism and global hegemony. For example, the 1955 photographic exhibition "The Family of Man," curated by Edward Steichen for the Museum of Modern Art in New York, exemplifies twentieth-century uses of the family as a metaphor for the imagined unification of global humanity, and featured over five-hundred photographs taken in sixty-eight countries. Christina Klein writes of the exhibition,

> In publicizing the idea that all humanity belonged to the same family, the show reinforced the terms through which the US explained and justified its reshaping of the international order. America's claims of global 'responsibilities,' 'obligations,' and 'commitments' became more acceptable when they were embedded in a logic of family.[24]

Like the multiracial marketing of the previous chapter or the multicolored global maps in this one, "The Family of Man" relied precisely on the visibility of racial, ethnic, and gendered difference in order to convey its message about human universalism and multiculturalism. And as Klein suggests, the language of family was used not only to frame integration and global humanitarianism as a positive good but also to justify United States paternalism and military intervention abroad. This "logic of family" thus set a precedent for contemporary neoliberal forms of multiculturalism and colorblindness that shape the meaning of ancestry tests like 23andMe. Today, the idea of shared human ancestry as a global project of universalism is less to justify United States military and political projects abroad (as Klein describes) and rather, has been mobilized by neoliberal political rationality for private companies to market consumer products for profit. The result, however, is similar: discourses of global ancestry and the kinship of humanity ultimately *obscure* the effects and social organization of racialized, gendered, and sexual power.

The contradictions between this globally framed narrative in 23andMe marketing and its embeddedness in the history of United States imperialism are thus also eclipsed by the visual and discursive universalization of genes and genetic testing. In other words, the presentation of 23andMe as a technically applicable service for all people obfuscates the ways in which it is situated within broader national logics shaped by racial difference and global politics. For example, 23andMe can only be shipped primarily to countries in North America and Europe, with a few exceptions including Hong Kong, Singapore, American Samoa, and the Northern Mariana Islands.[25] Notably, these exceptions have been historically colonized or are currently occupied by countries in North America or Europe, which is likely the reason they have access to the United States-based service.

In addition to the stratified access and use of the service, the racialization of genetic ancestry also hides in plain sight. Like the online dating and egg and sperm donation platforms, 23andMe does not use the language of race or racial difference and avoids racial terms like "White," "Black," "Latinx," etc. Many of the ancestry categories used by 23andMe are instead described as ethnic categories, or national or continental associations. This is certainly intentional because of historical associations with race science and eugenics, and the way race is associated with controversy and politics in contemporary popular culture. But as a result, 23andMe makes invisible the social and political meanings of racial difference, the way power and privilege are organized around it, and the role of genetics in influencing categories of racial difference in contemporary popular culture.

Uniquely, Asianness is one of the few exceptions where the geographic association with the continent of Asia coincides with the word "Asian" as a racial category or identity. While we might understand many who have ancestry connections designated as European would be racially categorized as White, 23andMe very purposefully and understandably uses the term European as a geographic reference distinct from White as a racial one. However, with Asian, we see the one word capturing both Asian as a geographic reference and as a racial one. In some ways, we could call this coincidental; 23andMe and the field of genetic science are not originating these multiple references to the word "Asian." However, in contemporary culture, this linguistic conflation functions as a kind of semiotic collapse with very real consequences: wherein Asian as a reference to someone's geographic ancestry or "national" origins is assumed to be the same as Asian American as a US racial category developed and utilized strategically as an identity of political solidarity.

Many of us within Asian Americans studies have witnessed the fallout from this issue: people unfamiliar with Asian American history or the Asian American Movement of the 1960s and 1970s that originated the term Asian American as a political identity don't identify with Asian American as an identity or misunderstand its origins and political uses. Rather, they assume it is imposed as an overgeneralized geographic grouping in the same way 23andMe tells you "what you are." Although not specifically referencing 23andMe or genetic tests, one vivid example of this in recent popular culture was a *New York Times* online interactive piece published in February 2023 titled "12 Asian Americans Discuss." In the focus group, Asian Americans were asked "How do you feel about the term 'Asian American'? Do you think it's a useful way to group Asians of different ethnicities?"[26] All four of the featured respondents replied as if it were a generalized geographic or ethnic category (similarly to the way it is used in 23andMe). One response included, "We are grouped together too often," while another pondered "It is weird, though, because you don't think of other people as South American or European." And a third posited, "It's a broad lump." Asian American studies scholar Paul Nadal offered a succinct and incisive critique from the field, tweeting in response,

> An important lesson in Asian American studies is that "Asian American" was a social movement before it was ever an identity. Which means that the term, as a mode of identification, then and now, ascriptive or otherwise, makes sense only with reference to its political content.[27]

Indeed, if any of the respondents, or whoever wrote the question, were aware of the political history of the term "Asian American," none of them let on. But how many of them are familiar with 23andMe and the use of geography and identities that it markets? While 23andMe is certainly not responsible for creating this collapse and misunderstanding of Asian racial identity, it continues to reflect, reproduce, and normalize these forms and expressions of depoliticization.

Global Genes and the Making of Identity

In addition to framing identity in geographic terms, the very subcategories that 23andMe and other US based genetic ancestry companies use are often specific to their national and racial context. For 23andMe, the breakdown of racial categories and ethnicities by currently existing nation-states are still American-based categories of ethnic and regional difference. Categories in 23andMe like "Chinese," "Vietnamese," or "British & Irish" are not universal, inherent, or even scientific, but rather provide a culturally and nationally legible interpretation of individuals' genetic information in comparison to broader population data. For example, whereas 23andMe presents a percentage for "Chinese" with a list of "administrative regions" (listed as provinces like Guangdong or Shandong) where they "found the strongest evidence" of ancestry, other testing services, in comparison, use different terms. For example, the Chinese-based genetic ancestry testing service WeGene breaks down ancestry into more specific categories within "Chinese" that are primarily legible within Chinese ethnic politics, such as Northern Han, Southern Han, Miao Yao, or Gaoshan.[28]

Despite the culturally specific interpretation used by 23andMe, the global ancestry connections the company advertises and offers span throughout the world. In one blog post, 23andMe describes,

> This report uses DNA you inherited from both sides of your family and tells you the proportion of your DNA that comes from each of forty-five worldwide genetic populations, offering a detailed view of your ancestry from before ocean-crossing ships and airplanes were on the scene. The report also compares your DNA to individuals of known ancestry from over 115 countries and territories in Europe, Africa, the Americas, Asia, and Oceania, telling you more about where your recent ancestors may have lived.[29]

Based on the information offered directly from 23andMe, the significance of the test and the meaning of ancestry are defined by inheritance, "genetic populations," and the comparison of an individual to a broader corpus of ancestral locations. In addition to assuming that families are

Figure 5.1. "Root for Your Roots." 23andMe Advertisement. May 2018.

genetically related, the quote also connects ancestry to the act of migration ("ocean-crossing ships and airplanes").

Through these perceived genetic connections to specific populations and nations, individual users, and their shared genes with imagined ancestors and kin from around the world, constitute this global "family." In one example during the 2018 FIFA World Cup, 23andMe launched an advertising campaign around the men's soccer competition (Figure 5.1). A print ad showed a Black soccer player in a green jersey on his knees in a packed stadium, cheering as if he had just scored a goal. Superimposed behind him was a shaded purple map of Africa with a small circle highlighting the region of Nigeria. The tagline on the bottom read, "Root for Your Roots" and underneath that, "It's in your DNA."

Evoking the playful nature of sports fan cultures and the use of 23andMe as a mix of leisure and self-discovery, the advertisement indeed suggests that 23andMe can help you decide what soccer team to cheer for. Upon learning that you have a certain amount of ancestry from various places around the world, like Nigeria for example, you might then root for their soccer team. In this context, the ad suggests that the genetic information that connects a person's ancestry to a geographical location that maps onto a current-day nation-state can and should be the grounds for cultural associations and actions. And the fantasy of the global family is further sustained, embraced, and substantiated by the social imagination and embodiment of an individual's global "roots" and the connections and actions inspired by them.

The 23andMe webpage advertising the specific ancestry service also similarly enfigures the individual using their connection to global ancestors (Figure 5.2). As of 2019, this webpage showed a brightly colored world map in the background. European countries were colored in various shades of blue while the shape of China was bright red and several Southeast Asian countries appeared in various hues of yellow and orange. A bright sticker-like logo declared "1000+ ancestry regions" next to an example of the ancestry composition format. A small circular image of a woman's face, much resembling a profile picture, was surrounded by a thick donut-like circle divided into various colors matching those of the countries in the background. Overlaid next to this pie chart was a table with the name "Jacqueline" at the top, presumably of the person pictured, with "100%" beside it, representing her entire ancestry makeup that has been accounted for by the subsequent data provided. The table includes two major headings—"European—50.1%" in blue and "East Asian and Native American—49.95" in red. Beneath the European category, various "regions" and corresponding percentages are offered, such as "British & Irish—39.7%," "French & German—7.0%," "Broadly Northwestern European "3.2%," and "Scandinavian 0.2%." In varying shades of red and orange beneath the second heading are "Vietnamese—46.3%," "Indonesian, Thai, Myanmar—1.5%," and "Chinese—0.5%." No explanation was offered regarding the combining of "East Asian" and "Native American." However, 23andMe explains each of the categories on an informational webpage titled "23andMe Reference Populations & Regions." Between 2019 and 2022, the content and explanations continued to be edited and updated. However, consistent throughout period is the claim that,

> The peoples of East Asia and the Americas have a shared genetic history. Their common ancestors left western Asia over 50,000 years ago, migrating east across the continent.[30]

Explanations of "shared genetic histories" and global migrations continue to be offered for various population groups for all the regions

Figure 5.2. Screenshot of "Our Services—Ancestry." 23andMe Website. Accessed May, 9 2019. https://www.23andme.com/en-ca/dna-ancestry/.

analyzed by 23andMe. Users are encouraged to imagine our "common ancestors" as individuals "leaving" western Asia and "migrating" east, as if an old family story. These fantasies further reinforce the conceptualization of humanity as a family that shares ancestors and "roots," migrated around the globe, and connected through the "DNA matches" that represent remnants of an inherited past.

The graphical representations of 23andMe also demonstrate the visual narration of these ideas of global connection, ethnic difference, and inherited genetic kinship. A person's ancestry is represented textually by numerical information, visually by the donut-like graph that encircles her face (half orange for East Asian and half blue for European), and geographically by the map in which European countries are highlighted in blues and the Asian countries in reds and oranges. Jacqueline's pie chart shows us how visually satisfying it can be to represent yourself as the sum of your ancestral parts, as if identity and being made whole was as simple as adding up to 100%. She is presented as the symbol of the complete self, the you that you were welcomed to by purchasing the kit.

And it is not a coincidence that the person chosen to demonstrate how ancestry composition works is multiracial. Using the genetic results of a multiracial person brings together this ethos of self-knowledge through ancestral connection with the contemporary version of multiculturalism that 23andMe espouses. As Michele Elam analyzes and critiques, multiracial people in public discourse are often held up as icons of multiculturalism and, "If once mulattos stood as testimony of racial inequity, now they are frequently invoked as fleshly confirmation of racial equality has arrived and, thereby, fulfilled part of the nation's providential destiny."[31] In 23andMe, the future is here. Racial mixing takes on this contemporary symbolism of futurity and the "discovery" that we are all already genetic mixtures of ancestral populations. As a result, the distillation of social identities like race into a set of locations offers the illusion of leaving behind historically constructed categories of an abject racist past.[32] Therein, 23andMe and its customers can embrace the (neo) liberal separation of ancestry from race, and the depoliticization of race, even as it reproduces categories of racialized difference and inculcates them into narratives of scientific and technological innovation through genetic research bringing about a better world.

The Multicultural Consumption of Kinship

In addition to picturing the world as one big diverse family, these offerings of an imagined identity of global ancestry also frame a particular kind of kinship as consumable. In the previous example, Jacqueline's background offers a visually striking image of what the ancestry test results claims to offer customers. Her composition spans multiple continents and countries visualized by the multi-colored design of the world map. And it is precisely through the deconstruction and superimposition of the world map onto the individual consumer that allows them to see themselves as a representation of the multicultural world. To become multicultural is as simple as purchasing the test and finding out what parts of the world you represent.

This is of course a fantasy or, more precisely, a version of Ellen Samuels's "fantasy of identification" that "is always far less concerned with individual identity than with placing that individual within a legible group."[33] In this context, these percentages only have meaning in relation to a broader population that has already been categorized and differentiated. And the "legible groups" within that population, with which identification is possible, constitute that image of contemporary multiculturalism. This fantasy of identification also reveals the relationality implied in the discursive construction of global ancestry. Like the profiles of the previous chapter, a person's ancestry information can only be meaningful through its individualization against a broader corpus of participants. Customers are presented individual genetic information, but it is framed as part of a larger diversity of human populations, and the marketed diversity is defined by shared ancestors and therefore shared genetic connections to others.

23andMe also offers another kind of "global family" through their social media-style platform for meeting and interacting with one's "DNA relatives." Using their accounts, customers are connected with hundreds of "relatives" that are both genetically related to them and envisioned as fellow global citizens with their own ancestry compositions and connections around the world (regardless of their actual physical location). The DNA Relatives section of 23andMe offers users a long, filterable list, not unlike the list of profiles on the online dating or egg and sperm donation interfaces, with hundreds of "relatives" that have also purchased the

23andMe service, sent in their DNA samples, and opted into this feature. This list offers varying connections as close as "parent" or "sibling" (if a user has close genetic relatives that have submitted DNA to 23andMe) and as distant as fifth cousins. Each is represented by a small circular profile picture (though many have opted not to include any image, and the space is filled by default with their initials), the individual's name, and information about their genetic relation to the logged-in user.

What does it mean to be related according to 23andMe? Connections made to others based on shared genetic segments are framed as kin relationships. For the platform, terms like sibling or cousin solely refer to genetic relatedness defined by information such as "37% DNA shared, 2 segments." Clicking on a person's profile shares the individual's name (as they have chosen to be listed on the site), their self-reported location, and the opportunity to "connect" with them (add them to your friend network) or message them. Below these options is further information about "your genetic relationship." For example, based on the number of shared DNA segments, an algorithm estimates that you might be fourth cousins with someone (Figure 5.3). In this case, under smaller text titled "Common lineage," 23andMe explains, "You and X may share a set of third-great-grandparents. You could also be from different generations (removed cousins) or share only one ancestor (half cousins)." Underneath this is a multicolored graphic of a family tree. A circle that represents the user is on the bottom left. Above that is a (genetic) "parent," and above this ascending diagonally, in graduated colors from yellow to red: "grandparent," "great-grandparent" and so forth until "third-great-grandparents." Directly below third-great-grandparents, four generations below in line with the circle representing me, is "fourth cousin" highlighted in purple. Underneath this image is a section titled "family background" with the text, "We recommend adding additional information about yourself and your family's ancestry to compare with your DNA relatives." There's space to input the user's maternal grandmother's birthplace, maternal grandfather's birthplace, paternal grandmother's birthplace, paternal grandfather's birthplace, other ancestor's birthplace, family surnames, and family tree.

The image of the family tree by 23andMe further demonstrates the convergence of social formations of family and kinship with genetic logics of relatedness. Catherine Nash's theorization of "genetic kinship" fur-

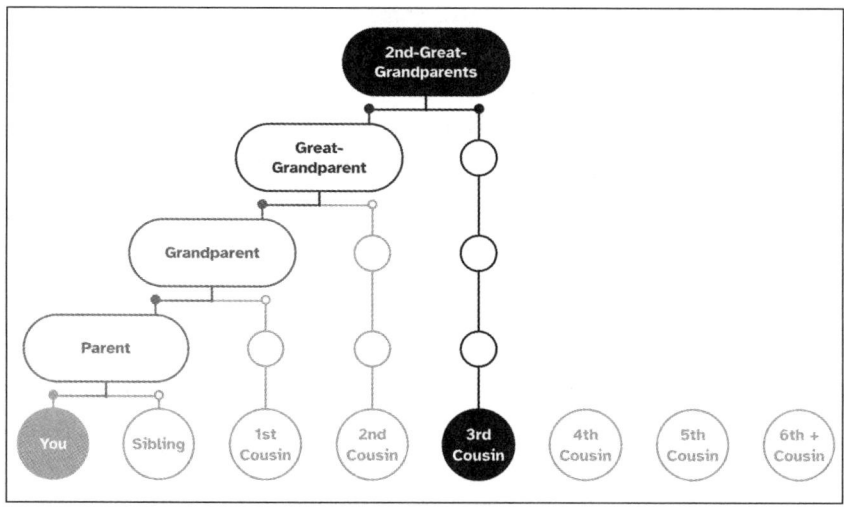

Figure 5.3. Screenshot example of a chart explaining common lineage. 23andMe Website. Accessed October 31, 2024.

ther draws connections between the history of family tree imagery and genetic technologies, writing, "Secular family trees drew on the model of sacred biblical pedigrees before the scientific appropriation of the family tree in evolutionary biology and anthropological diagrams of kinship."[34] As Nash suggests, and as the trees featured on 23andMe demonstrate, family trees do not simply reflect genetically based realities but rather shape the very meaning of those relationships. In this context, 23andMe uses the concept of ancestry and its relationship to inheritance and relatedness to articulate new images of kin networks constituted by fantasies of vast generations and global ancestry.

New Genetic Intimacies

While the variety of testimonials promoted through the 23andMe website suggests an embrace of individuals with limited knowledge about their genetic and family history, the interface itself and the opportunities for its use are founded on heteronormative ideologies of reproduction and the family as a genetic unit. The only definition of "relative" used by the service is that of a genetic relative. Using the language of kinship (relatives, cousins, relatedness, etc.), these direct-to-consumer genetic tests have pushed and put into question the boundaries of family and its relationship to genetics. In a contemporary culture where kinship is *not* reducible to genetics alone, how can we understand the growing significance and popularity of 23andMe and the connections it offers?

Despite the privileging of genetic relationships through the conflation of normative kinship discourse with biogenetic relatedness, the discovery of these genetic relatives offers new opportunities for the formation of social and embodied connections. Sociologists Margaret K. Nelson and Rosanna Hertz explore this tension in the context of "siblings" that are genetically related through a shared sperm donor. They write, "When parents choose to interact with the families of donor siblings, they are creating a kind of 'kin' that is both 'voluntary' and unusual. They and their children suddenly have a set of previously unexperienced 'relatives.'"[35] As they show, even as some people "completely dismiss the notion that genes create kinship[,] . . . when bonds do emerge[,] it is because people have gone beyond their ideas about the significance of genes as the taken-for-granted basis for the creation of kinship and moved on to use them to create intimacy."[36] They coin the term "genetic strangers" to explore the relationship between "something that usually connotes familiarity with something that symbolizes the opposite."[37] This intimacy that Nelson and Hertz reference, created from the discovery of a genetic connection but substantiated through social interaction, offers a framework for understanding the broader landscape of multicultural kinship-building using 23andMe and other direct-to-consumer genetic tests that offer the possibility to connect with previously anonymous DNA relatives.[38] What I refer to as "genetic intimacies," these social and affective relations framed in the language of kinship among previously "genetic strangers" constitutes a specific type of family formation produced by genetic technologies. This is certainly not exclusive to 23andMe, however 23andMe represents a popular and culturally normative platform that constructs these genetic intimacies as a particular iteration of kinship.

In the last decade, stories about individuals who were conceived through sperm donation and then found genetic half-siblings using 23andMe or other services like it have proliferated throughout local and national news. For example, as described in multiple national news outlets in 2019, a woman named Shauna Harrison used 23andMe to discover twenty-nine genetic half-siblings. In one media article, she was quoted discussing what this newfound kinship meant to her:

> Harrison said one of the benefits of meeting her new half-siblings is finding people who understand not only that "our dad is not our biological father," but they were birthed through a donor . . .
> [She said,] "That's a very different way to think about your identity and have to grapple with that. Having people who have been through the same thing and who can share not just that experience but literally share your DNA with you is very helpful."[39]

In this and other stories like it, kinship was initiated by the knowledge of genetic connection but subsequently embodied through social interaction and shared experience. Furthermore, the claim that "our dad is not our biological father" challenges the normalized uses of parental language in discussing genetic relatedness. Here, parenthood and genetic connection are distinct forms of kinship.

While this may seem evident, especially for those whose parents or kin are not the same people with whom they share genetic material (including but not limited to queer families, adoptive families, and families formed through sperm or egg donation), the hegemony of the heteronormative reproductive family is perpetuated through the continued conflation and essentialism of genetic relatedness and kinship. For example, in a *Forbes* article titled "Why Sperm Donor Privacy Is Under Threat from DNA Sites—Is There Anything They Can Do About It?" the piece uses the term "real parents" to refer to genetic parents:

> . . . people conceived through donor sperm could identify their father by looking for them directly or by finding siblings. And it's already happening. Numerous tales of children finding their real parents have emerged in the last year.[40]

The unqualified references to a sperm donor as a "father" and individuals that share a sperm donor as "siblings" assumes that, rather than by complex forms of relationality, kinship is defined by genetic connection. And the use of the term "real parents" to reference genetic parents reinforces the hegemony of genetics as the "real" way to form kinship.

This is also a familiar trope in adoption narratives, wherein adoptees are often asked if they know who their "real parents" are.[41] Kimberly Leighton has considered this issue for both adoptees and those that were donor-conceived in arguing that this assumption or diagnosis of "genealogical bewilderment," a term used in the psychology of adoption to refer to the presumed harm that "children suffer from not knowing— and not being raised by—their 'real parents . . . ,'" represents "a racially-based, heteronormative understanding of identity and a prejudicial view of the family."[42] 23andMe and other genetic ancestry services not only reinforce but actively capitalize on this normalization that genetic information is necessary for a complete (and healthy) identity. Leighton also highlights the importance of genetic genealogy in maintaining categories of race, writing, "Without clear and certain knowledge of genetic genealogy, the epistemology of race as a means of assigning categories of identity to groups of individuals, based on heredity, falls apart."[43]

Indeed, genealogy is crucial to the ideology of racial categorization. And thus, it makes sense that ancestry testing services not only promote these two aspects of identity (genetic genealogy and ethnic ancestry) as benefits of the product, but also that the services themselves rely on those aspects of identity to reinforce the importance of the other. Characteristic of the broader shift of neoliberalism from an ethos of exclusion to inclusion, 23andMe has indeed provided individual opportunities for adoptees and people who were conceived through gamete donation, that have been historically excluded by the absence of genetic knowledge, to be included in these normative explorations of personal genetics. However, this inclusion neither interrogates nor disrupts the underlying social power of the genetic. Rather, it is predicated on the continued normative valuation, monetization, and privileging of genetic relatedness and genealogy.

The popular and publicized use of these services by transracial adoptees clearly demonstrates this entanglement of racial, kinship, and genetic identity. For example, in March 2019, the *Philadelphia Inquirer* published a human-interest story titled "DNA helping Chinese adoptees do what was once impossible: Locate blood relatives in this country," chronicling Temple University student Stefanie Beard and her use of 23andMe to discover her genetic cousin and Bryn Mawr College student Claire Mitchell. The article narrates how the two college students were adopted as infants from the same orphanage in China two years apart and, through extraordinary coincidence, both submitted their DNA to 23andMe, discovered they were genetically related, and happened go to schools in the same city in the United States. According to the article, they exchanged phone numbers and eventually met in person for Chinese New Year. It describes, "Since [meeting], they've gone to dinner and to the movies. When they're together, laughter comes easily. Both will keep an eye out for additional blood relatives, as they get to know each other."[44] And photographs of the two women show them together in downtown Philadelphia on a fall day. They smile laughing and holding hands, walking down a stone path or on a bench in Washington Square. They look like family.

Later that year, their story was picked up by other local news outlets and eventually gained national attention when it was featured on the 23andMe Blog and other company-run social media platforms. The 23andMe Blog further explained Stefanie's initial motivation for using the service: a friendly debate with her sister Kristyn, who was also adopted from China, about "who had a higher percentage of Chinese ancestry in their DNA. (Stefanie turned out to be 77 percent Chinese and 13 percent Vietnamese to Kristyn's 99 percent Chinese.)"[45]

The story was indeed heartwarming and demonstrates the ways in which services like 23andMe can produce new forms of kinship, intimacy, and care. Already the motivation to purchase and take the test itself functioned as an act of kinship among two sisters who shared the experience of both having been adopted from China. And after discovering a genetic cousin through 23andMe, a new kinship was formed not only through the information itself but also through the social and affective bonds created through their embodied encounters with one another.

At the same time, the story encapsulates the different ideologies of race and kinship that have become internalized in our culture. The authority given to quantification and ancestry obfuscates the unarticulated meanings that being "X percent Chinese" represents. What does it mean to be 77% Chinese compared to 99% Chinese, especially for two Chinese adoptees that share American parents? In the United States context, these racial and genealogical numbers become a quantification of a racialized self that is defined by genetic relatedness to imagined Chinese ancestors, one that is further affirmed by the discovery of a cousin that (unsurprisingly) is also ethnically Chinese (a fact in accordance with her 23andMe report). This is not a critique of the individuals who use these services or craft their own meanings from them, but rather to highlight and locate the social and cultural assumptions about identity and kinship that have come to constitute this use of this technology: Chineseness in this context is assumed and made meaningful through these imagined and embodied forms of kinship defined by the genetic.

In addition to quantifying the language of identity through percentage breakdowns, these 23andMe stories of discovering genetic relatives in the transracial adoptive context also situate Asianness and Asian American kin formation in juxtaposition with adoptees' (most often) White families. For a Chinese adoptee raised by a White family, kinship has been defined by racial difference. And meeting a cousin or genetic relative through 23andMe may be the first time they experience kinship with someone who shares their racial or ethnic identity. Even for those that have adoptive kin that are also Asian (like Stefanie), within the transracially adoptive family, kinship and shared racial experience are not synonymous. As such, while the language of 23andMe imagines these affiliations to "Chineseness" or "Koreanness" in ethnic or geographic terms (and definitely not racial terms), the racialization of difference within the transracial family connects those ethnic terms to racial difference. Thus, the kinship between transracial adoptees founded on discovered genetic connection, indeed, could be defined through ethnic terms of shared "Chinese American" ancestry. However, it is also only made meaningful in a social and cultural context in which being Chinese American or being a Chinese adoptee is part of a racialized identity of difference. This is also not to say that this connection between ethnic and geographic categories of genetic tests and racial difference is exclusive to Asian American users. But rather to highlight how the seemingly depoliticized categories of geographic and ethnic difference in 23andMe cannot escape the specifically racialized experiences of those that find kinship within them. In this context, like the photograph in Deann Borshay Liem's film in Chapter 3, 23andMe is participating in the formation of Asian diasporic kinship that had not previously existed. Though, here, it is a kinship that is still imbricated in genetic essentialism and the neoliberal racial logics of consumer culture but that also offers individuals new opportunities to grapple with what these encounters mean.

While stories of adoptees finding and meeting genetic relatives have become a key marketing tool for 23andMe and other genetic ancestry services, they also have the potential to capture a more capacious understanding of how genetic kinship has become entangled in the gendered and racialized flows of migration and diaspora.[46] Within popular media, the 2015 documentary *Twinsters* and the 2021 documentary *Found* have both demonstrated the ways in which transnational forms of kinship have been produced by discovering genetic connections. *Twinsters* chronicles the experiences of Korean adoptees Anaïs Bordier in France and Samantha Futerman in the US, and their discovery that they are not only genetically related siblings but that they are twins. Although they did not discover one another through a genetic testing service, their relationship is predicated on the likelihood of their genetic relatedness (part of the climax of the film is the confirmation that they are indeed genetic twins) and what that means to each of them. The film captures their developing kinship from the uncanny recognition of their physical resemblance to their first physical meeting and then to contemplation of what their newfound relationship means for their futures. Their kinship is truly transnational as their shared (historical and genetic) origins in Korea found the basis of their meeting, and yet they are citizens of different countries as adults. And they must negotiate their burgeoning relationship mediated through the continued use of digital technologies (text and Skype) from their home countries and their eventual meeting in person in London.

Similarly, *Found* chronicles three teenaged Chinese adoptees in the United States that have discovered they are genetic cousins through 23andMe. Their kinship becomes further transnational when they travel to China together to explore their shared histories. They visit the sites where they were found and the orphanage in which they all stayed as infants. And they even meet a few potential birth families. Indeed, like other adoption narratives, the potential discovery of genetic parents is a central narrative theme.[47] However, more unique to this film is how the genetic relationships instigated by 23andMe have produced the conditions for each of the three individuals to explore other forms of kinship tied to their transnational history. At one point, they meet the orphanage workers and foster families that cared for them before they were adopted. And, like Borshay Liem's *In the Matter of Cha Jung Hee* discussed in Chapter 3, the film highlights how adoptive kinship need not only be constrained to relations between adoptive parents, genetic/birth parents, and adoptee (more commonly known as the adoption triad). But rather, in *Found*, kinship with other caretakers and other adoptees also inform the embodied experience of nationality, ethnicity, race, and transnationalism.

Whether discovering genetic relatives or quantifying ethnic ancestry, direct-to-consumer genetic ancestry tests have become a technology of kinship within contemporary American popular culture that represent the potential for new articulations of race, kinship, and belonging. In this context, genetic knowledge production functions as the site of race and kinship's co-constitution, and 23andMe functions as the system through which those articulations are made meaningful. Genetic knowledge production is a process of not only the discovery or articulation of genetic information that was already there (for example, whether two people are genetically related) but also the social context by which that information becomes *knowledge*, or meaningful information with which to make sense of oneself and the world. Emerging forms of kinship among individuals with so-called "alternative" family formation stories (using a sperm donor or through adoption) that find others to which they are genetically related exemplify how genetic technologies are shaping the meaning of kinship in contemporary culture. These intimacies may be rooted in the genetic connection articulated by 23andMe, but they are embodied through the interactions and intimacies crafted by those involved.

Like many digital worlds and consumer markers, the social and cultural landscape upon which direct-to-consumer genetic tests are purchased, used, and debated continues to change at a rapid pace. Controversies have arisen over the use of these services to solve criminal cases and concerns over data security. In 2025, 23andMe filed for bankruptcy, generating concerns and speculation about what will happen to users' data if the company were sold or acquired.[48] However, the broader consumer market for genetic ancestry information and analysis continues to thrive. As this chapter suggests, cultural narratives about what direct-to-consumer genetic tests can offer users reflect changing discourses of family and kinship and the intimacies that are produced and embodied when individuals share DNA. While the framing of new genetic connections solely as a positive good can obfuscate how services like 23andMe normalize genetic essentialism and the depoliticization of race, 23andMe is a product of a cultural moment in which family and kinship are defined in much broader terms than solely heteronormative, biological reproduction.

Conclusion

Futures of Kinship

In March 2020, technologies of kinship took on a whole new valence when the World Health Organization officially declared COVID-19 a pandemic, and communities across the world began to go into lockdown. From the closing of public businesses and services to curfews and quarantines, we all felt the constriction of our social and cultural worlds. In addition to widespread loss and economic precarity, the hegemony of the nuclear family and the organization of contemporary society into single-family units became even more solidified as stay-at-home orders were issued and transnational mobility was restricted. Many were separated from loved ones, extended family members, and nonbiological kin because of travel and gathering restrictions. During that time, we all learned how to reorganize our work, leisure, and family life to fit digital worlds. And while kinship stratified by race, class, and transnational borders has long been maintained in digitized ways, technology as the foundation for embodying social relations and kinship was amplified to an extreme during the height of COVID-19 lockdowns.[1]

From its origination, the cultural and political narratives around COVID-19 were also shaped by its racialized association with China alongside openly anti-Asian violence and racism. The pandemic amplified, reproduced, and transformed a number of the racial narratives that have been discussed in this book. Within the United States and our supposedly colorblind multicultural society, as Leslie Bow describes, "Racist love transforms into racist hate with dizzying speed."[2] For some, the solution to anti-Asian sentiment and violence might be found in the model minority logics discussed in Chapter 2: in April 2020, former democratic candidate for president Andrew Yang wrote an op-ed in the *Washington Post* titled "We Asian Americans are not the virus, but we can be part of the cure." The piece asserted, "We

Asian Americans need to embrace and show our Americanness in ways we never have before. We need to step up, help our neighbors, donate gear, vote, wear red white and blue, volunteer, fund aid organizations, and do everything in our power to accelerate the end of this crisis."[3] Yang explicitly referenced the history of Japanese American military duty in WWII and framed patriotic behavior as an appropriate response to racism. Predictably, the piece was met with controversy among Asian Americans, many of whom were quick to critique the underlying model minority narrative.

The influence of borders on families, kinship, and mobility was also deeply shaped by the pandemic. While the specific agency of the United States Immigration and Naturalization Service, established during Chinese exclusion and discussed in the first chapter of this book, officially ceased to exist in 2003, its originary regulatory functions have proliferated through the establishment of the three entities under the supervision of the Department of Homeland Security founded in 2003 to replace it: US Citizenship and Immigration Services (USCIS), US Immigration and Customs Enforcement (ICE), and US Customs and Border Protection (CPB). On January 31, 2020, the United States issued stringent travel restrictions that denied entry to all foreign nationals who had visited anywhere in China fourteen days prior. In a personal example, that same week, a friend of mine, a White American man, and his partner, a Chinese woman, were about to board a plane to the United States from Shanghai when she was denied entry on the flight. Despite having been together for months prior, with the same COVID-19 risks and lack of symptoms, he was allowed to travel back to the United States as an American citizen, but she was not as a Chinese national. He chose to stay in China with her and that summer they got legally married, in part to help facilitate future mobility amid the pandemic.

Stories like this one abounded throughout the pandemic. And despite those cultural fantasies that we're all part of a global family (as discussed in Chapter 5), during the pandemic, nation-state borders were reified and reasserted in formidable ways. Indeed, this particular iteration of travel restrictions had been rationalized by the global public health crisis, potential visa limitations, and the possibility of later difficulty traveling in accordance with them. And for my friend and his partner, differential constraints were based on differences of citizenship, rather than explicitly on race. However, their experience reflects the ways in which racialized boundaries and the naturalization of the privileged mobility of the White man against the exclusion of the Asian woman can be obfuscated and justified through institutions of public health, citizenship, and national borders. Furthermore, what appears to be a relatively common solution to the challenges of transnational mobility (legal marriage) also reflects a privileged form of legal kinship that is based in heteronormativity and not afforded to all.

In this context, the technologies of kinship discussed in this book and their co-constitution with Asian diasporic racialization continue to shape the formation and embodiment of kinship in the pandemic and "post-" pandemic eras. And the case studies of this book have offered a genealogical account of the ways in which social systems and technologies shape the racialization and gendering of that kinship. Together they have traced some of the contours of contemporary "kinship as a cultural system" (to borrow from David Schneider's original framing) in ways that attend to the historical entanglements of Asian American racialization, the emergence of neoliberal multiculturalism, and the rise of the digital.[4] Theorizing technologies of kinship offers a reconciliation of kinship as constituted not only by the individual and the "private" worlds of civil life but also by the regulatory, affective, and interactive systems through which kinship is produced and made meaningful.

To consider the role of technology in the construction of racialized forms of kinship, one cannot start with the emergence of in vitro fertilization or other forms of "modern" assistive reproductive technologies. Rather, in Asian American studies we might begin by looking earlier, as the first chapter does, to consider the early twentieth century mobilization of government immigration bureaucracy to produce Chinese (American) paper families. These paper families and the immigration bureaucracy designed to identify and eliminate them persisted until 1965, at which point the Chinese Confession Program had detected thousands of paper families and the priorities of immigration legislation shifted. The second chapter further chronicles this cultural turning point marked by the convergence of growing immigration from Asia and the emergence of the figure of the Asian American family as model minority. The third chapter builds on these racial narratives established in the previous chapter to consider the use of photography in Chinese transnational adoption communities in the 1990s and 2000s. This was a historical moment where transnational adoptive families were quickly gaining visibility and normalcy, and the meaning of race was thrown into question in new ways.

The final two chapters use the emergence of the digital as a means of examining new norms of family formation predicated on digital technologies and their use of race as a consumable product of individual identity. The fourth chapter, focusing on the use of profiles in online dating and egg and sperm donation websites, frames profile technology as producing new forms of kinship. While dating and the use of donor eggs and sperm certainly predate the digital, the profile interface transforms race into a filterable characteristic rather than a collective or political identity. The final chapter considers the moving target of 23andMe as an example of direct-to-consumer genetic tests and the new forms of kinship they produce and promote. Intersecting narratives of scientific development and digitization entangle race and kinship in new and complex ways. As these case studies show, even in sites where family is literally conceived through normative forms of reproduction, it is still always *conceived of* through a complex of narratives, cultural scripts, and affects. Identifying and analyzing the different technologies of kinship that people use to create family and make sense of their worlds helps us remain attuned to the social and cultural organization of power that shape the world, while also recognizing and honoring the agency of those involved.

Furthermore, in the contemporary moment, the ideology of family continues to be fought over, contested, and produced in stratified ways, and the racialization of Asian Americans is further imbricated into the multiculuralizing of culture and ethnicity. In the realm of representation and narrative possibility, in August 2021, Netflix released comedy-drama series *The Chair* starring Sandra Oh as Professor Ji-Yoon Kim, the newly appointed first woman and non-White chair of the English Department at the fictional Pembroke University. Throughout the episodes, Ji-Yoon is forced to manage her department's dwindling enrollment numbers, her senior colleagues whose antiquated views are often thrown into comic relief by their students, and the precarious tenure case of her Black junior colleague Yaz McKay, whose retention is continually put at risk by said senior colleagues. Woven into these threads of academic life, Ji-Yoon is also a single mother raising her rambunctious seven-year-old daughter JuJu with the help of her father and the occasional babysitter when they aren't scared away. Endearing, funny, and painfully realistic at times, the show made a splash in academia where many could relate to Ji-Yoon's struggle to negotiate departmental politics, racism and sexism in the academy, and the tensions of campus activism, all while trying to manage her own personal life.

In addition to all there is to say about the show's depiction of life as a woman of color in academia, *The Chair* offers a unique image of Asian American family and kinship. Over the course of the show, it is revealed that Ji-Yoon, as a single woman, adopted JuJu as an infant and named her after her late mother Ju-Hee. Throughout the series, Ji-Yoon and JuJu are seen struggling (in sometimes dramatized ways) to negotiate the nuances of transracial adoption given that JuJu is Mexican American, with a Korean name no less. JuJu spends much of her time at home being looked after by Ji-Yoon's father Habi who only speaks Korean, and she occasionally acts out in school. At one point JuJu is shown refusing to speak Korean, and at another, she painfully declares that Ji-Yoon isn't her "real mother" which is revealed to be parroted after an insensitive comment from a classmate. However, in other moments, she is seen running off to trade Pokemon cards at a family birthday party and cheering on her baby cousin at the infant's *doljabi* ceremony, a Korean tradition celebrated on a child's first birthday. The tension between mother and daughter ebbs and flows as JuJu sometimes lacks affection towards her mother and Ji-Yoon must often leave JuJu to go to work.

After a series of mishaps that gesture to the gap between them, a moment of tenderness is found when Ji-Yoon arrives home after a long day at work, undoubtedly after JuJu has already gone to sleep. JuJu has been working on a school presentation on Día de los Muertos (Day of the Dead) for several episodes as an attempt to explore her Mexican heritage. As Ji-Yoon approaches the front door of their house, candles line the walkway leading inside to the living room where a small *ofrenda* sits on the coffee table. The alter built to honor kin that have passed away shows photographs of Ji-Yoon's mother who, as she had shared with JuJu in an earlier episode, had died when Ji-Yoon was fourteen. Through tears Ji-Yoon tenderly examines the offering JuJu has made in honor of her own namesake, reveling in a moment of intergenerational kinship. However, the next morning, it's back to reality when Ji-Yoon hurriedly drops JuJu off at school for the presentation with Habi, who has dressed in a full mariachi suit and sombrero in a sweet display of grandfatherly commitment. After glancing at another Latinx child from school dressed up for the presentation with her two Latinx parents, JuJu begs Ji-Yoon to come with them. But Ji-Yoon refuses, wrapped up in the professional drama at the university that beckons her back to work.

The Chair offers a version of family and kinship not explicitly occupied with the question of *what* constitutes an "Asian American family," but rather shows that the more important question might be: *how* can Asian American (and multiracial) kinship be lived and embodied? And asking whether JuJu is or isn't Asian American because of her imbrication within this Asian American family despite her lack of biological or genetic relation to her Asian (American) mother and grandfather tells us much less about what race and kinship mean in United States culture than asking, how does race shape what kinship can be? And how might kinship itself challenge the boundaries of racial categories and meanings? As Ji-Yoon, JuJu, and Habi demonstrate, kinship can be constructed, not by the biological givens of reproduction or heteronormativity, but rather, by negotiating what it means to be someone's "real parent," embodying the cultural traditions that shape identity, and offering tender moments of love and care. And while the series does not explore the power structures or technologies that undeniably made this kinship possible, underlying the racial specificity of this narrative are the immigration policies and bureaucracies that situated Habi and Ji-Yoon in the United States, the adoption processes and practices that brought JuJu into their family, and the material opportunities for JuJu to seek genetic relatives in the future.

While media representations of Asian American family and kinship, like *The Chair*, television sitcom *Fresh of the Boat*, and films like *Crazy Rich Asians, The Farewell, After Yang,* and *Everything Everywhere All at Once* have been gaining traction in recent years, representations of race and kinship continue to be transformed and obscured by discourses of "culture." Growing from the narratives of neoliberal multicultural consumption and the right to "preference" discussed in the final chapters of this book, "culture" has become an object (or set of objects) of consumption for those with the means to do so. In 2019, 23andMe announced a collaboration with popular travel housing service Airbnb.[5] Promoting what they call "heritage travel," users who receive an ancestry report from 23andMe could "click through to their ancestral populations and find Airbnb homes and experiences in their native countries," according to the Airbnb press release.[6] What does it mean to "explore your heritage" in this way? What are people expecting to find when they go to these nations in which they have discovered ancestry? The cofounder and Chief Product Officer of Airbnb, Joe Gebbia, offered answers to these questions with the belief that "authentic travel experiences help you connect with local cultures and create a sense of belonging anywhere in the world—and what better way to do that than traveling to your roots."[7] As Gebbia makes clear, ancestry and "roots" have now become the impetus for global tourism. While written in earnest, for Airbnb and 23andMe, this meant the comfort of global capitalist consumption *everywhere* in the world for those privileged enough to do so.

While the companies could not have predicted the pandemic ahead that would change global travel for years to come, the promotion was an invitation, advertisement, and encouragement for colonial forms of tourism in ways unattuned to the complexities of power that shape inequity on a global scale.[8] Furthermore, it reproduced an ethos of leisure and privileged mobility that is in spectacular contradiction to the reality of borders throughout United States history and into the global present. Current crises in the militarization of borders and the violent treatment of the people detained at them demonstrate the precise violence of "belonging" *nowhere* in the world.[9] And family and kinship are imbricated in this framing precisely through the literal regulation of and violence against families combined with the figurative image of the family as a metaphor for the nation.

As this book has suggested, neither the privatized rights to create family nor the family as a justification for individual consumption offer the pathway to collective justice. However, as we more deeply understand how family and kinship are produced, sustained, and transformed within systems of power, perhaps we can find ways of honoring personhood, reducing suffering, and crafting new forms of intimacy and connection. By examining Asian American racialization to understand the role of technology in the construction of kinship, we can also more deeply understand how race is defined and articulated in contemporary culture. And in a historical moment when racial categories and the social construction of race are continually contested, it is more important than ever to critically interrogate the racialized and gendered contexts in which access to narratives of family are built and offer the tools to reimagine those boundaries.

ACKNOWLEDGMENTS

This book in all its iterations has traversed many institutions, states, countries, and periods of my life. And I am grateful to all who I have encountered and learned from on this journey.

The first version of this project originated at Yale University where I was privileged to work with advisors, mentors, and peers that inspired and challenged me. I am deeply indebted to Mary Lui who read countless drafts and chapters, always gave the most thoughtful and generous advice and feedback, and introduced me to what kind of scholar I could be. I am also so grateful to Laura Wexler and Kathryn Dudley, who fostered my interdisciplinary nature and continually offered unique and exciting intellectual connections.

I would not be the person or scholar I am today without the intellectual communities of American Studies; Women's, Gender & Sexuality Studies; Ethnicity, Race, and Migration; the Asian American Studies Working Group; and the Ethnography and Oral History Working Group at Yale. I especially want to thank Gary Okihiro, Margaret Homans, Inderpal Grewal, Greta LaFleur, Susan Shand, Susie An, Janis Jin, Yahel Matalon, Jacinda Tran, Sasha Sabherwal, Randa Tawil, Ashanti Shih, Madeleine Han, Yuhe Faye Wang, Melissa Redwood, Kristin Hankins, Megan Asaka, and Juliet Nebolon. Beginning at Yale but extending far beyond, I am also indebted to Thy Phu for her mentorship, guidance, and collaboration over many years, from my first dissertation chapter on paper family photography through the present.

During my time at Yale, research on this project was generously supported by the Mellon Foundation, the American Studies Summer Research Fellowship, and conferences hosted by the Yale Photographic Memory Workshop, Toronto Photography Seminar, and the Alliance for the Study of Adoption and Culture. I also want to gratefully acknowledge the Yale Asian American Cultural Center, the student staff there who shared their passion, enthusiasm, and encouragement with me in a space we all came to call home, and Saveena Dhall who showed me what true leadership is and what it can do.

I want to express my deepest gratitude to my friends, mentors, and colleagues at University of Wisconsin-Madison. I am profoundly grateful to Leslie Bow and Cindy I-Fen Cheng who guided, advised, and inspired me in so many ways, from reading chapters and giving rigorous yet compassionate feedback, to offering advice in every area of intellectual and professional life, to helping me envision what this book (and more) could be. Special thank you as well to Lori Kido Lopez for her mentorship, encouragement, and advocacy for this work.

This book would not be what it is today without the UW-Madison Center for the Humanities and its First Book Workshop. I am indebted to Russ Castronovo and Megan Massino for their support as well as Leslie Bow, Cindy I-Fen Cheng, Lori Kido Lopez, Lisa Nakamura, and David Eng who provided invaluable and incisive feedback as readers. I also owe so much to the communities in Asian American Studies, Gender & Women's Studies, the Holtz Center for Science and Technology Studies, and the Ethics of Care Initiative at UW-Madison. Many thanks to Timothy Yu, Peggy Choy, Judith Houck, Pernille Ipsen, Sara Chadwick, Anna Campbell, Jill Casid, Finn Enke, Christine Garlough, Ruth Goldstein, Maria Lepowsky, Keisha Lindsay, Annie Menzel, Sami Schalk, Kelly Marie Ward, Rodlyn-mae Banting, Su Ann Rose, Jamie Gratrix, Nina Valeo Cooke, Sainath Suryanarayanan, and Noah Weeth Feinstein. Thank you to my research assistant Keegan McCance, and all my students in Asian American Studies, Gender & Women's Studies, and the APIDA Student Center.

Amid revising this project through and beyond the pandemic (and other big life transitions), some of my fondest memories are of writing group sessions, exchanging feedback, sharing meals, and going for walks and adventures with Nadia Chana, Jennifer Nelson, Kristina Huang, Juliet Huynh, Eileen Lagman, and Yanie Fécu. And within this group, I especially want to thank James McMaster for being my person as we went on what often felt like twin journeys of writing, teaching, grieving, and figuring out what it means to be academics. I also have profound gratitude for Emi Frerichs and Ruth Llana Fernández with whom I have been able to share commiseration, consultation, and care in all the best ways.

The Department of English and the Program in Gender and Women's Studies at Dalhousie University has been my home as I completed work on this book. Many thanks to Jennifer Andrews and Lindsay DuBois for their mentorship and support, and who ensured the resources I needed to finish this book. And I am grateful for the advice, friendship, and guidance of Asha Jeffers, Erin Wunker, Elizabeth Fitting, Liesl Gambold, Bart Vautour, Kathy Cawsey, Heather Jessup, Alice Brittan, Karen Foster, Eric Schmaltz, Justina Spencer, Rohan Maitzen, Jason Haslam, Julia Wright, Anthony Enns, Margaret Robinson, Trevor Ross, and Lyn Bennett.

This research would not exist without the people who generously shared their stories, archives, and labors with me. And I give my heartfelt thanks to the adoptees with whom I interviewed, Families with Children from China New York, Kathy Urbina and Tim Stoenner, Deann Borshay Liem, Angela Tudico from the National Archives in New York City, and Li Wei Yang from the Huntington Library.

It has been an honor and a dream to work with NYU Press. I have the utmost gratitude to Eric Zinner for believing in and advocating for the project. Many thanks also to Furqan Sayeed, Ainee Jeong, and Dolma Ombadykow for helping shepherd both the book and me through this process, and to the anonymous reviewers for providing thoughtful and generative feedback that helped elevate the manuscript into the book it is now. Earlier portions of this manuscript have appeared as "A Technology of Family: Photography and Kinship Formation in Transnational Adoption from Asia," *American Quarterly* 74, no. 4 (December 2022): 921–943; and "Paper Family Photography: Photography and the State in the Era of Paper Families and Chinese Exclusion (1882–1943)," *Photography and Culture* 10, no. 2 (2017): 105–119. Thank you to Sarah Parsons who offered critical guidance on the journal article based on my research from Chapter 1.

I want to thank all my friends and kin that have filled my life with love, support, care, joy, and refuge throughout the ups and downs of this project. I am grateful to Betsy Smith, Berit Pratt, Lily Pratt, Mei Lin Pratt, Hanni Beyer Lee, Kim Chang, Margaret Cerullo, Carollee Bengelsdorf, Jiang Hong, Liming Liu, Julia Porter, Hannah Tessler, Marjorie Berman, Kelsie Lo-Pelletier, Sam Early, Megan Sutherland, Matisse Madden, Ann Cowlin, Mary Lou Martin, Michelle Higgins,

Lara MacLean, Jillian MacDonald, Elizabeth Carbonneau, Meredith Kalaman, Tania Saliba, Denise Cantu, Drew Weatherhead, Sarah Cruickshanks, Sophia Lourme, Nicole Snow, and Jill Hackett. Special thank you to Joy Lieberthal Rho for her care, labor, and perspective on good days and bad. I also want to express my profound appreciation for my other soulmate Courtney Sato for her unwavering, compassionate, and lifelong friendship in all areas of life, regardless of whether we are near or far.

Many thanks to my family Bill Grohmann, Jesse Johnson, Mutong Guo, Elena Ritter, and the cats who have seen me through this project, Shushu, Baobao, and Sesame. I am full of gratitude for my partner Andrew Brown, who inspires me and brings joy and meaning to all aspects of life, and for our little one Darcy.

Finally, I dedicate this book to my mother Kay Ann Johnson, who passed away in 2019, and who wrote her own books to teach me and so many others. From her, I learned. And for her, I created.

NOTES

INTRODUCTION

1 Omi and Winant, *Racial Formation in the United States*.
2 For more, see Morley and Robins's early theorization of techno-Orientalism in *Spaces of Identity*; Roh, Huang, and Niu's *Techno-Orientalism*; and Bui's *Model Machines*.
3 Bow, *Racist Love*, 111.
4 For more on inscrutability, Asian racialization, and affect, see Sunny Xiang's *Tonal Intelligence* and Xine Yao's *Disaffected*.
5 Ninh, *Ingratitude*, 9. Emphasis in original.
6 While conducting my research on the public websites of commercial egg and sperm cryobanks for Chapter 4, representations of Asian donors or customers was almost completely absent. However, according to one study commenting on the use of reproductive assistive services, "With other variables controlled, Asian women remain similar to white women in terms of receiving medical services for infertility." Arthur L. Greil et al., "Race-Ethnicity and Medical Services for Infertility," 502.
7 Foucault, "Technologies of the Self," 18.
8 Saussure, *Course in General Linguistics*, 66.
9 As Sarah Franklin writes in *Biological Relatives*, IVF is "doubly reproductive": "it successfully reproduces reproduction, and its reproductive success biologically is what confirms, or proves, that it works technologically," 6. See also Strathern, *After Nature* and *Reproducing the Future*; and Becker, *The Elusive Embryo*.
10 For further examples, see Hertz, *Single by Chance*; Lewin, *Gay Fatherhood*; Mamo, *Queering Reproduction*; and Roberts, *Killing the Black Body*.
11 Roberts, "Race, Gender, and Genetic Technologies," 791.
12 See Nakamura, *Cybertypes*; Chun, "Introduction: Race and/as Technology"; and Nakamura and Chow-White, *Race After the Internet*.
13 Williams, *Keywords*, 249.
14 Azoulay, "What is a photograph? What is photography?"
15 For discussions theorizing race and photography see, Campt, *Image Matters* and *Listening to Images*, Hartman *Wayward Lives, Beautiful Experiments*, and Mani, *Unseeing Empire*.
16 Phu, *Picturing Model Citizens*, 47.
17 Lowe, *Immigrant Acts*, 11. Emphasis in original.

18 Chen, *Trans Exploits*, 4.
19 Foucault, *The History of Sexuality Volume I*, 92–93.
20 Ibid., 127.
21 Teresa de Lauretis defines technologies of gender as "the techniques and discursive strategies by which gender is constructed and hence . . . violence is engendered (38)." de Lauretis, *Technologies of Gender*, 38.
22 For example, it could be argued that all technologies of sex are also technologies of power precisely because power is imbricated within the very construction of sex and sexuality in the first place (as *The History of Sexuality* posits).
23 Foucault, "Technologies of the Self," 18.
24 Deleuze and Guattari, *A Thousand Plateaus*, 7.
25 Brown, "Thing Theory," 4.
26 Autry, "Jessica Krug, Rachel Dolezal and America's white women who want to be black."
27 Greenfieldboyce, "Race Doesn't Exist. Or Does It?," Adelman, *Race: The Power of an Illusion*.
28 For more on the role of genetics in defining kinship in American culture see, Finkler, "The Kin in the Gene." Additionally, in "The Traffic in Women," Gayle Rubin offers a historiography of the role of kinship in the organization of sex/gender systems, wherein she asserts, "Kinship systems are and do many things. But they are made up of, and reproduce, concrete forms of socially organized sexuality. Kinship systems are observable and empirical forms of sex/gender systems," 169.
29 Schneider, *American Kinship*, 1.
30 For more specific analysis of the intersections of belonging, queer theory, and kinship, see Freeman, "Queer Belongings."
31 Bradway and Freeman, *Queer Kinship*, 2.
32 Ibid., 3.
33 Samuels, *Fantasies of Identification*, 2.
34 Ibid., 3.
35 Kim, *The Racial Mundane*, 3.
36 Ibid. Emphasis in original.
37 Thompson, *Making Parents*, 8.
38 Eng, *The Feeling of Kinship*, 10.
39 Kang, *Compositional Subjects*, 142. Emphasis in original.
40 For more on the 1875 Page Act see Luibhéid, *Entry Denied* and Chan, "The Exclusion of Chinese Women, 1870–1943." For more on Bachelor Societies see Chan, *Asian Americans: An Interpretive History* and Nee and Nee, *Longtime Californ'*.
41 Lee, *Fictive Kinship*, 50.
42 See Lau, *Paper Families*.
43 Stoler, *Along the Archival Grain*, 2.
44 See Leonard, *Making Ethnic Choices* and Bald, *Bengali Harlem*.
45 Ngai, *Impossible Subjects*, 3. Emphasis in the original.
46 Klein, *Cold War Orientalism*, 189.

47 Ibid., 146.
48 Bonilla-Silva, *Racism without Racists*, 18.
49 See Wu, *The Color of Success*.
50 William Petersen, "Success Story, Japanese-American Style."
51 Melamed, "The Spirit of Neoliberalism," 14.
52 Eng, *The Feeling of Kinship*, 9–10.
53 Ad Council, "Love Has No Labels—Diversity & Inclusion."

CHAPTER 1. PAPER FAMILIES AND FAMILY PAPERS

1 The primary case files of this research are housed by National Archives, New York City, in the Chinese Exclusion Act Case Files of the Immigration and Naturalization Service. For the period between 1882 when the Chinese Exclusion Act passed and 1943 when it was repealed by the Magnuson Act, there are over 18,500 files of Chinese and Chinese American individuals that had moved through the New York branch of the INS. Additionally, I corroborated my observations about the immigration bureaucracy and treatment of paper families with archival case files from the legal papers of You Chung Hong housed at Huntington Library.
2 Box 538. Case file 171/76, Wong Tung Yee, Chinese Exclusion Act Case Files. National Archives, New York.
3 As Erika Lee argues in *At America's Gates*, the era of Chinese exclusion was not a monolithic period of uniform immigration regulation but a period encompassing a range of uneven processes and changing implementations of the law. In emphasizing this fraught negotiation as fundamentally racialized, Lee articulates Chinese exclusion as "an institution that produced and reinforced a system of racial hierarchy in immigration law, a process that both immigrants and immigration officials shaped, and a site of unequal power relations and resistance" (7).
4 Lau, *Paper Families* and Lee, *At America's Gates*. Both Lee and Lau provide extensive historical accounts of Chinese immigration during this period. Forming paper families was not only a strategy employed within a bureaucracy, but they were also embodied, felt, and lived. Some individuals spent the rest of their lives living with these identities.
5 For examples of this process and coaching books, see Lee, *At America's Gates*; Lau, *Paper Families*; and Yung, *Unbound Voices*.
6 Ngai, *Impossible Subjects*, 218.
7 Ibid., 220.
8 Putting terms like "paper family" and "paper son" in quotation marks helps to emphasize the constructed nature of these concepts. However, these were also the terms that were and are used to describe this type of family formation and, for the sake of removing distraction, I remove the quotations from this point onwards.
9 Luibhéid, *Entry Denied*, 54.
10 Lew-Williams, "Paper Lives of Chinese Migrants and the History of the Undocumented," 112.
11 Ibid., 116.

12 Lau, *Paper Families*, 4. Emphasis in original.
13 For example, Sharon Luk theorizes paper in the context of Chinese exclusion, specifically examining the role of letters in *The Life of Paper*.
14 Luibhéid, *Entry Denied*, 43.
15 Out of 321 files mentioning "paper" or "confession," 27 were the files of women. By the start of the twentieth century, the Page Act of 1875 had effectively stopped all immigration of Chinese women to the United States except those that could show substantial evidence that they were not prostitutes. This was often done through a series of often arbitrary and always stringent examinations and testimonies, and was almost always connected to the women's family status. Then, with the passing of the Chinese Exclusion Act in 1882, it became even more difficult for Chinese women to enter the United States, effectively narrowing the population of women immigrating to those that could show derivative United States citizenship through relation to United States-born husbands or fathers. See more in Luibhéid's *Entry Denied*.
16 As Erika Lee and Madeline Hsu describe, many Chinese during this period did go back and forth between China and the United States. See Erika Lee, *At America's Gates* and Hsu, *Dreaming of Gold, Dreaming of Home*.
17 Box 37, Case file 6/1728, Yee On, Chinese Exclusion Act Case Files, National Archives, New York.
18 "Testimony from Yee On," May 23, 1914, Box 37, Case file 6/1728, Yee On, Chinese Exclusion Act Case Files, National Archives, New York.
19 Ibid.
20 "Letter to the Commissioner of Immigration & Naturalization," May 9, 1936, Box 37, Case file 6/1728, Yee On, Chinese Exclusion Act Case Files, National Archives, New York.
21 Jasanoff, *States of Knowledge*, 2–3. Emphasis in original.
22 Ngai, *Impossible Subjects*, 205.
23 Luibhéid, *Entry Denied*, 50.
24 Foucault, *Discipline and Punish*, 190.
25 See more on the body and the archive in Sekula, "The Body and the Archive."
26 Many of the files that I examined had a reference sheet. Some of them had no family members listed like that of Jew Fook, who only had himself listed (with Relationship listed as "Self"). Others had anywhere between two and ten family members and witnesses included. "Reference Sheet," Box 452, Case file 165/717, Jew Fook, Chinese Exclusion Act Case Files, National Archives, New York.
27 See Lee, *At America's Gates*; Lau, *Paper Families*; and Luk, *Life of Paper* for more extensive narration of these practices.
28 In *Paper Families*, Lau chronicles the complexity and meticulousness with which questions about family and kinship were asked: "Applicants had to recall the ages (sometimes even the birth dates), occupations, and physical appearance of all family members—uncles, aunts, cousins, grandparents, and spouses of any of these family members. The type of foot—bound or natural—was asked for each

woman in the family. Applicants were asked the last time they had seen each person and where they were now and what they were doing" (48). For the files from the Chinese Exclusion Act Case Files that I examined, the official testimony usually comprised the greatest number of continuous pages. Ranging from three to twenty pages, official transcripts were usually printed on thin, almost translucent paper and case files often contained at least two copies. The official paginated document usually included testimonies from both the applicant and one to three witnesses interviewed individually. The names of the state employees were always recorded and usually included two inspectors, a secretary or stenographer, and an interpreter. At the end of the document, a ruling was made and seconded by the inspectors and it was noted when an applicant was admitted.

29 For more on coaching books see Lee, *At America's Gates* and Lau, *Paper Families*.
30 Yung, *Unbound Voices*, 32–56.
31 Luk, *Life of Paper*, 59.
32 In *The Presentation of Self in Everyday Life*, Erving Goffman defines the "performance" of everyday life as "all the activity of a given participant on a given occasion which serves to influence in any way any of the other participants" (15).
33 Bernstein, "Dances with Things," 75.
34 For more on embodiment and performativity, see Butler, *Gender Trouble* and Foster, "Choreographies of Gender."
35 "Testimony of Lum Lim Jung," November 8, 1929, Box 426, Case file 149/95, Lum Yuet Gay, Chinese Exclusion Act Case Files, National Archives, New York. 6.
36 "Testimony of Lum Yuet Gay," November 8, 1929, Box 426, Case file 149/95, Lum Yuet Gay, Chinese Exclusion Act Case Files, National Archives, New York. 12-13.
37 Azoulay, "What is a photograph? What is photography?" 12. Emphasis in original.
38 Foucault, *Discipline & Punish*, 191. Emphasis in original.
39 Sekula, "The Body and the Archive," 345. Emphasis in original.
40 Ibid. Emphasis in original.
41 For more on the Page Act, see Pegler-Gordon, *In Sight of America* and Luibhéid, *Entry Denied*.
42 Robertson, *The Passport in America*, 173.
43 Pegler-Gordon, *In Sight of America*, 71–72.
44 Tagg, *Burden Of Representation*, 5.
45 Yung, *Unbound Feet*, 68–69.
46 "Testimony of Moy Ham," May 4, 1927. Box 363. Case file 125/68 Moy Sue. Chinese Exclusion Act Case Files, National Archives, New York. 9.
47 Azoulay, "What is a photograph? What is photography?," 12.
48 Pegler-Gordon, *In Sight of America*, 82–88.
49 Thirty-six of 110 files included these family photograph collages.
50 Barthes, *Camera Lucida*, 77. Emphasis in original.
51 Wexler, "Techniques of the Imaginary Nation: Engendering Family Photography," 374. See also Thy Phu's discussion of Chinese American commercial portraiture in the early twentieth century in *Picturing Model Citizens*, 44–46.

52 Sucheng Chan, "The Exclusion of Chinese Women, 1870–1943," 95.
53 Luibhéid, *Entry Denied*, xxvi.
54 Lee, *At America's Gates*, 202.
55 I examined the files of Moy Hand Fun (first generation, father), Moy Di Yick (second generation, son), Moy Di Quay (second generation, son), and Moy Di Shew (File 170/518, second generation, daughter) in order to piece together this family history. Box 247, Case file 47/227, Moy Hand Fun; Box 515, Case file 169/706, Moy Di Yick; Box 519, Case file 169/998, Moy Di Quay; Box 529, Case file 170/518, Moy Di Shew. Chinese Exclusion Act Case Files, National Archives, New York.
56 Moy Di Wing was the first to arrive in New York City on Christmas Eve of 1935, on the SS Ansonia. The following year, Moy Di Wing served as the witness for his brother, Moy Di Wah, to come to the United States and three more brothers followed, Moy Di Nen, Moy Di Foo, and Moy Di Bin. In 1937, three more brothers arrived in the United States, Moy Di Yick, Moy Di Yin, and Moy Di Gway. The last to arrive, in New York City on February 23, 1938, ten years after Moy Hand Fun's death, was eighteen-year-old Moy Di Shew.
57 "Testimony of Investigation of Moy Di Foo," September 17, 1963. Box 529. Case file 170/518, Moy Di Shew. Chinese Exclusion Act Case Files, National Archives, New York.
58 Box 33. Case file 6/1533, Lung Guey. Chinese Exclusion Act Case Files, National Archives, New York.
59 Box 255. Case file 56/62, Louie Wing Chun. Chinese Exclusion Act Case Files, National Archives, New York.
60 Box 366. Case file 125/172 Chin Gook Ying. Chinese Exclusion Act Case Files, National Archives, New York.
61 Box 470. Case file 167/399, Moy Mee. Chinese Exclusion Act Case Files, National Archives, New York.
62 Box 531. Case file 170/665, Wong Yuet Shim. Chinese Exclusion Act Case Files, National Archives, New York.
63 Box 538. Case file 171/76, Wong Tung Yee. Chinese Exclusion Act Case Files, National Archives, New York.
64 Box 548. Case file 171/693, Young Wun Kau. Chinese Exclusion Act Case Files, National Archives, New York.
65 "Confession of Eng Kee On," May 26, 1965. Box 561. Case file 172/640, Jew Shee. Chinese Exclusion Act Case Files, National Archives, New York.
66 Carter, "Table Ad149–161 Immigrants, by country of birth—Asia: 1941–1997," *Historical Statistics of the United States*, 1-570.

CHAPTER 2. THE MAKING OF THE MODEL MINORITY FAMILY

1 See Lee, *Orientals*; Lui, *The Chinatown Trunk Mystery*; and Tchen, *New York before Chinatown*.
2 Ramirez, "America's Super Minority," 149.
3 Ninh, *Ingratitude*, 9. Emphasis in original.

4 Lowe, *Immigrant Acts*, 63. Emphasis added. This is not to say there have not been critical examinations of Asian American family and kinship that have explored these themes with nuance. For example, see Yanagisako, *Transforming the Past*.
5 Shibusawa, *America's Geisha Ally*, 4.
6 See, for example, Klein, *Cold War Orientalism*.
7 See also Palumbo-Liu, *Asian/American*.
8 Yu, *Thinking Orientals*, 6.
9 Wu, *The Color of Success*, 9.
10 Cheng, *Citizens of Asian America*, 3.
11 Wu, *The Color of Success*, 171–172.
12 Moynihan, "The Negro Family: The Case for National Action," 9-12.
13 Ferguson, *Aberrations in Black*, 18.
14 Ibid., 121.
15 Petersen, "Success Story, Japanese-American Style," 41.
16 U.S. News & World Report, "Success Story of One Minority Group in U.S.," 8.
17 Ibid.
18 Tachiki, "Introduction," *Roots: An Asian American Reader*, 1.
19 For other examples of later news media pieces challenging the model minority, see Sung-Hee Suh, "The Cost of Being an Asian-American Superachiever"; Janice Arkatov, "Breaking Down the Asian Stereotype"; and Ronald Takaki, "The Harmful Myth of Asian Superiority."
20 Ferguson, *Aberrations in Black*, 123. Lipsitz, *The Possessive Investment in Whiteness*, 24.
21 Nguyen, *Race and Resistance*, 144.
22 Anna Quindlen, "The Drive to Excel," *New York Times*, February 22, 11987, sec. 6, 32.
23 Lee, *Fictive Kinship*, 6.
24 These statistics represent all immigration and not just from Asia. Carter, "Table Ad950–954 Immigrants admitted under the Quota System: 1925–1968," *Historical Statistics of the United States*, 1-627.
25 Ngai, *Impossible Subjects*, 259.
26 Ibid., 230.
27 An Act to Amend the Immigration and Nationality Act and for Other Purposes. Public Law 89–236. US Statutes at Large 79 (1965), 913. In the text, I also refer to this act as the Immigration and Nationality Act of 1965 or the Hart-Celler Act of 1965.
28 "50,000 Enter U.S. Under New Law," 4.
29 Ngai, *Impossible Subjects*, 261–262.
30 Carter, "Table Ad955–965 Immigrants admitted under the Preference System: 1966–1991," *Historical Statistics of the United States*, 1-628.
31 Schmeck, "Asia Biggest Source of Brain Drain to US," 28.
32 Choy, *Empire of Care*, 5.
33 Lowe, *Immigrant Acts*, 16.
34 Ibid., 189–190.

35 Ibid., 22. Emphasis in original.
36 An Act to amend the Immigration and Nationality Act to revise the procedures for the admission of refugees, to amend the Migration and Refugee Assistance Act of 1962 to establish a more uniform basis for the provision of assistance to refugees, and for other purposes, 102. In the text, I also refer to this act as the Refugee Act of 1980.
37 Based on immigration data, 1981, 1982, and 1983 saw the highest numbers and percentage of refugee admissions from Asia. After 1983, refugee immigration from Asia began to decrease, even as total numbers of refugee immigration increased. Carter, "Table Ad1005–1013 Refugee and asylees admitted and granted permanent status, by continent of birth: 1948–1997," *Historical Statistics of the United States*, 1-635.
38 In this data set, Southeast Asia included Brunei, Burma, Cambodia, Indonesia, Laos, Malaysia, Singapore, Thailand, and Vietnam. Carter, "Table Ad149–161 Immigrants, by country of birth—Asia: 1941–1997," *Historical Statistics of the United States*, 1-569.
39 Espiritu, *Body Counts*, 10.
40 An Act to amend the Immigration and Nationality Act to revise the procedures for the admission of refugees, to amend the Migration and Refugee Assistance Act of 1962 to establish a more uniform basis for the provision of assistance to refugees, and for other purposes, 104.
41 This phrase occurs three times in the Refugee Act of 1980.
42 Nguyễn, "'Loving Couples and Families,'" 2.
43 Ibid.
44 Wang, "Asian Poor Neglected."
45 Ramirez, "America's Super Minority."
46 Blanksteen, "'Boat People' Find a Haven in the State: Haven for Refugees," NJ1.
47 Hume, "Indochinese Refugees Adapt Quickly in U.S., Using Survival Skills."
48 Ramirez, "America's Super Minority."
49 Editorial Board, "An Interview with S.I Hayakawa," 22–23.
50 For more discussion of these debates and activism within the Asian American community during this period see, Lopez, "The Yellow Press."
51 In the interview, Hayakawa also critiques Asian Americans and yellow power for aligning itself with the Black Panthers and black liberation struggles.
52 Nguyen, *The Gift of Freedom*, 3.
53 Ibid., 7.
54 Ibid., 8. Emphasis in original.
55 Ibid., 10.
56 Ninh, *Ingratitude*, 11.
57 Brown, "Neoliberalism and the End of Liberal Democracy," 39–40.

CHAPTER 3. PHOTOGRAPHIC CONCEPTIONS
1 US Department of State Bureau of Consular Affairs, "Adoption Statistics."
2 Eng, *The Feeling of Kinship*, 97–103.
3 Choy, *Global Families*, 9.

4   As Choy discusses, there were adoptions from Taiwan and Hong Kong in relatively small numbers. However, until the 1990s, Korea was the top sending country for transnational adoption.
5   See also Graves, *A War Born Family* and Woo, *Framed by War*.
6   Klein, *Cold War Orientalism*.
7   Johnson, China's Hidden Children, 17.
8   Ibid., 12.
9   Melamed, "The Spirit of Neoliberalism."
10 Brown, "Neoliberalism and the End of Liberal Democracy," 38–39.
11 Tu, *The Beautiful Generation*, 23. Tu's specific period of reference was 1995–2005, which was the era of fashion that she examined to unpack the dynamics of "Asian chic" emerging during this period.
12 While transnational adoption from China may seem disparate from the rise of Asian American fashion designers, Tu's articulation of the global dynamics of consumption, visuality, and the growing forms of intimacy between the United States and Asia provide a helpful cultural landscape for understanding the context of family formation during this period. Furthermore, on the ground, Tu's ethnographic work on fashion designers in New York City is directly situated in the same geographical place and connected cultural worlds as the middle and upper middleclass parents represented by FCCNY that were living in New York City (and the tri-state area) and adopting from China during the same years.
13 Kim, "An 'Orphan' with Two Mothers."
14 Kim, *Adopted Territory*. Dorow, *Transnational Adoption*. Louie, *How Chinese Are You?*.
15 See Nelson, *Invisible Asians*; McKee, *Disrupting Kinship*; and Pate, *From Orphan to Adoptee*.
16 Hirsch, *Family Frames*, 8.
17 In this context, I gesture to "thing theory" and scholarship in new materialisms, in which nonliving objects are conceived of agentive "things," to consider what Bill Brown calls "less an object than a particular subject-object relation" (4). See also Chen, *Animacies* and Bennett, *Vibrant Matter*.
18 In 2022, following leadership changes that reflected a shift from a Board of Directors comprising of mostly adoptive parents to one of majority Chinese adoptees, FCCNY changed their name to Chinese Adoptee Alliance.
19 These oral history interviews included more extensive discussion beyond the subject of referral photography including discussion of their own family formation narratives, their racialized and gendered experiences growing up, and their relationship to FCCNY.
20 Families with Children from China of Greater New York, Connecticut, and New Jersey Newsletters, private collection, in author's possession.
21 The conference was the Adoptive Parents Committee Conference, a national conference for both domestic and international adoptive families run by an organization by the same name.
22 Telfer, "Relationships with No Body?" 149.

23 Ibid.
24 Dorow, *Transnational Adoption*, 110–111.
25 Ibid.
26 I use pseudonyms for the names of all individual adoptees since they do not have public roles within the community.
27 Barthes, *Camera Lucida*, 66.
28 Azoulay, "What is a photograph? What is photography?," 12.
29 Petchesky, "Fetal Images," 279.
30 Dorow, 109.
31 Campt, *Image Matters*, 17.
32 For more on the process, see Kawakami, *Picture Bride Stories*.
33 Phu, *Picturing Model Citizens*, 47.
34 Ibid., 49.
35 Eng, *The Feeling of Kinship*, 107.
36 Baden, "Do You Know Your *Real* Parents?"
37 McKee, *Disrupting Kinship*, 13.
38 For more on early adoption from Korea see Oh, *To Save the Children of Korea*. For more on adoption from Vietnam see Varzally, *Children of Reunion*.
39 Klein, *Cold War Orientalism*. Guterl, *Seeing Race in Modern America*.
40 For discussion of the "as-if-biological" discourse, see Modell, *Kinship with Strangers*. For more on contemporary adoption narratives, see Homans, *The Imprint of Another Life*.
41 For more on the gendered abandonment and adoption of Chinese girls, see Johnson, *Wanting a Daughter, Needing a Son*.
42 Yuh, *Beyond the Shadow of Camptown*, 2.
43 Woo, *Framed by War*, 17.
44 Klein, *Cold War Orientalism*, 146.
45 Anagnost, "Scenes of Misrecognition," 390.
46 Louie, *How Chinese Are You?*, 8–9. See also Dorow, "Bringing Transnationalism Home" and Traver, "Home(land) Décor."
47 For more on accounts of these upbringings see Nelson, *Invisible Asians* and Kim, *Adopted Territory*.
48 In *How Chinese Are You?*, Louie references this mentorship of parents adopting from China. I also found evidence for this kind of exchange in transcripts of panel discussions featuring Korea adoptee speakers hosted by FCCNY.
49 Yngvesson, *Belonging in an Adopted World*, 28.
50 Kim, "An 'Orphan' with Two Mothers," 857.
51 Johnson, "Transnational Family Photographs and Adoption from Asia."
52 Cartwright, "Photographs of 'Waiting Children,'" 84.
53 McKee, *Disrupting Kinship*, 2.
54 Kim, "An 'Orphan' with Two Mothers," 862–864. Cultural analyses of *First Person Plural* can also be found in Eng's *The Feeling of Kinship* and Choy's *Global Families*.

55 Choy, *Global Families*, 132
56 Ibid., 146.
57 Phu, *Picturing Model Citizens*.

CHAPTER 4. MAKING RACIAL CHOICES

1 There is a marked lack of research on the specific modes of presentation of egg and sperm donors, including on the differences between earlier use of binders compared to online databases. However, further study on the material and regulative power of databases can be found in Bowker and Star, *Sorting Things Out*.
2 Fogg-Davis, "Navigating Race in the Market for Human Gametes," 14.
3 In addition to considering the general use of the profile interface for many online dating websites, I also examined the profile systems for Match.com and OkCupid. Both are particularly rich sites because they have remained two of the most popular dating websites since online dating gained mainstream popularity in the late 2000s. Founded in 1995, Match.com is the longest running dating website and continues to be the most popular with an estimated 35 million monthly visitors. And significantly for this research, OkCupid, which launched in 2004, has been at the forefront of public conversations about race and online dating. Among egg and sperm donation companies, I analyzed the websites of eight different large cryobanks across the United States, five of which were highlighted in a 2017 *Huffington Post* article as "big banks." These sites featured a range of styles and narratives about their services, but all offered a publicly available preview of their donor catalog and user profiles to highlight their substantial donor selections. In contrast to dating websites, these donor catalogs were available publicly without registration, though personal information of donors was redacted to some degree. Wendy Kramer, "Choosing a Sperm Bank . . . What to Know."
4 Daniels and Heidt-Forsythe, "Gendered Eugenics and the Problematic Free Market Reproductive Technologies." Curington, Lundquist, and Lin, *The Dating Divide*.
5 Nakamura, *Cybertypes*, 104.
6 Further studies include Noble, *Algorithms of Oppression* and Eubanks, *Automating Inequality*.
7 Nakamura, *Cybertypes*, 120.
8 Brown, "Neoliberalism and the End of Democracy," 44.
9 Melamed, "The Spirit of Neoliberalism," 3.
10 Kaplan, Loyer, and Daniels, "Precision Targets."
11 Rajan, *Lively Capital*, 8.
12 Chun, *Updating to Remain the Same*, 1.
13 For more of this history, see Ahuvia and Adelman, "Formal Intermediaries in the Marriage Market."
14 Almeling, *Sex Cells*, 34.
15 Ibid., 38.

16 Murphy, *The Economization of Life*, 6.
17 See Turkle, *Life on the Screen* and Boellstorff, *Coming of Age in Second Life* for early analyses of the identity and exchange online. More recent studies that engage with themes of marketplace and choice include Chun, *Updating to Remain the Same* and Rettberg, *Seeing Ourselves Through Technology*.
18 Frost, Chance, Norton, and Ariely, "People are Experience Goods," 52.
19 Ibid.
20 For sperm donors, surrounding this search bar are pulldown menus for thirteen different categories: anonymity, hair color, CMV status, race, ICI/IUI status, height, standard, ethnicity, blood type, weight, profile, eye color, and motility. The tab for egg donors shows nine categories: race, blood type, ethnicity, height, standard, eye color, weight, anonymity, and hair color. Cryos International Sperm and Egg Bank, "Find Donor."
21 California Cryobank, "Why Us?"
22 For example, in 2020, queer dating apps Grindr, Scruff, and Jack'd all announced they would be removing their ethnicity filter. See Garel, "Grindr, Scruff Removed Ethnicity Filers In Its Gay Dating Apps."
23 Sekula discusses the relationality of photography in a similar way in his discussion of Bertillon and the use of photography in categorizing criminality. Sekula writes, "Thus even the nominalist Bertillon was forced to recognize the higher reality of the 'average man.' The individual could be identified only by invoking the powers of this genie. And the individual existed *as an individual* only by being identified. Individuality as such had no meaning. Viewed 'objectively,' the self occupied a position that was wholly relative." Sekula, "The Body and the Archive," 363. Emphasis in original.
24 Ibid., 353.
25 Cvetkovich observes the phrase "structure of feeling" "is a good example of the use of the vocabulary of feeling to describe how social conditions are manifest in everyday life and how felt experience can be the foundation for emergent social formations." Cvetkovich, "Affect," 14.
26 Garde-Hansen and Gorton, *Emotion Online*, 13.
27 For more on affect online see, Garde-Hansen and Forton, *Emotion Online* and Paasonen, *Carnal Resonance*.
28 Almeling, *Sex Cells*, 61.
29 Lisa Nakamura's *Cybertypes* critiques early arguments of the Internet as a democratic space and highlights the reproduction of racism and racial stereotypes online. Nakamura raises questions of participation and access for racial, gender, and sexual minorities within the space of the Internet.
30 Nakamura, *Digitizing Race*, 16.
31 HoSang, *Racial Propositions*, 266.
32 See also, Saito, *The Politics of Exclusion*; Lipsitz, *The Possessive Investment in Whiteness*; and Ferguson, *Aberrations in Black*.

33 Match.com offers the following categories: Asian, Black/African descent, East Indian, Latino/Hispanic, Middle Eastern, Native American, Pacific Islander, White/Caucasian, and Other. OkCupid offers: Asian, Black, Hispanic/Latin, Indian, Middle Eastern, Native American, Pacific Islander, White, and Other.
34 Bonus, "Ethnicity," 79.
35 Almeling, *Sex Cells*, 32–33.
36 For more on the history of anti-miscegenation legislation, see Pascoe, *What Comes Naturally*.
37 East Meets East, "Homepage."
38 Weston, "Kinship, Controversy, and the Sharing of Substance," 168. Emphasis in original.
39 Roberts, *God's Laboratory*, 113.
40 Ibid., 115.
41 Almeling, *Sex Cells*, 69.
42 Li, "Asian women command premium prices for egg donation in US."
43 Ryan, "Want to Sell You Eggs to Pay for College? Be Asian."
44 Bever, "White woman sues sperm bank after she mistakenly gets black donor's sperm." Bellware, "White Woman Who Sued Sperm Bank Over Black Baby Says It's Not About Race."
45 Associated Press, "White parents who had Asian baby allege sperm mix-up by clinic." CBS News, "White couple gives birth to Asian daughter after alleged fertility clinic mix-up."
46 Fogg-Davis, "Navigating Race in the Market for Human Gametes," 13.
47 Daniels and Heidt-Forsythe, "Gendered Eugenics," 720. They define gendered eugenics as "the social practice of ascribing superior human traits to those who most closely match Western ideals of masculinity and femininity for the purpose of human reproduction." Ibid.
48 Ibid., 743–744.
49 OkCupid, "Race and Attraction." Brackets in original.
50 See Shim, "OkCupid Data Reveals the Disturbing Truth About How People Pick Their Partners"; Kleinman, "Black People And Asian Men Have A Much Harder Time Dating On OkCupid"; and Brown, "'Least Desirable'? How Racial Discrimination Plays Out In Online Dating."
51 OkCupid, "Race and Attraction."
52 Curington, Lundquist, and Lin, *The Dating Divide*, 4.
53 Nakamura, *Digitizing Race*, 5.
54 Shimizu, *The Hypersexuality of Race*. Cheng, *Ornamentalism*.
55 Bow, *Racist Love*, 154.
56 For more, see Wood, "Rape as a Practice of War"; Weaver, *Ideologies of Forgetting*; and Yuh, *Beyond the Shadow of Camptown*.
57 Constantino, "Atlanta spa shooter who targeted Asian women pleads guilty to four of eight murders."

58 For examples, see Tsjeng, "Asian Women's Bodies Are Not Playgrounds For White People" and Chou, "You Know What I Say About Men Who F—Asian Women?"
59 In *The Dating Divide*, Curington, Lundquist, and Lin discuss their interviews with Asian women in online dating and their experiences with stereotypes about Asian women's sexuality. Kip Fulbeck's *Part Asian, 100% Hapa* also features some discussion of multiracial Asian women's experiences of race and dating.
60 Bow, *Racist Love*, 156. Emphasis in original.
61 Melamed, "The Spirit of Neoliberalism," 2.
62 The study was funded by Match.com and conducted by global online market research firm Dynata. *Match*, "Singles in America."
63 Fairfax Cryobank, "Homepage."
64 Mekanism, "OkCupid: Every Single Person."
65 The theme of the 2019 Met Gala Ball and accompanying art exhibition at the Costume Institute of the Metropolitan Museum of Art was titled "Camp: Notes on Fashion," directly evoking Susan Sontag's 1964 essay "Notes on 'Camp.'" However, as one of the most exclusive events in the celebrity and fashion world, the theme elicited confusion for many in the mainstream who were not familiar with camp, and critical reception among many who pointed out its marginalized origins. News outlets like *New York Times*, *NBC News*, *CNN*, and *Vogue* published articles explaining and debating what constitutes camp. Pointing out the contradiction, Lena Waithe attended the Gala in a suit with the statement, "Black Drag Queens Inventend Camp," including the talked-about typo. I elaborate on this context because like the Met Gala, the camp aesthetics of the OkCupid campaign fits within a larger genealogy of tension between aesthetics born out of marginalization and their appropriation to privileged (or in this case marketing for profit) contexts. Whether the OkCupid campaign fits as an example could certainly be debated.
66 Mekanism (@mekanism), "We're proud to unveil our latest work for @OkCupid today . . . ," Instagram post.
67 Melissa Hobley (@melissahobley), "Proud that this campaign from @okcupid might be the first to celebrate nonbinary individuals. . . ." Instagram post.
68 See Clark, "After a record quarter OkCupid debuts 'provocative' new campaign championing inclusivity"; Faierman, "OkCupid Launches an Expansive Campaign for Almost Every Single Kind of Dater"; Print Mag, "OkCupid Gets a Little Naughty With Their Latest Ad Campaign"; and Tsangarakis, "OkCupid is 'for Every Single Person' in Colorful, Inclusive Ads."
69 For more on Asian inscrutability, see Xiang, *Tonal Intelligence* and Sianne Ngai's discussion of Animatedness in *Ugly Feelings*.
70 Admittedly, this did not prevent controversy regarding some of the images from the campaign, as the New York City Metropolitan Transportation Authority rejected several previously accepted posters due to its recent ban on cannabis ads and expanded restrictions on sex-related advertising. See Bain, "MTA rejects OkCupid ads that were previously OK'd."
71 Cryos International Sperm and Egg Bank, "Homepage."

CHAPTER 5. 23ANDME AND THE RACIALIZATION OF GENETIC ANCESTRY TESTING

1. 23andMe Blog, "23andMe+ Premium: An ongoing approach to your genetics."
2. Nelson, *The Social Life of DNA*, 3.
3. Nelkin and Lindee, *The DNA Mystique*, xxi.
4. Ibid., 2. While Nelkin and Lindee theorize the concept of genetic essentialism in the context of cultural images of DNA, the term was first used by Sarah Franklin in the context of gay and lesbian identities, reproduction, and kinship in "Essentialism, Which Essentialism?"
5. Nelkin and Lindee, *The DNA Mystique*, 6.
6. See more on the digitization of user data and data information in Chun, *Programmed Visions* and Nakamura and Chow-White, *Race After the Internet*.
7. Wailoo, Nelson, and Lee, *Genetics and the Unsettled Past*, 4.
8. TallBear, *Native American DNA*.
9. Nelson, *The Social Life of DNA*, 28–32.
10. For more on genetics and race, see also, Koenig, Lee, and Richardson, *Revisiting Race in the Genomic Age*; Wailoo, Nelson, and Lee, *Genetics and the Unsettled Past*; El-Haj, "The Genetic Reinscription of Race."
11. Nash, "Genetic Kinship," 4.
12. Hamilton, "Best Inventions of 2008: 1. The Retail DNA Test."
13. *23andMe*, "About."
14. According to the website, 23andMe can be used by individuals with more than 23 pairs of chromosomes, including individuals with Down Syndrome (trisomy 21) or Klinefelter syndrome (XXY). However, the company admits that their service will not be able to analyze information specific to the additional chromosomes. See for more info at 23andMe, "What Health Conditions Are Not Included in 23andMe."
15. 23andMe, "Ancestry Service." 23andMe, "Health Service."
16. 23andMe Blog, "A Totally New 23andMe Health Membership: Total Health."
17. In April 2018, news media described a case in which the direct-to-consumer genetic testing service FamilyTreeDNA worked with the FBI to identify a serial killer known as the Golden State Killer, using DNA from the case to look for genetic relatives of the suspect. On their website, in their Privacy and Data Protection page, 23andMe states that they "will not release any individual-level personal information to law enforcement without your explicit consent unless required by law." However, it is currently the responsibility of the company to decide and manage their own policies regarding the data and information of customers. See Zhang, "A DNA Company Wants You to Help Catch Criminals" and Bonvillian, "'Golden State Killer' suspect tracked down using DNA on genealogy website, officials say." 23andMe, "Privacy and Data Protection."
18. 23andMe, "Research."

19 23andMe, "23andMe Improves Research Consent Process." According to their website, "23anMe's IRB is an Association for the Accreditation of Human Research Protection Programs (AAHRPP)-accredited company, Ethical and Independent Review Services, Inc. (Independence, MO and San Anselmo, CA). 23andMe, "Surveys and Quick Questions: Does 23andMe have IRB approval?"
20 23andMe, "The Science Behind 23andMe."
21 As of August 2022, thirty-six percent of company employees were categorized as "Asian or Pacific Islander." 23andMe, "Our Workplace Diversity," Diversity, Equity, and Inclusion Webpage.
22 Briggs, "Science," 217. Emphasis in original.
23 As discussed in previous chapters, Choy defines global family making as the "process involving the decisions made and actions taken by people who create and sustain a family by consciously crossing national and often racial borders." Choy, *Global Families*, 9.
24 Klein, *Cold War Orientalism*, 188.
25 The full list is available at 23andMe, "What Countries Do You Ship To?"
26 *New York Times*, "12 Asian Americans Discuss."
27 Paul Nadal (@paulnadal_), "An important lesson in Asian American Studies is that 'Asian American' was a social movement before it was ever an identity . . ." Twitter post.
28 While my research did not include quantitative data from customers, this example is a real comparison using my own genetic data submitted to 23andMe and imported to WeGene. On 23andMe, my report says I am 92.8% Chinese with no percentage breakdowns for the ten associated regions listed. On WeGene, I am listed as 89.94% Chinese and within that includes 44.73% Northern Han, 31.50% Southern Han, and 3.8% Miao.
29 23andMe, "What Ancestry-Related Information Can I Learn From 23andMe?"
30 In 2019, the page read, "The peoples of East Asia and the Americas have a shared genetic history. Their common ancestors left western Asia over 50,000 years ago, migrating east across the continent. Sometimes a piece of DNA matches a regional population but cannot be assigned to a more specific population. In such a case we assign the DNA 'broadly' to that regional population rather than a specific one. Broadly East Asian & Native American DNA is a relic of this ancient population split, and reflects shared roots in central and northern Asia." In 2021, the page had been edited to read, "The peoples of East Asia and the Americas have a shared genetic history. Their common ancestors left western Asia over 50,000 years ago, migrating east across the continent. The ancestors of Native Americans began to cross into the Americas 12,000 to 15,000 years ago. Broadly East Asian & Native American DNA is a relic of this ancient population split, and reflects shared roots in central and northern Asia." 23andMe, "Reference Populations."
31 Elam, *The Souls of Mixed Folk*, 9. See also, DaCosta, *Making Multiracials*.

32. Sturgis and Joseph more specifically describe 23andMe's approach to racial mixing, writing "the company participates in fixing the meaning of a racially ambiguous look that narratively frames mixed-race Blackness as an ailment in need of an antidote—as if racial mixture can cure or neutralize the ostensible harms of Blackness." Sturgis and Joseph, "Visualizing Mixed Race and Genetics," 41.
33. Samuels, *Fantasies of Identification*, 6.
34. Nash, "Genetic Kinship," 3. See also Bouquet, "Family trees and their affinities."
35. Nelson and Hertz, *Random Families*, 8.
36. Ibid., 4.
37. Ibid., 4.
38. One significant difference between the networks that Nelson and Hertz discuss and websites like 23andMe is the intent with which individuals participate in direct-to-consumer genetic tests. While many popular accounts have highlighted the potentiality of connection with genetic relatives, 23andMe advertises that as only one aspect of the service.
39. See Molina, "Woman discovers she has 29 siblings after taking DNA test. And counting"; Holcombe, "A DNA testing site turned this woman from an only child to one of 30 siblings"; and Hassan, "2 Bay Area women linked to 28 siblings following DNA test."
40. Brewster, "Why Sperm Donor Privacy Is Under Threat From DNA Sites—Is There Anything They Can Do About It?"
41. For more on adoption narratives, including discussion on how adoptees are "peculiarly burdened . . . with this obligation to find, know, and grasp material origins" (114), see Homans, *The Imprint of Another Life*.
42. Leighton, "Addressing the Harms of Not Knowing One's Heredity," 65, 70.
43. Ibid., 68.
44. Gammage, "DNA helping Chinese adoptees do what was once impossible: Locate blood relatives in this country." 23andMe, "Searching for family in China, Stefanie ended up finding a cousin through 23andMe that only lived 12 miles away from her," Facebook post.
45. Rifkin, "Adopted Separately in China, Cousins Wind Up Almost Next Door."
46. The adoption tag has over fifty different stories of adoptees discovering genetic relatives.
47. For more analysis on the hegemony of narratives of searches and origins in adoption narrative see, Homans, *The Imprint of Another Life*. Other documentary examples include *First Person Plural* and *Somewhere Between*, directed by Linda Goldstein Knowlton (2011).
48. Eddy, "23andMe Just Filed for Bankruptcy. You Should Delete Your Data Now."

CONCLUSION

1. For example, see Parreñas, *The Force of Domesticity*.
2. Bow, *Racist Love*, 195.

3 Yang, "We Asian Americans are not the virus, but we can be part of the cure."
4 Schneider, *American Kinship*.
5 Martin, "AirBnB Partners With 23andMe To Recommend Heritage Inspired Vacations."
6 AirBnB, "Heritage Travel on the Rise: AirBnB and 23andMe Team Up to Make it Even Easier."
7 Ibid.
8 Pratt, *Imperial Eyes*.
9 See Cacho, *Social Death* and Yuval-Davis, *The Politics of Belonging*.

BIBLIOGRAPHY

"12 Asian Americans Discuss." *New York Times*. February 21, 2023. https://www.nytimes.com/interactive/2023/02/21/opinion/asian-americans-focus-group.html.

23andMe. "Reference Populations." Accessed June 2, 2019 and October 5, 2021. https://customercare.23andme.com/hc/en-us/articles/212169298-23andMe-Reference-Populations-Regions.

———. "What Ancestry-Related Information Can I Learn From 23andMe?" Accessed June 3, 2019. https://customercare.23andme.com/hc/en-us/articles/115013846688-What-Ancestry-Information-Can-I-Learn-from-23andMe.

———. "What Health Conditions Are Not Included in 23andMe." Accessed July 14, 2019. https://customercare.23andme.com/hc/en-us/articles/236409067-Conditions-NOT-Included-In-23andMe.

———. "What Countries Do You Ship To?" Accessed September 25, 2021. https://int.customercare.23andme.com/hc/en-us/articles/214806628-What-Countries-Do-You-Ship-To.

———. "Ancestry Service." Accessed October 5, 2021. https://www.23andme.com/dna-ancestry.

———. "Research." Accessed October 5, 2021. https://www.23andme.com/research/.

———. The Science Behind 23andMe." Accessed August 2, 2022. https://www.23andme.com/genetic-science/.

———. "Our Workplace Diversity." Accessed August 2, 2022. https://www.23andme.com/en-ca/diversity-equity-inclusion/.

———. "About." Accessed November 10, 2024. https://www.23andme.com/about.

———. "Surveys and Quick Questions: Does 23andMe have IRB approval?" Accessed April 16, 2025. https://int.customercare.23andme.com/hc/en-us/articles/215296358-Surveys-and-Quick-Questions.

23andMe Blog. "23andMe Improves Research Consent Process." June 24, 2020. https://blog.23andme.com.

———. "23andMe+ Premium: An ongoing approach to your genetics." October 1, 2020. https://blog.23andme.com/articles/23andmeplus.

———. "A Totally New 23andMe Health Membership: Total Health." October 25, 2023. https://blog.23andme.com/articles/total-health.

23andMe Facebook. "Searching for family in China, Stefanie ended up finding a cousin through 23andMe that only lived 12 miles away from her." Facebook post. May 6, 2019. https://www.facebook.com/23andMe/posts/10158382623962802.

"50,000 Enter U.S. Under New Law." *New York Times*. October 8, 1966. ProQuest Historical Newspapers.

Ad Council. "Love Has No Labels—Diversity & Inclusion." Posted March 3, 2015, by Ad Council. YouTube, 3 min. 19 sec. https://www.youtube.com/watch?v=PnDgZuGIhHs.

Adelman, Larry, creator. *Race: The Power of an Illusion*. 2003; California Newsreel, https://www.racepowerofanillusion.org/.

Ahuvia, Aaron C. and Mara B. Adelman. "Formal Intermediaries in the Marriage Market: A Typology and Review." *Journal of Marriage and Family* 54, no. 2 (May 1992): 452–463.

Airbnb. "Heritage Travel on the Rise: Airbnb and 23andMe Team Up to Make it Even Easier." May 21, 2019. https://press.airbnb.com/heritage-travel-on-the-rise/.

Almeling, Rene. *Sex Cells: The Medical Market for Eggs and Sperm*. Berkeley: University of California Press, 2011.

Anagnost, Ann. "Scenes of Misrecognition: Maternal Citizenship in the Age of Transnational Adoption." *Positions: East Asia Cultures Critique* 8, no. 2 (2000): 389–421.

An Act to Amend the Immigration and Nationality Act and for Other Purposes. Public Law 89-236. US Statutes at Large 79 (1965): 911–922.

An Act to amend the Immigration and Nationality Act to revise the procedures for the admission of refugees, to amend the Migration and Refugee Assistance Act of 1962 to establish a more uniform basis for the provision of assistance to refugees, and for other purposes. Public Law 96-212. US Statutes at Large 94 (1980): 102–118

Associated Press. "White parents who had Asian baby allege sperm mix-up by clinic." *Los Angeles Times*. September 13, 2019. https://www.latimes.com/world-nation/story/2019-09-12/white-parents-asian-baby-sperm-mix-up-alleged.

Arkatov, Janice. "Breaking Down the Asian Stereotype." *Los Angeles Times*. April 1, 1990: F60. ProQuest Historical Newspapers.

Autry, Robyn. "Jessica Krug, Rachel Dolezal and America's white women who want to be black." *NBC News*. September 7, 2020. https://www.nbcnews.com/think/opinion/jessica-krug-rachel-dolezal-america-s-white-women-who-want-ncna1239418.

Azoulay, Ariella. "What is a photograph? What is photography?" *Philosophy of Photography* 1, no. 1 (2010): 9–13.

Baden, Amanda L. "'Do You Know Your *Real* Parents?' and Other Adoption Microaggressions." *Adoption Quarterly* 19, no. 1 (2016): 1–25.

Bain, Phoebe. "MTA rejects OkCupid ads that were previously OK'd." *Marketing Brew*. January 24, 2021. https://www.marketingbrew.com/stories/2022/01/24/mta-rejects-okcupid-ads-that-were-previously-ok-d.

Bald, Vivek. *Bengali Harlem and the Lost Histories of South Asian America*. Cambridge, MA: Harvard University Press, 2015.

Barthes, Roland. *Camera Lucida: Reflections on Photography*. Translated by Richard Howard. New York: Hill and Wang, 1981.

Becker, Gay. *The Elusive Embryo: How Women and Men Approach New Reproductive Technologies*. Berkeley: University of California Press, 2000.

Bellware, Kim. "White Woman Who Sued Sperm Bank Over Black Baby Says It's Not About Race." *HuffPost*. October 2, 2014. https://www.huffpost.com/entry/black-sperm-lawsuit_n_5922180.

Bennett, Jane. *Vibrant Matter: A Political Ecology of Things*. Durham, NC: Duke University Press, 2010

Bernstein, Robin. "Dances with Things: Material Culture and the Performance of Race." *Social Text* 27, no. 4 (2009): 67–94.

Bever, Lindsey. "White woman sues sperm bank after she mistakenly gets black donor's sperm." *Washington Post*. October 2, 2014. https://www.washingtonpost.com/news/morning-mix/wp/2014/10/02/white-woman-sues-sperm-bank-after-she-mistakenly-gets-black-donors-sperm/.

Blanksteen, Jane. "'Boat People' Find a Haven in the State: Haven for Refugees." *New York Times*. August 12, 1979: NJ1. ProQuest Historical Newspapers.

Boellstorff, Tom. *Coming of Age in Second Life: An Anthropologist Explores the Virtually Human*, revised edition. Princeton: Princeton University Press, 2015.

Bonilla-Silva, Eduardo. *Racism without Racists: Color-Blind Racism and the Persistence of Racial Inequality in America*. Lanham, MD: Rowman & Littlefield Publishers, 2017.

Bonus, Rick. "Ethnicity." *Keywords for Asian American Studies*, edited by Cathy J. Schlund-Vials, K. Scott Wong, and Linda Trinh Võ. New York: New York University Press, 2015.

Borshay Liem, Deann, director. First Person Plural. Center for Asian American Media, 2000. 1 hr. DVD.

———. In the Matter of Cha Jung Hee. New Day Films, 2010. 1 hr., 1 min. DVD.

Bouquet, Mary. "Family trees and their affinities: the visual imperative of the genealogical diagram." *Journal of Royal Anthropological Institute* 2 (1994): 43–66.

Bow, Leslie. *Racist Love: Asian Abstraction and the Pleasures of Fantasy*. Durham, NC: Duke University Press, 2022.

Bowker, Geoffrey C. and Susan Leigh Star. *Sorting Things Out: Classification and Its Consequences*. Cambridge, MA: The MIT Press, 1999.

Bradway, Tyler and Elizabeth Freeman. *Queer Kinship: Race, Sex, Belonging, Form*. Durham, NC: Duke University Press, 2022.

Brewster, Thomas. "Why Sperm Donor Privacy Is Under Threat From DNA Sites—Is There Anything They Can Do About It?" *Forbes*. April 23, 2019. https://www.forbes.com/sites/thomasbrewster/2019/04/23/why-sperm-donor-privacy-is-under-threat-from-dna-sites--is-there-anything-they-can-do-about-it/.

Briggs, Laura. "Science." In *Keywords for American Cultural Studies*, first edition, edited by Bruce Burgett and Glenn Hendler. New York: New York University Press, 2007.

Brown, Ashley. "'Least Desirable'? How Racial Discrimination Plays Out In Online Dating." *NPR*. January 9, 2018. https://www.npr.org/2018/01/09/575352051/least-desirable-how-racial-discrimination-plays-out-in-online-dating.

Brown, Bill. "Thing Theory." *Critical Inquiry* 28, no. 1, Things (Autumn 2001): 1–22.

Brown, Wendy. "Neoliberalism and the End of Liberal Democracy." In *Edgework: Critical Essays on Knowledge and Politics*. Princeton: Princeton University Press, 2006.

Bui, Long T. *Model Machines: A History of the Asian as Automation*. Philadelphia: Temple University Press, 2022.

Butler, Judith. *Gender Trouble: Feminism and the Subversion of Identity*. New York: Routledge, 1990.

Cacho, Lisa Marie. *Social Death: Racialized Rightlessness and the Criminalization of the Unprotected*. New York: New York University Press, 2012.

California Cryobank. "Why Us?" Accessed January 4, 2019. https://www.cryobank.com/why-use-us/.

Campt, Tina M., *Listening to Images*. Durham, NC: Duke University Press, 2017.

———. *Image Matters: Archive, Photography, and the African Diaspora in Europe*. Durham, NC: Duke University Press, 2012.

Carter, Susan B., Scott Sigmund Gartner, Michael R. Haines, Alan L. Olmstead, Richard Sutch, and Gavin Wright, editors. *Historical Statistics of the United States: Millennial Edition Online*. New York: Cambridge University Press, 2006.

Cartwright, Lisa. "Photographs of 'Waiting Children': The Transnational Adoption Market." *Social Text* 21 no. 1 (Spring 2003): 83–109.

CBS News. "White couple gives birth to Asian daughter after alleged fertility clinic mix-up." *CBS News*. September 12, 2019. https://www.cbsnews.com/news/fertility-clinic-sperm-donor-mixup-white-couple-give-birth-to-asian-daughter/.

Chan, Sucheng. *Asian Americans: An Interpretive History*, Woodbridge, CT: Twayne Publishers, 1991.

———. "The Exclusion of Chinese Women, 1870–1943" in *Entry Denied: Exclusion and the Chinese Community in American 1882–1943*, edited by Sucheng Chan. Philadelphia: Temple University Press, 1994.

Chen, Jian Neo. *Trans Exploits: Trans of Color Cultures & Technologies in Movement*. Durham, NC: Duke University Press, 2019.

Chen, Mel Y. *Animacies: Biopolitics, Racial Mattering, and Queer Affect*. Durham, NC: Duke University Press, 2012.

Cheng, Anne Anlin. *Ornamentalism*. Oxford: Oxford University Press, 2019.

Cheng, Cindy I-Fen. *Citizens of Asian America: Democracy and Race during the Cold War*. New York: New York University Press, 2013.

Chinese Exclusion Act Case Files, RG 85, Records of the Immigration and Naturalization Service. National Archives, New York.

Chou, Elaine Hsieh. "You Know What I Say About Men Who F—Asian Women?" *Vanity Fair*. June 16, 2022. https://www.vanityfair.com/hollywood/2022/06/asian-women-movies-tv-stereotypes?srsltid=AfmBOoq6Crno4GQBz-f_VPzqxdm9gLjx4UpN19Dxtjqmjcq7aGmO4tB7.

Choy, Catherine Ceniza. *Empire of Care: Nursing and Migration in Filipino American History*. Durham, NC: Duke University Press, 2003.

———. *Global Families: A History of Asian International Adoption in America*. New York: New York University Press, 2013.

Chun, Wendy Hui Kyong. *Updating to Remain the Same.* Cambridge, MA: The MIT Press, 2016.

———. *Programmed Visions: Software and Memory.* Cambridge, MA: The MIT Press, 2011.

———. "Introduction: Race and/as Technology; or, How to Do Things to Race." *Camera Obscura* 24, no. 1 (2009): 6–35.

Clark, Kendra. "After a record quarter OkCupid debuts 'provocative' new campaign championing inclusivity." *The Drum.* August 2, 2021. https://www.thedrum.com/news/2021/08/02/after-record-quarter-okcupid-debuts-provocative-new-campaign-championing-inclusivity.

Constantino, Annika Kim. "Atlanta spa shooter who targeted Asian women pleads guilty to four of eight murders." *CNBC.com.* July 27, 2021. https://www.cnbc.com/2021/07/27/atlanta-spa-shooter-who-targeted-asian-women-pleads-guilty-to-four-counts-of-murder.html.

Cryos International Sperm and Egg Bank. "Homepage." Accessed March 11, 2019, https://www.cryosinternational.com/.

———. "Find Donor." Accessed April 13, 2025. https://www.cryosinternational.com/en-us/us-shop/client/find-donor/search-sperm-donors/.

Curington, Celeste Vaughan, Jennifer H. Lundquist, and Ken-Hou Lin, *The Dating Divide: Race and Desire in the Era of Online Romance.* Oakland: University of California Press, 2021.

Cvetkovich, Ann. "Affect." In *Keywords for American Cultural Studies,* second edition, edited by Bruce Burgett and Glenn Hendler. New York: NYU Press, 2014, 13–16.

DaCosta, Kimberly McClain. *Making Multiracials: State, Family, and Market in the Redrawing of the Color Line.* Stanford: Stanford University Press, 2007.

Daniels, Cynthia and Erin Heidt-Forsythe. "Gendered Eugenics and the Problematic Free Market Reproductive Technologies: Sperm and Egg Donation in the United States." *Signs* 37 no. 3 (Spring 2012): 719–747.

de Lauretis, Teresa. *Technologies of Gender: Essays on Theory, Film, and Fiction.* Bloomington: Indiana University Press, 1987.

Deleuze, Gilles and Felix Guattari. *A Thousand Plateaus: Capitalism and Schizophrenia.* Translated by Brian Massumi. Minneapolis: University of Minnesota Press, 1987.

Dorow, Sara K. *Transnational Adoption: A Cultural Economy of Race, Gender, and Kinship.* New York: New York University Press, 2006.

———. "Bringing Transnationalism Home: Mobility and Locality in China-Canada Adoption." In *Trans-Pacific Mobilities: The Chinese and Canada,* edited by Lloyd L. Wong. Vancouver: University of British Columbia Press, 2017.

East Meets East. "Homepage." Accessed January 7, 2019. https://www.eastmeeteast.com/.

Eddy, Max. "23andMe Just Filed for Bankruptcy. You Should Delete Your Data Now." *New York Times.* March 25, 2025. https://www.nytimes.com/wirecutter/reviews/23andme-data-bankrupt/.

Editorial Board, "An Interview S.I. Hayakawa." *Roots: An Asian American Reader*, edited by Amy Tachiki. Los Angeles: UCLA Asian American Studies Center Press, 1971.

Elam, Michele. *The Souls of Mixed Folk: Race, Politics, and Aesthetics in the New Millennium*. Stanford: Stanford University Press, 2011.

El-Haj, Nadia Abu. "The Genetic Reinscription of Race." *Annual Review of Anthropology* 36 no. 1 (September 2007): 283–300.

Eng, David. *The Feeling of Kinship: Queer Liberalism and the Racialization of Intimacy*. Durham, NC: Duke University Press, 2010.

Espiritu, Yến Lê. *Body Counts: The Vietnam War and Militarized Refugees*. Oakland: University of California Press, 2014.

Eubanks, Virginia. *Automating Inequality: How High-Tech Tools Profile, Police, and Punish the Poor*. New York: St. Martin's Press, 2017.

Faierman, Leonardo. "OkCupid Launches an Expansive Campaign for Almost Every Single Kind of Dater." *Ad Week*. August 2, 2021. https://www.adweek.com/creativity/okcupid-launches-an-expansive-campaign-for-almost-every-single-kind-of-dater/.

Fairfax Cryobank. "Homepage." Accessed July 22, 2022. https://fairfaxcryobank.com/.

Families with Children from China of Greater New York, Connecticut, and New Jersey Newsletters, private collection, in author's possession.

Ferguson, Roderick A. *Aberrations in Black: Toward a Queer of Color Critique*. Minneapolis: University of Minnesota Press, 2003.

Finkler, Kaja. "The Kin in the Gene: The Medicalization of Family and Kinship in American Society." *Current Anthropology* 42, no. 11 (April 2001): 235–263.

Fogg-Davis, Heath. "Navigating Race in the Market for Human Gametes." *Hastings Center Report* 31, no. 5 (2001): 13–21.

Foster, Susan Leigh. "Choreographies of Gender." *Signs* 24, no. 1 (Autumn 1998): 1–33.

Foucault, Michel. *The History of Sexuality, Volume I: An Introduction*. Translated by Robert Hurley. New York: Vintage Books, 1980.

———. "Technologies of the Self." In *Technologies of the Self: A Seminar with Michel Foucault*, edited by Luther H. Martin, Huck Gutman, and Patrick H. Hutton, 16–49. London: Tavistock Publications, 1988.

———. *Discipline and Punish: The Birth of the Prison*, second edition. Translated by Alan Sheridan. New York: Vintage Books, 1995.

Franklin, Sarah. "Essentialism, Which Essentialism? Some Implications of Reproductive and Genetic Technoscience." 27–39. In *Issues in Biological Essentialism versus Social Construction in Gay and Lesbian Identities*, edited by John Dececco and John Elia. London: Harrington Park Press, 1993.

———. *Biological Relatives: IVF, Stem Cells, and the Future of Kinship*. Durham, NC: Duke University Press, 2013.

Freeman, Elizabeth. "Queer Belongings: Kinship Theory and Queer Theory." *A Companion to Lesbian, Gay, Bisexual, Transgender, and Queer Studies*, edited by George. E. Haggerty and Molly McGarry. Oxford: Blackwell Publishing, 2007.

Frost, Jeana H., Zoe Chance, Michael I. Norton, and Dan Ariely. "People are Experience Goods: Improving Online Dating with Virtual Dates." *Journal of Interactive Marketing* 22, no. 1 (Winter 2008).

Fulbeck, Kip. *Part Asian/100% Hapa*. San Francisco: Chronicle Books, 2006.

Futerman, Samantha and Ryan Miyamoto, directors. *Twinsters*. Netflix, 2015. 1 hr., 29 min.

Gammage, Jeff. "DNA helping Chinese adoptees do what was once impossible: Locate blood relatives in this country." *Philadelphia Inquirer*. May 15, 2019. https://www.inquirer.com/news/china-adoption-adoptee-dna-temple-university-20190315.html.

Garde-Hansen, Joanne and Kristyn Gorton. *Emotion Online: Theorizing Affect on the Internet*. London: Palgrave Macmillan, 2013.

Garel, Connor. "Grindr, Scruff Removed Ethnicity Filers In Its Gay Dating Apps. The Racists Stayed." June 5, 2020. *HuffPost.com*. https://www.huffpost.com/archive/ca/entry/grindr-ethnicity-gay-dating-apps_ca_5eda7ccdc5b695fc9e8f9e02.

Goffman, Erving. *The Presentation of Self in Everyday Life*. New York: Anchor Books, 1959.

Graves, Kori A. *A War Born Family: African American Adoption in the Wake of the Korean War*. New York: New York University Press, 2020.

Greenfieldboyce, Nell, host. Radiolab. "Race Doesn't Exist. Or Does It?," WNYC Studios, April 15, 2014. Podcast, 22 min., 5 sec. https://radiolab.org/podcast/91654-race-doesnt-exist-or-does-it.

Greil, Arthur L., Julia McQuillan, Karina M. Shreffler, Katherine M. Johnson, and Kathleen S. Slauson-Blevins. "Race-Ethnicity and Medical Services for Infertility: Stratified Reproduction in a Population-based Sample of U.S. Women." *Journal of Health and Social Behavior* 52, no. 4 (December 2011): 493–509.

Guterl, Matthew. *Seeing Race in Modern America*. Chapel Hill: The University of North Carolina Press, 2013.

Hamilton, Anita. "Best Inventions of 2008: 1. The Retail DNA Test." *Time*. October 29, 2008. https://content.time.com/time/specials/packages/article/0,28804,1852747_1854493_1854113,00.html#:~:text=And%20so%20for%20pioneering%20retail,business%20and%20a%20status%20symbol.

Hartman, Saidiya. *Wayward Lives, Beautiful Experiments: Intimate Histories of Riotous Black Girls, Troublesome Women and Queer Radicals*. New York: WW Norton, 2020.

Hassan, Anser. "2 Bay Area women linked to 28 siblings following DNA test." *ABC 30 News*. March 30, 2019. https://abc30.com/dna-23andme-siblings-baya-rea/5226592/.

Hertz, Rosanna. *Single by Chance, Mothers by Choice: How Women Are Choosing Parenthood Without Marriage and Creating the New American Family*. New York: Oxford University Press, 2006.

Hirsch, Marianne. *Family Frames: Photography, Narrative and Postmemory*. Cambridge: Harvard University Press, 1997.

Hobley, Melissa. "Proud that this campaign from @okcupid might be the first to celebrate nonbinary individuals . . ." @melissahobley Instagram post. September 9, 2021. https://www.instagram.com/p/CTnix_7LSDg/.

Holcombe, Madeline. "A DNA testing site turned this woman from an only child to one of 30 siblings." *CNN*. April 4, 2019. https://www.cnn.com/2019/04/04/us/30-siblings-united-dna-testing-trnd.

Homans, Margaret. *The Imprint of Another Life: Adoption Narratives and Human Possibility*. Ann Arbor: University of Michigan Press, 2013.

HoSang, Daniel Martinez. *Racial Propositions: Ballot Initiatives and the Making of Postwar California*. Berkeley: University of California Press, 2010.

Hsu, Madeline. *Dreaming of Gold, Dreaming of Home: Transnationalism and Migration Between the United States and South China, 1882–1943*. Stanford: Stanford University Press, 2000.

Hume, Ellen. "Indochinese Refugees Adapt Quickly in U.S., Using Survival Skills." *Wall Street Journal*. March 21, 1985: 1. ProQuest Historical Newspapers.

Jasanoff, Sheila. *States of Knowledge: The Co-Production of Science and the Social Order*. Edited by Sheila Jasanoff. New York: Routledge, 2004.

Johnson, Kay Ann. *Wanting a Daughter, Needing a Son: Abandonment, Adoption, and Orphanage Care in China*. St. Paul: Yeong & Yeong Book Company, 2004.

———. *China's Hidden Children: Abandonment, Adoption, and the Human Cost of the One-Child Policy*. Chicago: University of Chicago Press, 2016.

Johnson, LiLi, "Transnational Family Photographs and Adoption From Asia." *Trans-Asia Photography Review* 11, no. 1 (Spring 2021).

Kang, Laura Hyun Yi. *Compositional Subjects: Enfiguring Asian/American Women*. Durham, NC: Duke University Press, 2002.

Kaplan, Caren, Erik Loyer, and Ezra Claytan Daniels. "Precision Targets: GPS and the Militarization of Everyday Life." *Canadian Journal of Communication* 38 (2013): 397–420.

Kawakami, Barbara F. *Picture Bride Stories*. Honolulu: University of Hawaii Press, 2016.

Kim, Eleana J. *Adopted Territory: Transnational Korean Adoptees and the Politics of Belonging*. Durham: Duke University Press Books, 2010.

Kim, Jodi. "An 'Orphan' with Two Mothers: Transnational and Transracial Adoption, the Cold War, and Contemporary Asian American Cultural Politics." *American Quarterly* 61, no. 4 (2009): 855–880.

Kim, Ju Yon. *The Racial Mundane: Asian American Performance and the Embodied Everyday*. New York: New York University Press, 2015.

Klein, Christina. *Cold War Orientalism: Asia in the Middlebrow Imagination, 1945–1961*. Berkeley: University of California Press, 2003.

Kleinman, Alexis. "Black People And Asian Men Have A Much Harder Time Dating On OkCupid." *Huffington Post*. Published September 12, 2014. Updated December 6, 2017. https://www.huffpost.com/entry/okcupid-race_n_5811840.

Knowlton, Linda Goldstein, dir. Somewhere Between. Long Shot Factory, 2011. 1hr., 28 min. https://somewherebetweenmovie.com/.

Koenig, Barbara A., Sandra Soo-Jin Lee, and Sarah S. Richardson, editors. *Revisiting Race in the Genomic Age*. New Brunswick: Rutgers University Press, 2008.

Kogonada, dir. After Yang. A24, 2021.

Kramer, Wendy. "Choosing a Sperm Bank . . . What to Know." *Huffington Post.* August 23, 2017. https://www.huffpost.com/entry/choosing-a-sperm-bankwhat-to-know_b_599d7cdde4b02289f7619150.

Lau, Estelle. *Paper Families: Identity, Immigration Administration, and Chinese Exclusion.* Durham, NC: Duke University Press, 2007.

Lee, Catherine. *Fictive Kinship: Family Reunification and the Meaning of Race and Nation in American Imagination.* New York: Russell Sage Foundation, 2013.

Lee, Erika. *At America's Gates: Chinese Immigration during the Exclusion Era, 1882–1943.* Chapel Hill: The University of North Carolina Press, 2003.

Lee, Robert G. *Orientals: Asian Americans in Popular Culture.* Philadelphia: Temple University, 1999.

Leighton, Kimberly. "Addressing the Harms of Not Knowing One's Heredity: Lessons from Genealogical Bewilderment." *Adoption & Culture* 3 (2012): 63–107.

Leonard, Karen. *Making Ethnic Choices: California's Punjabi Mexican Americans.* Philadelphia: Temple University Press, 1994.

Lew-Williams, Beth. "Paper Lives of Chinese Migrants and the History of the Undocumented." *Modern American History* 4 (2021): 109–130.

Lewin, Ellen. *Gay Fatherhood: Narratives of Family and Citizenship in America.* Chicago: University of Chicago Press, 2009.

Li, Shan. "Asian women command premium prices for egg donation in US." *Los Angeles Times,* May 4, 2012. https://www.latimes.com/health/la-xpm-2012-may-04-la-fi-egg-donation-20120504-story.html.

Lipitz, Amanda, dir. *Found.* Netflix, 2021. 1hr., 37 min. https://www.netflix.com/ca/title/81476857.

Lipsitz, George. *The Possessive Investment in Whiteness: How White People Profit from Identity Politics.* Philadelphia: Temple University Press, 1998.

Louie, Andrea. *How Chinese Are You?: Adopted Chinese Youth and Their Families Negotiate Identity and Culture.* New York: New York University Press, 2015.

Lowe, Lisa. *Immigrant Acts: On Asian American Cultural Politics.* Durham, NC: Duke University Press Books, 1996.

Lopez, Lori Kido. "The Yellow Press: Asian American Radicalism and Conflict in *Gidra.*" *Journal of Communication Inquiry* 35, no. 3 (2011): 235–251.

Lui, Mary Ting Yi. *The Chinatown Trunk Mystery: Murder, Miscegenation, and Other Dangerous Encounters in Turn-of-the-Century New York City.* Princeton: Princeton University Press, 2007.

Luibhéid, Eithne. *Entry Denied: Controlling Sexuality at the Border.* Minneapolis: University of Minnesota Press, 2015.

Luk, Sharon. *The Life of Paper: Letters and a Poetics of Living Beyond Captivity.* Oakland: University of California Press, 2018.

Mamo, Laura. *Queering Reproduction: Achieving Pregnancy in the Age of Technoscience.* Durham, NC: Duke University Press, 2007.

Mani, Bakirathi. *Unseeing Empire: Photography, Representation, South Asian America.* Durham, NC: Duke University Press, 2020.

Martin, Nicole. "Airbnb Partners With 23andMe To Recommend Heritage Inspired Vacations." *Forbes*. June 5, 2019. https://www.forbes.com/sites/nicolemartin1/2019/06/05/airbnb-partners-with-23andme-to-recommend-heritage-inspired-vacations/.

Match. "Singles in America." *Match.com*. November 2021. https://www.singlesinamerica.com/home

McKee, Kimberly. *Transnational Politics of Korean Adoption in the United States*. Urbana: University of Illinois Press, 2019.

Mekanism. "We're proud to unveil our latest work for @OkCupid today . . ." @mekanism Instagram post. August 2, 2021. https://www.instagram.com/p/CSFcjYYpFfI/.

———. "OkCupid: Every Single Person." Accessed October 24, 2024. https://mekanism.com/work/okcupid-every-single-person.

Melamed, Jodi. "The Spirit of Neoliberalism: From Racial Liberalism to Neoliberal Multiculturalism." *Social Text* 24, No. 4 (Winter 2006): 1–24.

Modell, Judith S. *Kinship with Strangers: Adoption and Interpretations of Kinship in American Culture*. Berkeley: University of California Press, 1994.

Molina, Brett. "Woman discovers she has 29 siblings after taking DNA test. And counting." *USA Today*. April 8, 2019. https://www.usatoday.com/story/news/nation/2019/04/08/23-andme-dna-test-30-siblings-sperm-donor-facebook-group/3373958002/.

Morley, David and Kevin Robbins. *Spaces of Identity: Global Media, Electronic Landscapes and Cultural Boundaries*. London: Routledge, 1995.

Moynihan, Daniel Patrick. "The Negro Family: The Case for National Action." Office of Policy Planning and Research. United States Department of Labor. March 1965.

Murphy, Michelle. *The Economization of Life*. Durham, NC: Duke University Press, 2017.

Nadal, Paul. "An important lesson in Asian American Studies is that 'Asian American' was a social movement before it was ever an identity . . ." @paulnadal_ Twitter post. February 21, 2023. https://x.com/paulnadal_/status/1628028631879483393.

Nakamura, Lisa. *Cybertypes: Race, Ethnicity, and Identity on the Internet*. New York: Routledge, 2002.

———. *Digitizing Race: Visual Cultures of the Internet*. Minneapolis: University of Minnesota Press, 2008.

Nakamura, Lisa and Peter A. Chow-White, editors. *Race After the Internet*. New York: Routledge, 2012.

Nash, Catherine. "Genetic Kinship." *Cultural Studies* 18, no. 1 (2004): 1–33.

Nee, Victor G. and Brett De Bary Nee. *Longtime Californ': A Documentary Study of an American Chinatown*. New York: Pantheon Books, 1973.

Nelkin, Dorothy and M. Lindee. *The DNA Mystique: The Gene as a Cultural Icon*. Ann Arbor: University of Michigan Press, 1995.

Nelson, Alondra. *The Social Life of DNA: Race, Reparations, and Reconciliation After the Genome*. Boston: Beacon Press, 2016.

Nelson, Kim Park. *Invisible Asians: Korean American Adoptees, Asian American Experiences, and Racial Exceptionalism*. New Brunswick: Rutgers University Press, 2016.
Nelson, Margaret K. and Rosanna Hertz. *Random Families: Genetic Strangers, Sperm Donor Siblings, and the Creation of New Kin*. Oxford: Oxford University Press, 2019.
Ngai, Mae M. *Impossible Subjects: Illegal Aliens and the Making of Modern America*. Princeton: Princeton University Press, 2014.
Ngai, Sianne. *Ugly Feelings*. Cambridge, MA: Harvard University Press, 2007.
Nguyễn, Linh Thủy. "'Loving Couples and Families:' Assimilation as Honorary Whiteness and the Making of the Vietnamese Refugee Family." *Social Sciences* 10, no. 6 (2021): 209. https://doi.org/10.3390/socsci10060209.
Nguyen, Mimi Thi. *The Gift of Freedom: War, Debt, and Other Refugee Passages*. Durham, NC: Duke University Press Books, 2012.
Nguyen, Viet Thanh. *Race and Resistance: Literature and Politics in Asian American*. Oxford: Oxford University Press, 2002.
Ninh, erin Khuê. *Ingratitude: The Debt-Bound Daughter in Asian American Literature*. New York: New York University Press, 2011.
Noble, Safiya Umoja. *Algorithms of Oppression: How Search Engines Reinforce Racism*. New York: New York University Press, 2018.
Oh, Arissa H. *To Save the Children of Korea: The Cold War Origins of International Adoption*. Stanford: Stanford University Press, 2015.
The OkCupid Blog. "Race and Attraction." OkCupid.com. September 10, 2014. http://blog.okcupid.com/index.php/race-attraction-2009-2014/.
Omi, Michael, and Howard Winant. *Racial Formation in the United States: From the 1960s to the 1990s*, second edition. New York: Routledge, 1994.
Paasonen, Susanna. *Carnal Resonance: Affect and Online Pornography*. Cambridge, MA: The MIT Press, 2011.
Palumbo-Liu, David. *Asian/American: Historical Crossings of a Racial Frontier*. Stanford: Stanford University Press, 1999.
Parreñas, Rhacel. *The Force of Domesticity: Filipina Migrants and Globalization*. New York: New York University Press, 2008.
Pascoe, Peggy. *What Comes Naturally: Miscegenation Law and the Making of Race in America*. Oxford: Oxford University Press, 2010.
Pate, SooJin. *From Orphan to Adoptee: U.S. Empire and Genealogies of Korean Adoption*. Minneapolis: University of Minnesota Press, 2014.
Peet, Amanda and Julia Wyman, creators. *The Chair*. 2021. Netflix. https://www.netflix.com/ca/title/81206259.
Pegler-Gordon, Anna. *In Sight of America: Photography and the Development of US Immigration Policy*. Berkeley: University of California Press, 2009.
Petchesky, Rosalind Pollack. "Fetal Images: The Power of Visual Culture in the Politics of Reproduction." *Feminist Studies* 13, no. 2 (Summer 1987): 263–92.
Petersen, William. "Success Story, Japanese-American Style." *New York Times*. January 9, 1966. ProQuest Historical Newspapers.

Phu, Thy. *Picturing Model Citizens: Civility in Asian American Visual Culture.* Philadelphia: Temple University Press, 2011.
Pratt, Mary Louise. *Imperial Eyes: Travel Writing and Transculturation.* New York: Routledge, 1992.
Print Mag. "OkCupid Gets a Little Naughty With Their Latest Ad Campaign." *Print Mag.* August 4, 2021. https://www.printmag.com/advertising/okcupid-gets-a-little-naughty-with-their-latest-ad-campaign/.
Rajan, Kaushik Sunder. *Lively Capital: Biotechnologies, Ethics, and Governance in Global Markets.* Durham, NC: Duke University Press, 2012.
Ramirez, Anthony. "America's Super Minority." *Fortune Magazine.* November 24, 1986. CNN Fortune Magazine Archive. https://money.cnn.com/magazines/fortune/fortune_archive/1986/11/24/68318/index.htm.
Rettberg, Jill Walker. *Seeing Ourselves Through Technology: How We Use Selfies, Blogs and Wearable Devices to See and Shape Ourselves.* New York: Palgrave Macmillan, 2014.
Rifkin, Rachael. "Adopted Separately in China, Cousins Wind Up Almost Next Door." *23andMe Blog.* November 26, 2019. https://blog.23andme.com/articles/national-adoption-awareness-chinese-adoptees.
Roberts, Dorothy. *Killing the Black Body: Race, Reproduction, and the Meaning of Liberty.* New York: Pantheon Books, 1997.
———. "Race, Gender, and Genetic Technologies: A New Reproductive Dystopia?" *Signs* 34 no. 4 (Summer 2009): 783–804.
Roberts, Elizabeth. *God's Laboratory: Assisted Reproduction in the Andes.* Berkeley: University of California Press, 2012.
Robertson, Craig. *The Passport in America: The History of a Document.* Cambridge: Oxford University Press, 2010.
Roh, David S., Betsy Huang, and Greta A. Niu, *Techno-Orientalism: Imagining Asia in Speculative Fiction, History, and Media.* New Brunswick: Rutgers University Press, 2015.
Rubin, Gayle. "The Traffic in Women: Notes on the 'Political Economy' of Sex." In *Toward an Anthropology of Women,* edited by Rayna R. Reiter. New York: Monthly Review Press, 1975. 157–210.
Ryan, Erin Gloria. "Want to Sell Your Eggs to Pay for College? Be Asian." *Jezebel.* May 4, 2012. https://jezebel.com. Accessed January 7, 2019.
Saito, Leland. *The Politics of Exclusion: The Failure of Race-Neutral Policies in Urban America.* Stanford: Stanford University Press, 2009.
Samuels, Ellen. *Fantasies of Identification: Disability, Gender, Race.* New York: New York University Press, 2014.
Saussure, Ferdinand de. *Course in General Linguistics.* Translated and Annotated by Roy Harris. Chicago: Open Court, 1986.
Schmeck Jr, Harold M. "Asia Biggest Source of Brain Drain to US." *New York Times.* January 13, 1973: 28. ProQuest Historical Newspapers.
Schneider, David M. *American Kinship: A Cultural Account.* Chicago: University Of Chicago Press, 1968.

Sekula, Allan. "The Body and the Archive." In *The Contest of Meaning: Critical Histories of Photography*, edited by Richard Bolton. Cambridge, MA: The MIT Press, 1992. 343–388.

Shibusawa, Naoko. *America's Geisha Ally: Reimagining the Japanese Enemy*. Cambridge, MA: Harvard University Press, 2006.

Shim, Eileen. "OkCupid Data Reveals the Disturbing Truth About How People Pick Their Partners." *Mic.com*. September 15, 2014. https://www.mic.com/articles/98864/ok-cupid-just-release-five-years-of-data-on-race-and-dating.

Shimizu, Celine Parreñas. *The Hypersexuality of Race: Performing Asian/American Women on Screen and Scene*. Durham, NC: Duke University Press, 2007.

Stoler, Ann Laura. *Along the Archival Grain: Epistemic Anxieties and Colonial Common Sense*. Princeton: Princeton University Press, 2009.

Strathern, Marilyn. *After Nature: English Kinship in the Late Twentieth Century*. Cambridge, UK: Cambridge University Press, 1992.

———. *Reproducing the Future: Anthropology, Kinship, and the New Reproductive Technologies*. New York: Routledge, 1992.

Sturgis, Meshell and Ralina L. Joseph. "Visualizing Mixed Race and Genetics." In *Race and Media: Critical Approaches*. Edited by Lori Kido Lopez. New York: New York University Press, 2020.

Suh, Sung-Hee. "The Cost of Being an Asian-American Superachiever." Letter to the Editor published in *New York Times*. August 15, 1986: A26. ProQuest Historical Newspapers.

Tachiki, Amy. "Introduction." *Roots: An Asian American Reader*, edited by Amy Tachiki, Eddie Wong, Franklin Odo, and Buck Wong. Los Angeles: UCLA Asian American Studies Center Press, 1971.

Tagg, John. *Burden Of Representation: Essays on Photographies and Histories*. Amherst: University of Massachusetts Press, 1988.

TallBear, Kim. *Native American DNA: Tribal Belonging and the False Promise of Genetic Science*. Minneapolis: University of Minnesota Press, 2013.

Takaki, Ronald. "The Harmful Myth of Asian Superiority." *New York Times*. June 16, 1990: L21. ProQuest Historical Newspapers.

Tchen, John Kuo Wei. *New York before Chinatown: Orientalism and the Shaping of American Culture, 1776–1882*. Baltimore: The Johns Hopkins University Press, 1999.

Telfer, Jon. "Relationships with No Body?—'Adoption' Photographs, Intuition and Emotion." *Social Analysis* 4, No. 3 (November 1999): 144–158.

Thompson, Charis. *Making Parents: The Ontological Choreography of Reproductive Technologies*. Cambridge, MA: The MIT Press, 2007.

Traver, Amy E. "Home(land) Décor: China Adoptive Parents' Consumption of Chinese Cultural Objects for Display in their Homes." *Qualitative Sociology* 30 (2007): 201–220.

Tsangarakis, Maria. "OkCupid is 'for Every Single Person' in Colorful, Inclusive Ads." *Muse by Clio*. August 4, 2021. https://musebyclios.com/advertising/okcupid-every-single-person-colorful-inclusive-ads/.

Tsjeng, Zing. "Asian Women's Bodies Are Not Playgrounds For White People." *Vogue UK*. March 19, 2021. https://www.vogue.co.uk/arts-and-lifestyle/article/atlanta-shootings-racism.

Tu, Thuy Linh Nguyen. *The Beautiful Generation: Asian Americans and the Cultural Economy of Fashion*. Durham, NC: Duke University Press, 2011.

Turkle, Sherry. *Life on the Screen: Identity in the Age of the Internet*. New York: Simon & Schuster, 1995.

US Department of State Bureau of Consular Affairs. "Adoption Statistics." Accessed July 14, 2019. https://travel.state.gov/content/travel/en/Intercountry-Adoption/adopt_ref/adoption-statistics.html.

U.S. News & World Report. "Success Story of One Minority Group in U.S." December 26, 1966. Reprinted in *Roots: An Asian American Reader*. Edited by Amy Tachiki, Eddie Wong, Franklin Odo, and Buck Wong. Los Angeles: UCLA Asian American Studies Center Press, 1971: 6–10.

Varzally, Allison. *Children of Reunion: Vietnamese Adoptions and the Politics of Family Migrations*. Chapel Hill: The University of North Carolina Press, 2017.

Wailoo, Keith, Alondra Nelson, and Catherine Lee, editors. *Genetics and the Unsettled Past: The Collision of DNA, Race, and History*. New Brunswick: Rutgers University Press, 2012.

Wang, K. Connie. "Asian Poor Neglected." *Los Angeles Times*. December 2, 1993: WB1. ProQuest Historical Newspapers.

Weaver, Gina Marie. *Ideologies of Forgetting: Rape in the Vietnam War*. Albany: State University of New York Press, 2010.

Weston, Kath. "Kinship, Controversy, and the Sharing of Substance: The Race/Class Politics of Blood Transfusion." In *Relative Values: Reconfiguring Kinship Studies*. Edited by Sarah Franklin and Susan McKinnon. Durham, NC: Duke University Press, 2001.

Wexler, Laura. "Techniques of the Imaginary Nation: Engendering Family Photography." In *Race and the Production of Modern American Nationalism*, edited by Reynolds J. Scott-Childress. New York: Routledge Press, 1999. 359–381.

Williams, Raymond. *Keywords: A Vocabulary of Culture and Society*. 1976. Revised Edition. Oxford: Oxford University Press, 2015.

Woo, Susie. *Framed by War: Korean Children and Women at the Crossroads of US Empire*. New York: New York University Press, 2019.

Wood, Elisabeth Jean. "Rape as a Practice of War: Toward a Typology of Political Violence." *Politics & Society* 46 no. 4 (2018): 513–537.

Wu, Ellen D. *The Color of Success: Asian Americans and the Origin of the Model Minority*. Princeton: Princeton University Press: 2014.

Yanagisako, Sylvia Junko. *Transforming the Past: Tradition and Kinship Among Japanese Americans*. Stanford: Stanford University Press, 1992.

Yang, Andrew. "We Asian Americans are not the virus, but we can be part of the cure." *Washington Post*. April 1, 2020. https://www.washingtonpost.com/opinions/2020/04/01/andrew-yang-coronavirus-discrimination/.

Yao, Xine. *Disaffected: The Cultural Politics of Unfeeling in Nineteenth-Century America*. Durham, NC: Duke University Press, 2021.

Yngvesson, Barbara. *Belonging in an Adopted World: Race, Identity, and Transnational Adoption*. Chicago: University of Chicago Press, 2010.

Yu, Henry. *Thinking Orientals: Migration, Contact, and Exoticism in Modern America*. Oxford: Oxford University Press, 2001.

Yuh, Ji-Yeon. *Beyond the Shadow of Camptown: Korean Military Brides in America*. New York: New York University Press, 2004.

Yung, Judy. *Unbound Feet: A Social History of Chinese Women in San Francisco*. Berkeley: University of California Press, 1995.

———. *Unbound Voices: A Documentary History of Chinese Women in San Francisco*. Berkeley: University of California Press, 1999.

Yuval-Davis, Nira. *The Politics of Belonging: Intersectional Contestations*. London: SAGE Publications, 2011.

Xiang, Sunny. *Tonal Intelligence: The Aesthetics of Asian Inscrutability During the Long Cold War*. New York: Columbia University Press, 2020.

INDEX

Page numbers in italics indicate Figures.

AAHRPP. *See* Association for the Accreditation of Human Research Protection Programs
A24, 1
academic life, 185
achievement, model minority and, 63–64
Ad Council, 25–26
adoptees, 1, 107, 175. *See also* transnational adoption
adoption. *See* transnational adoption; transracial adoption
Adoption Law of the People's Republic of China, 92–93
adoptive kinship, 24, 95, 97, 101
Adoptive Parents Committee Conference, 201n21
African Americans, 68–69, 156
African diaspora, 102
After Yang (film), 1–3
Airbnb, 23andMe and, 187
Almeling, Rene, 124–25, 131, 133
American culture, 3, 5, 15, 18, 91
American exceptionalism, 24, 78
American Kinship (Schneider), 15
"America's Super Minority," 82
Anagnost, Ann, 106
Ancestry.com, 157
And Just Like That (television show), 91–92
androgyny, 149
anti-Asian racism, 181–82
anti-miscegenation, 131

Appalachian Whites, 82–83
archival documents, 21
Ariely, Dan, 125
armed forces, naturalization relation to, 32
ARTs. *See* assistive reproductive technologies
Asian American family, 18, 186; model minority relation to, 23–24, 64–65, 78–79, 84–85, 183–84; naturalization of, 5, 66; racialization of, 19, 69, 73; racial power and, 13–14; reproduction and, 89
Asian American history, 164
Asian American identity, 24, 64, 163–64
Asian American labor, 80, 88–89
Asian American racial formation, 17, 20
Asian Americans. *See specific topics*
Asian cyborg, 4
Asian diaspora, 6, 29, 62, 71, 82; demographic makeup of, 72–74; genetic ancestry testing relation to, 156; intergenerational struggle of, 66; nuclear family relation to, 68; racialization of, 19–20, 22; as refugees, 23–24
Asianness, 26–27, 67–68, 120, 177; femininity relation to, 142; model minority and, 24, 65; neoliberalism relation to, 121; pansexual identity relation to, 149; 23andMe relation to, 163
"Asian Poor Neglected," 82
"Asian women command premium prices for egg donation in US," 133

228 | INDEX

Asiatic Barred Zone Act (1917). *See* Immigration Act (1917)
assistive reproductive technologies (ARTs), 5, 8, 132–33, 135. *See also* in vitro fertilization
Association for the Accreditation of Human Research Protection Programs (AAHRPP), 208n19
asylees, 81
At America's Gates (Lee, E.), 195nn3–4
Attorney General, 81–82
Azoulay, Ariella, 10, 48, 101

baby shower, 108
"bachelor societies," 20
Barthes, Roland, 55, 100
Beard, Stefanie, 175–76
belonging, 13–14, 16–18
benevolence, in colonialism, 86
Bernstein, Robin, 44
biological parent, 14–15
birthright citizenship, 36, 61
Black communities, stereotypes of, 23
BlackPeopleMeet, 131
"'Boat People' Find a Haven in the State," 83–84
the body, racialization of, 17–18, 152
Bonilla-Silva, Eduardo, 23
Bordier, Anaïs, 178
Borshay Liem, Deann, 24, 96, 110, 112–16, 177
Bow, Leslie, 4, 141, 181
Bradway, Tyler, 16
Briggs, Laura, 160
Brown, Bill, 13, 201n17
Brown, Louise, 8
Brown, Wendy, 88, 93, 122

California Cryobank, 117, *118*
Camera Lucida (Barthes), 100
Campt, Tina, 102
capitalism, 79, 123, 154, 161; consumption relation to, 147; immigration preference system relation to, 80; multiculturalism relation to, 25, 159; racial contradictions in, 134
Cartwright, Lisa, 107, 112
case file system, 41
Cattelan, Maurizio, 144–45
Certificate of Identity, 31
The Chair (comedy-drama series), 184–86
Chan, Sucheng, 57
Chance, Zoë, 125
ChatGPT, 123
Cheng, Anne Anlin, 140
Cheng, Cindy I-Fen, 68
China, adoption from, 1–2, 24, 91–93, 95–98, 102, 105–6, 108–10. *See also* transnational adoption
Chinese Adoptee Alliance, 201n18
Chinese American family formation, 21, 58
Chinese American Portraits (McCunn), 57
Chinese Confession Program, INS, 31–33, 35–37, 48, 60–61, 183; Moy Hand Fun and, 59; photography relation to, 53–54
Chinese Consolidated Benevolent Association, 70
Chinese culture, performance of, 106
"Chinese Detention Station," 37
Chinese diaspora, 29–30, 32
Chinese exclusion, 29, 40, 49–50, 57, 58, 195n3
Chinese Exclusion Act (1882), 20, 31, 36, 195n1, 196n15; family reunification relation to, 73–74; Magnuson Act relation to, 60
Chinese male laborers, 20
Chinese women, immigration of, 57–58, 196n15
Chin family, 60
Choy, Catherine Ceniza, 77–78, 92, 111, 161, 208n23
citizenship, 36, 39, 61
civility, model minority and, 113
class bifurcation, model minority and, 80

class normativity, 82–83
coaching books, of paper families, 43–44
collectivist culture, 70
Collins, Albert A., 29–30
colonialism, 79, 80, 86, 163, 187
colorblindness, 162; multiculturalism and, 90, 130–31; neoliberalism and, 25–26, 138; visuality and, 147, 148; WMAF relation to, 140
commercialization, of egg and sperm donation, 124–25
commodification, 26, 109–10, 119
community building, 9
Compositional Subjects (Kang), 20
Confession Program, 21
consumer choice, 127, 142–43, 161
consumer culture, 122, 178; dating culture relation to, 124; genetic ancestry testing relation to, 27, 154; racialization in, 26, 120, 130
consumer identity, 121–22
consumption, 129, 143; capitalism relation to, 147; family and, 186–87; neoliberalism and, 159, 161
"contrapuntal intrusions," 21
COVID-19 pandemic, 123, 151, 181–83
CPB. *See* Customs and Border Protection
Cramblett, Jennifer, 134–35
cultural background, 131
cultural essentialism, Asian American, 64, 67, 72, 79, 82, 122
cultural identity, 14
Curington, Celeste Vaughan, 120, 138
Customs and Border Protection (CPB), US, 182
Cvetkovich, Ann, 204n25

Daniels, Cynthia R., 120, 135
data, 158–59, 179
dating culture, 124
The Dating Divide (Curington, Lundquist, and Lin), 138
"debt-bound daughter," 85

debt-bound racialization, 88–89
Deleuze, Gilles, 13
demographic makeup, of Asian diaspora, 72–74
Department of Homeland Security, 182
deregulation, 122–23
differentiation, photography and, 53
digital-sexual racism, 138
digital technology, 9, 122–23
digitization, 122–24, 155, 181
Digitizing Race (Nakamura), 129
disciplinary society, case file system and, 41
discrimination, 71, 117, 137–38, 139, 147
diversity, 139–40, 143; egg and sperm donation and, 133; genetic ancestry testing relation to, 155; OkCupid relation to, 145, 147; 23andMe and, 153, 159–60
"DNA Day 2010," 157
"DNA helping Chinese adoptees do what was once impossible: Locate blood relatives in this country," 175–76
The DNA Mystique (Nelkin and Lindee), 155
"DNA Relatives," 153, 170–71
Dolezal, Rachel, 14
Donahue, P. A., 51–52
donor siblings, 173–74
Dorow, Sara K., 94, 98
Down Syndrome, 207n14
"The Drive to Excel," 71–72

EastMeetsEast, 131
educational achievement, immigration preference system relation to, 79
egg and sperm donation, 8, 9, 139, 144, 151, 193n6; commercialization of, 124–25; consumer culture relation to, 122; donor siblings and, 173–74; kinship relation to, 128–29; online dating compared to, 117, 203n3; profile interface for, 26, 126–28, 184; race relation to, 119, 131–33, 134–35; 23andMe compared to, 163, 170–71

230 | INDEX

Elam, Michelle, 169
Ellis Island, 29–30, 45
Empire of Care (Choy), 77–78
employment-based preferences, 77
Eng, David, 19, 25, 91, 103
Espiritu, Yến Lê, 81
essentialism, 72–73
essentialization, of family, 64
ethnic awareness, 106
ethnicity, 130–31, 204n22
eugenics, 135, 163, 205n47
"event of photography," 10
"Every Single Non-Monogamist" campaign advertisement, 149, *150*, 150–51
"Every Single Pansexual" campaign advertisement, 148, *148*
exclusion, 6, 147; Chinese, 29, 40, 49–50, 57, 58, 195n3; racialization and, 20–21, 33, 34, 103
experience goods, 125–26

Families with Children from China of Greater New York, Connecticut, and New Jersey (FCCNY), 95–96, 97–98, 108–9, 201nn18–19, 202n48
family, 35, 41, 43, 67, 162; consumption and, 186–87; essentialization of, 64; global, 92, 161, 166–67, 169, 170–71, 182–83; heterosexual reproductive normativity relation to, 184; model minority relation to, 71–72; neoliberal multiculturalism relation to, 26; nuclear, 4, 65, 68–69, 80, 181; power of, 19. *See also* Asian American family
family formation, 8–9, 13–14, 18, 40, 134–35, 201n12; Chinese American, 21, 58; digitization and, 123–24; FCCNY relation to, 96, 97–98; photography and, 10, 99–102; racialization of, 117, 119; referral photograph and, 92, 201n19; transnational adoption and, 103–4
"The Family Man," 162
"family of man," 27

family photo collage, 55, *56*, 57
family reunification, 23–24, 65, 79, 104; immigration and, 21, 22, 77; in immigration policy, 73–74, 81–82, 83–84; immigration preference system and, 76, 80–81, 90
family traditions, 106
Family Tree DNA, 157, 207n17
family trees, 171, 172, *172*
"fantasy of identification," 170
Farrell, Colin, 2
fashion designers, 201n12
FCCNY. *See* Families with Children from China of Greater New York, Connecticut, and New Jersey
The Feeling of Kinship (Eng), 91
femininity, 142, 205n47
Ferguson, Roderick, 68–69, 71
Ferrari, Pierpaolo, 144–45
"50,000 Enter US Under New Law," 76
filial obligation, 88
filial piety, 70
filtering system, of profile interface, 117, 127, 131
First Person Plural (film), 96, 110–11
Fogg-Davis, Heath, 119, 135
Fook, Jew, 196n26
"For Every Single Person" campaign, 144–45, *146*, 146–47, 206n70; "Every Single Non-Monogamist," 149, *150*, 150–51; "Every Single Pansexual," 148, *148*
Fortune (magazine), 82, 84
Foucault, Michel, 7, 11–12, 41, 49
Found (documentary), 178
Franklin, Sarah, 193n9, 207n4
Freeman, Elizabeth, 16
free market choice, 133, 151
Frost, Jeana H., 125
Futerman, Samantha, 178
futurism, multiculturalism and, 2

gamete economy, 135
Garde-Hansen, Joanne, 128

Gebbia, Joe, 187
gender, 58, 103, 147, 194n21, 205n47; immigration relation to, 36, 40, 60; transnational adoption relation to, 94, 105
"genealogical bewilderment," 175
genetic ancestry testing, 3, 9, 13, 154, 157, 163; kinship relation to, 27, 172–74, 179; law enforcement and, 158, 207n17; as meaning-making processes, 155–56, 161–62; racial categorization in, 165; transnational adoption and, 175–76. *See also* 23andMe
genetic essentialism, 177–78, 180, 207n4
genetic identity, genetic ancestry testing relation to, 27
genetic intimacies, 27, 173, 179
genetic kinship, 171, 172
genetic relatedness, 157; kinship relation to, 171, 172–73, 174–75, 178–79; quantification and, 176–77
Genetics and the Unsettled Past (Wailoo, Nelson, and Lee, C.), 156
genetic strangers, 173
Gentlemen's Agreement, 10, 22, 73, 102
"gift of freedom," 84–85, 87–88
Gilder, George, 123
global ancestors, 167, 169, 172
global family, 92, 161, 166–67, 169, 171; COVID-19 pandemic relation to, 182–83; kinship and, 170
global industry, transnational adoption as, 111
globalization, 93–94
global supply chains, 123
global tourism, 187
Goffman, Erving, 44, 197n32
Golden State Killer, 207n17
Gorton, Kristyn, 128
government bureaucracy, 3, 6, 13, 41, 48, 60; kinship relation to, 33, 34, 39, 61–62; paper families relation to, 21–22, 39–40; photography relation to, 52, 54;

realities relation to, 34, 36; temporality and, 35
Gow Mo Chun, 47
gratitude, model minority and, 86–87
"green card" marriage, 89
Guattari, Félix, 13
Guterl, Matthew, 104

habeas corpus, 40
Harrison, Shauna, 173–74
Hart-Celler Act. *See* Immigration and Nationality Act (1965)
Hayakawa, S. I, 85–87
healthcare, 158
Heidt-Forsythe, Erin, 120, 135
Hertz, Rosanna, 173
heteronormativity, 61, 68, 72, 78, 104
heteropatriarchal norms, 69
heterosexual reproductive normativity, 4–5, 72, 174–75, 184; kinship relation to, 15, 180; 23andMe relation to, 172
Hirsch, Marianne, 94–95
The History of Sexuality (Foucault), 11
Hmong refugees, 82
Hobley, Melissa, 145
home videos, 101–3
Hom Shee, 47
Hong, You Chung, 29, 195n1
Hong-Kee Min, Justin, 2
HoSang, Daniel, 130
Hui Kyong Chun, Wendy, 9, 123
Hui She, 47
Human Genome Diversity Project, 159
humanitarianism, 92, 162
humanity, 162, 169
human universalism, 162
Huntington Library, 29
Huynh, Ai-Linh, 83–84
hypervisibility, of Asian American family, 66

ICE. *See* Immigration and Customs Enforcement

identity, 14, 27, 79, 121–22, 141, 170; Asian American, 24, 64, 163–64; in "For Every Single Person" campaign, 145, 146–47; OkCupid relation to, 145; pansexual, 148–49; quantification of, 176–77; 23andMe relation to, 163, 169. *See also* racial identity
Immigrant Acts (Lowe), 66
immigrant parent sacrifice, 88
immigration, 31, 35, 41, 79, 81–83, 103; of Chinese women, 57–58, 196n15; citizenship relation to, 39, 61; family reunification and, 21, 22, 77; gender relation to, 36, 40, 60; interviews for, 45–49, 51–52, 196n28; photography relation to, 51–52, 53–55
Immigration Act (1917), 22, 77
Immigration and Customs Enforcement (ICE), US, 182
Immigration and Nationality Act (1965), 22, 61, 65, 81, 199n27, 200n36, 200n40; national origin quotas relation to, 74–75; visas relation to, 75–76
Immigration and Naturalization Service (INS), 20–21, 29, 182, 195n1; Asian diaspora relation to, 62; Chinese Confession Program of, 31–33, 35–37, 48, 53–54, 59, 60–61, 183
immigration case files, of Chinese diaspora, 29–30
immigration policy, 77, 80, 89–90, 186, 200n37; Asian American family relation to, 65–66; family reunification in, 73–74, 81–82, 83–84; liberalization of, 22, 61, 78; national origin quotas in, 74–76
immigration preference system, 77; educational achievement relation to, 79; family reunification in, 76, 80–81, 90; kinship relation to, 64–65, 78
imperialism, 162–63
inclusion, 13, 23–24, 27, 78, 145; liberalism and, 119; multiculturalism and, 67, 150; 23andMe and, 159

Indigenous land claims, 156
individualism, 121, 124
"Indochinese Refugees Adapt Quickly in US, Using Survival Skills," 84
inheritance, 14, 15, 154, 165, 166
INS. *See* Immigration and Naturalization Service
intergenerational struggle, of Asian diaspora, 66
interracial marriage, 23
interviews, for immigration, 45–49, 51–52, 196n28
In the Matter of Cha Jung Hee (film), 24, 96, 110–11, 112–16, 179
intimacy, 9, 16, 120, 129, 187–88; genetic, 27, 173, 179; racialization of, 19, 25
in vitro fertilization, 5, 8, 183, 193n9

Japan, 60, 66–67
Japanese Americans, 68–69
Jasanoff, Sheila, 39–40
Jew Law Ying, 43–44
Jezebel (website), 133
Johnson, Kay, 92–93
Johnson-Reed Act (1924), 22

Kang, Laura Hyun Yi, 20
Kim, Eleana J., 94
Kim, Jodi, 107, 110
Kim, Ju Yon, 17
"kincoherence," 16
kinship, 1, 7–8, 76, 103, 180, 181; adoptive, 24, 95, 97, 101; American culture and, 3, 15, 18; Asian American racial formation and, 20; COVID-19 pandemic relation to, 182–83; egg and sperm donation relation to, 128–29; genetic ancestry testing relation to, 27, 172–74, 179; genetic relatedness relation to, 171, 172–73, 174–75, 178–79; global family and, 170; government bureaucracy relation to, 33, 34, 39, 61–62; in immigration interviews,

47–48; immigration policy relation to, 77; immigration preference system relation to, 64–65, 78; immigration relation to, 41; online dating relation to, 120; paper families relation to, 31–32, 35, 38–39, 196n28; photography and, 13, 51, 55, 94–96, 100–102, 108–9, 110, 116; profile interface relation to, 119, 138, 143, 151–52; queer, 16, 104; race relation to, 4, 17, 28, 133, 186–88; racial identity relation to, 131; racialization and, 2–3, 6, 90, 183; reference sheet relation to, 43; sexuality relation to, 194n28; subject-object relation in, 13; transnational adoption and, 177; 23andMe relation to, 154–56, 157, 162, 176; visuality of, 107
Klein, Christina, 22–23, 104, 105, 162
knowledge production, 179
Kogonada, 1
Korea, 105; transnational adoption from, 23, 24, 92, 106, 112–13, 201n4; US relation to, 115–16
Krug, Jessica, 14
Kuo, David, 71–72

labor, 20, 77, 79, 80, 88–89
Lau, Estelle, 31, 195n4, 196n28
Lauretis, Teresa de, 12, 194n21
law enforcement, genetic ancestry testing and, 158, 207n17
Lee, Catherine, 21, 73, 156
Lee, Erika, 31, 58, 195nn3–4
Lee Fee Leung, 38
Lee Jung Leung, 38
Lee Mon Leung, 38
Lee Ock Leung, 38
Lee Yin Leung, 38
legal entry, kinship relation to, 43
legality, performance of, 46
Leighton, Kimberly, 175
Lewis, Michael, 123
Lew-Williams, Beth, 34

liberalism, 23, 67, 87, 119, 130. *See also* neoliberalism
liberalization, of immigration policy, 22, 61, 78
lifestyle choices, 147
Lin, Ken-Hou, 120, 138
Lindee, M. Susan, 155
Ling, Di, 108–10
Lipsitz, George, 71
Lively Capital (Rajan), 123
"logic of family," 162
Los Angeles Times (newspaper), 82, 133
Louie, Andrea, 94, 202n48
"Love Has No Labels" campaign, 25–26
Loving v. Virginia (1967), 23
Lowe, Lisa, 11, 66, 79–80
Luibhéid, Eithne, 33, 35, 41, 57–58
Luk, Sharon, 44
Lum Chee Dye, 48
Lum Kao Ngon, 47
Lum Lim Jung, 45, 46, 48, 50
Lum Shu Kwong, 45
Lum Soon Doo, 46
Lum Yuet Gay, 45–48, 50
Lundquist, Jennifer H., 120, 138
Lung family, 60

Magnuson Act (1943), 60, 195n1
mainstream media, 71
marginalization, 206n65
marketplace ideologies, 124, 125, 136, 139, 142
marriage, 16, 23, 61, 66, 89, 183
masculinity, 142, 205n47
Match.com, 126, 130, 144, 203n3, 205n33. *See also* online dating
Match Group, 135–36
May Fook, 52
McCunn, Ruthanne Lum, 57
McKee, Kimberly D., 94, 104, 109
meaning-making processes, 152, 155–56, 161–62
media representations, 186–87

media technology, 7, 9, 128
Mekanism, 144–45
Melamed, Jodi, 93, 122, 143
menu-driven identities, 120–21
Met Gala Ball, 206n65
Migration and Refugee Assistance Act (1962), 81
militarism, US, 81, 86
military brides, 105, 142
minoritization, in popular culture, 147
Mitchell, Claire, 175–76
mixed race, 209n32
model minority, 6, 26, 70, 77, 90, 113; achievement and, 63–64; anti-Asian racism relation to, 181–82; Asian American family relation to, 23–24, 64–65, 78–79, 84–85, 183–84; Asian American racial formation and, 17; class bifurcation and, 80; family relation to, 71–72; gratitude and, 86–87; neoliberalism relation to, 88–89; racialization relation to, 5, 64–66, 72–73, 82; racial liberalism relation to, 67; radical politics relation to, 86; refugees relation to, 83–84; tiger parents and, 4
morality, 161
Moy, Carter, 59
Moy, Dorothy, 59
Moy family, 58–59, 198n56
Moy Fook, 53, 54
Moy Ham, 51–52
Moy Hand Fun, 58–59
Moy Look, 53, 54
Moynihan, Daniel Patrick, 68–69, 85
Moynihan Report. *See The Negro Family*
Moy Sue, 51–52, 53, 54
Moy Wong Lai, 59
multicultural families, 19, 143
multiculturalism, 6, 22; American exceptionalism and, 24; capitalism relation to, 25, 159; colorblindness and, 90, 130–31; futurism and, 2; inclusion and, 67, 150; interracial marriage and, 23; kinship and, 162; online dating relation to, 140, 144–45; racialization and, 184; self-knowledge and, 169; transnational adoption relation to, 93, 104, 105–6; 23andMe relation to, 153, 154–55, 159–61, 170; visuality of, 145; WMAF relation to, 139. *See also* neoliberal multiculturalism
Murphy, Michelle, 125

Nadal, Paul, 164
Nakamura, Lisa, 9, 120–21, 129, 138, 204n29
Nash, Catherine, 171, 172
national identity, 79
national origin quotas, 22, 74–76
Native Americans, 167, 208n30
naturalization, 5, 17, 32, 66, 74
The Negro Family (Moynihan), 68–69, 71
Nelkin, Dorothy, 155
Nelson, Alondra, 154, 156
Nelson, Kim Park, 94
Nelson, Margaret K., 173
Neo Chen, Jian, 11
neoliberalism, 6, 8, 88–89, 109, 139, 162; colorblindness and, 25–26, 138; consumption and, 159, 161; profile interface relation to, 119, 125; race relation to, 133, 141, 169; 23andMe relation to, 154–55, 175
neoliberal multiculturalism, 25–26, 121–22, 134, 147, 148–49, 154–55; consumption and, 186–87; race relation to, 139, 143–44, 156, 183; transnational adoption and, 93, 119
neoliberal political rationality, 6, 93, 122–23
new materialisms, 201n17
New York City Metropolitan Transportation Authority, 206n70
New York Times (newspaper), 71–72, 76, 164; "'Boat People' Find a Haven in the

State," 83–84; "Success Story, Japanese American Style," 23, 63, 69
Ngai, Mae, 22, 32, 40, 74–75, 76
Ng Foon Bon, 47
Ng She, 47
Nguyễn, Linh Thủy, 82
Nguyen, Mimi Thi, 84–85, 87
Ninh, erin Khuê, 5, 64, 85, 88, 89
nonbinary identity, 145, 147
Norton, Michael I., 125
"Notes on 'Camp,'" 206n65
nuclear family, 4, 65, 68–69, 80, 181

Oh, Sandra, 184–85
OkCupid, 130, 135, *137*, 137–38, 203n3, 205n33; "For Every Single Person" campaign of, 144–45, *146*, 146–47, 148, *148*, 149, *150*, 150–51, 206n70; marginalization and, 206n65; 23andMe compared to, 153. *See also* online dating
Omi, Michael, 3
online dating, 9, 120, 134–36, 139, 151, 206n59; discrimination in, 137–38; egg and sperm donation compared to, 117, 203n3; ethnicity and, 204n22; multiculturalism relation to, 140, 144–45; profile interface and, 26, 119, 125, 128, 184; race and, 126, 127, 141; 23andMe compared to, 163, 170–71
"Online dating is a personal nightmare. But very good for society," 140
online profiles. *See* profile interface
"Our Services-Ancestry," 23andMe, 167, *168*, 169
Ozawa v. United States (1922), 74

Page Act (1875), 20, 31, 49, 57, 103, 196n15
pansexual identity, 148–49
paper families, 34, 53, 58, 76, 195n4; Chinese Confession Program relation to, 31–33, 35–37, 54, 60–61, 183; coaching books of, 43–44; government bureaucracy relation to, 21–22, 39–40; kinship relation to, 31–32, 35, 38–39, 196n28; photography relation to, 50–52; of Yee On, 37–39
Paper Families (Lau), 195n4, 196n28
parental supervision, 70
Parkinson's disease, 157
Parreñas-Shimizu, Celine, 140
The Passport in America (Robertson), 50
Pate, SooJin, 94, 105
paternalism, 104, 105, 162
patriarchal cultural values, 57, 72
Pegler-Gordon, Anna, 50
performance, 44, 46, 106, 197n32
"performance competence," 44
Petchesky, Rosaline, 101
Petersen, William, 63, 69
Philadelphia Inquirer (newspaper), 175–76
photography, 3, 6, 45–46, 103, 112–13; Chinese Confession Program relation to, 53–54; Chinese exclusion relation to, 49–50, 57; family formation and, 10, 99–102; in immigration interviews, 48–49; kinship and, 13, 51, 55, 94–96, 100–102, 108–9, 110, 116; paper families relation to, 50–52; in physiognomic methods, 127; racialization relation to, 106–7; relationality of, 204n23; as testimony, 51–52, *53*; transnational adoption and, 24–25, 92, 94–96, 98–101, 107–8, 201n19. *See also* referral photograph
Phu, Thy, 10, 103
physiognomic methods, 127
picture brides, 10, 22, 73, 102–3, 105
Picturing Model Citizens (Phu), 103
popular culture, 19, 121–22, 138, 147, 156, 163
power, 7, 16, 19, 87, 92, 102; capitalism relation to, 161; of government bureaucracy, 48; photography and, 45–46; racial, 13–14, 72; sexuality and, 12, 194n22; systemization of, 10–11

preference, racial bias compared to, 137–38
pregnancy, 101
The Presentation of Self in Everyday Life (Goffman), 197n32
privatization, neoliberalism and, 8
production, technologies of, 12
professional class migration, 77–79, 83
professional skills, 65
profile interface, 120, 134, 203n3; for egg and sperm donation, 26, 126–28, 184; filtering system of, 117, 127, 131; kinship relation to, 119, 138, 143, 151–52; marketplace ideologies in, 139, 142; neoliberalism and, 119, 125; race and, 126, 127–28, 141, 151, 184

quantification, 176–77
queer kinship, 16, 104
queer studies, 16–17
QuickMatch Scores, 135–36, 137, 137–38

race, 67, 94, 129, 130, 140, 147; consumer choice and, 127, 142–43; egg and sperm donation relation to, 119, 131–33, 134–35; genetic ancestry testing relation to, 27, 157; kinship relation to, 4, 17, 28, 133, 186–88; neoliberalism relation to, 133, 141, 169; neoliberal multiculturalism relation to, 139, 143–44, 156, 183; online dating and, 126, 127, 141; in popular culture, 121–22, 138, 163; profile interface and, 126, 127–28, 141, 151, 184; as social construction, 14–15, 152, 188; 23andMe relation to, 154, 169; visuality of, 50, 53, 121, 159
Race (documentary), 14
"Race and Attraction, 2009–2014," 135–36, 137, 137–38
"Race Doesn't Exist. Or Does it?," 14
racial bias, preference compared to, 137–38
racial categorization, 14, 121, 135–36, 165, 175

racial contradictions, in profile interface, 134
racial difference, commodification of, 26
racial fetishization, 140–41
racial formation, 3–4, 17, 20
racial hierarchies, 116, 195n3
racial identity, 14, 18, 120–21, 131, 151, 161; consumer choice and, 142–43; marketplace ideologies and, 136; model minority relation to, 64; profile interface relation to, 26; transnational adoption and, 177
racialization, 4, 40, 60, 84, 88–89, 184; adoptive kinship relation to, 95, 97; of Asian American family, 19, 69, 73; of Asian diaspora, 19–20, 22; of the body, 17–18, 152; in consumer culture, 26, 120, 130; exclusion and, 20–21, 33, 34, 103; of family formation, 117, 119; genetic ancestry testing and, 163; "gift of freedom" relation to, 87–88; of intimacy, 19, 25; kinship and, 2–3, 6, 90, 183; model minority relation to, 5, 64–66, 72–73, 82; photography relation to, 106–7; transnational adoption and, 92, 98, 116
racialized gendered relations, immigration preference system and, 80
racialized interchangeability, 108–10, 113–15
racial liberalism, 23, 67
racial logics, paper families and, 53
racial mixing, 169, 209n32
racial order, family relation to, 67
racial power, 13–14, 72
racial privilege, in family formation, 134–35
racial restrictions, on naturalization, 74
racism: in academic life, 185; anti-Asian, 181–82; digital-sexual, 138; online dating relation to, 134; sexualized, 141; stereotypes and, 204n29; WMAF relation to, 139

Racist Love (Bow), 141
radical politics, 86
Radiolab, 14
Rajan, Kaushik Sunder, 123
Reagan, Ronald, 83, 123
realities: government bureaucracy relation to, 34, 36; photography relation to, 101–2, 108, 112–13
reference sheet, 41, 42, 43, 196n26
referral photograph, 98–103, 106; family formation and, 92, 201n19; kinship and, 94–97, 108, 110, 116; racialization and, 107; visuality and, 24
Refugee Act (1980), 81–82, 200n36
refugees, 85, 89; Asian diaspora as, 23–24; Immigration and Nationality Act and, 200n40; immigration policy and, 80–81, 200n37; model minority relation to, 83–84; second-wave, 82–83; subjectification of, 87–88. *See also* immigration
regulation, 23andMe and, 159
relationality: of photography, 204n23; power and, 16
reproduction, 61, 193n9, 205n47; Asian American family and, 89; heteronormativity and, 72; transnational adoption compared to, 98, 100
reproductive assistive services, 193n6
reproductive justice, 135
resettlement programs, 81
Roberts, Dorothy, 8
Roberts, Elizabeth, 132
Robertson, Craig, 50
"Root for Your Roots," 166, *166*
Roots (Tachiki), 70, 85–86

Samuels, Ellen, 17, 170
San Francisco Earthquake (1906), 32
Saussurean tradition, 7
Schneider, David, 15, 183
science, 160–61
scientific research, 158–59, 160
search goods, 125–26

second-wave refugees, 82–83
Sekula, Allan, 49, 127, 204n23
self-knowledge, 169
Sex and the City (television show), 91
sexual expression, 9
sexuality, 11–12; kinship relation to, 194n28; power and, 194n22
sexualized racism, 141
sexual regulation, 57–58
sexual stereotypes, 140–41
sexual violence, 141
"shared genetic histories," 167, 169
Shibusawa, Naoko, 66
signifiers, 7–8, 10
sign systems, technologies of, 12
"Singles in America" study, 144
skilled labor: capitalism relation to, 79; immigration policy and, 77
slavery, 156
social construction, 14–16, 152, 188
social good, 160
social meaning, consumer choice and, 161
social media, 9, 125; multiculturalism relation to, 144; profile interface on, 26; 23andMe compared to, 170–71
social ordering, 122, 131–32
social personhood, 107
social science, 67
socioeconomic means, 151
soft power, 92
sojourner mentality, 57
"son preference," 92–93
Sontag, Susan, 206n65
"sound-image," 7
South America, 132
"special needs" children, 107, 108
Steichen, Edward, 162
stereotypes, 135; of Black communities, 23; online dating and, 206n59; racism and, 204n29; sexual, 140–41. *See also* model minority
Stoler, Ann Laura, 21
"structure of feeling," 204n25

subject formation, 103, 107
subjectification, of refugees, 87–88
subject-object relation, 13
"Success Story, Japanese American Style," 23, 63, 69
"Success Story of One Minority Group," 69–70
"The Super Minority's Poor Cousins," 84
surrogacy, 5, 8
systemization, of power, 10–11

Tachiki, Amy, 70
Tagg, John, 50
TallBear, Kim, 156
Tang, Ji, 108–10
technique, 9
technological representation, 103
technologies of kinship, definition of, 3, 7–8. *See also specific topics*
"Technologies of Self" (Foucault), 12
technology. *See specific topics*
techno-Orientalism, 4, 149
Telfer, Jon, 98
temporality, government bureaucracy and, 35
testimony, photography as, 51–52, 53
"thing theory," 201n17
Thompson, Charis, 18
tiger parents, model minority and, 4
Time (magazine), 63, 157
transnational adoption, 14, 22, 91, 116, 201n12, 202n48; commodification relation to, 109–10, 119; family formation and, 103–4; FCCNY and, 96–98; genetic ancestry testing and, 175–76; as global industry, 111; kinship and, 177; from Korea, 23, 24, 92, 106, 112–13, 201n4; multiculturalism relation to, 93, 104, 105–6; photography and, 24–25, 92, 94–96, 98–101, 107–8, 201n19; picture brides compared to, 103; racialized interchangeability and, 114–15; 23andMe and, 178–79

transracial adoption, 92–93, 141, 175, 185; biological parent relation to, 14; family formation and, 96, 119; kinship and, 94, 131, 177; racialization and, 106–7
Tu, Thuy Linh Nguyen, 93
Turner-Smith, Jodie, 2
"12 Asian Americans Discuss," 164
23andMe, 27, 172, 175, 207n14, 208n30; AAHRPP and, 208n19; Airbnb and, 187; Asian American identity relation to, 163–64; donor siblings and, 173–74; genetic essentialism and, 180; global family and, 166–67; healthcare relation to, 158; heterosexual reproductive normativity relation to, 172; kinship relation to, 154–56, 157, 162, 176; multiculturalism relation to, 153, 154–55, 159–61, 170; "Our Services-Ancestry," 167, 168, 169; racial categorization of, 165; racial mixing and, 209n32; social media compared to, 170–71; transnational adoption and, 178–79; WeGene compared to, 208n28
23andMe+ Total Health™, 158
Twinsters (documentary), 178
The two Cha Jung Hees, 112

ultrasound images, 101–2
Unbound Feet (Yung), 51
United States (US), 182, 187; antimiscegenation in, 131; Asian diaspora in, 19–20, 22, 23–24, 29, 68, 71, 72–74; colonialism of, 79; globalization and, 93–94; imperialism and, 162–63; inclusion in, 13; Japan relation to, 66–67; Korea relation to, 115–16; militarism, 81, 86; racialization in, 3, 5; refugees in, 81, 85, 88–89. *See also* Immigration and Naturalization Service; paper families
United States v. Bhagat Singh Thind (1923), 74
upward mobility, 78, 83

US. *See* United States
US Citizenship and Immigration Services (USCIS), 182
US News & World Report (news outlet), 69

Vietnam, 23, 92
Vietnam War, 86
Viet Thanh Nguyen, 71
visas, Immigration and Nationality Act relation to, 75–76
visual culture, 10
visuality: colorblindness and, 147, 148; immigration interviews relation to, 48; of kinship, 107; of multiculturalism, 145; photography and, 10; of race, 50, 53, 121, 159; of racial identity, 161; referral photograph and, 24

Wailoo, Keith, 156
Waithe, Lena, 206n65
Wall Street Journal (newspaper), 84
"Want to Sell Your Eggs to Pay for College? Be Asian.," 133
war orphans, 92
Washington Post (newspaper), 140
WeGene, 165, 208n28
welfare, 82–83
Weston, Kath, 131–32
Wexler, Laura, 57
"white-collar proletariat," 79

White male, Asian female couple (WMAF), 139–42
Whiteness, 130; class normativity and, 82–83; egg and sperm donation relation to, 151; masculinity relation to, 142
whitening, 132
Williams, Raymond, 9
Winant, Howard, 3
WMAF. *See* White male, Asian female couple
Wong, Victor, 70
Wong Gong, 60
Wong Sik Koey, 31, 55
Wong Tung Gee, 29–31, 54–55
Wong Tung Yee, 29–31, 33, 54–55, 56
Wong Wing Yick, 29–31, 54, 60
Woo, Susie, 105, 115
work ethic, 71–72
World Health Organization, 181
World War II, 60
Wu, Ellen, 67

Yang, Andrew, 181–82
Yee Bok On, 38
Yee On, 37–39
yellow peril, 4, 17, 71
Yngvesson, Barbara, 106–7
Yu, Henry, 67
Yung, Judy, 43

Zhou, Youyou, 140
Zucker, W. J., 45–49

ABOUT THE AUTHOR

LiLi Johnson is Assistant Professor of English and Gender and Women's Studies at Dalhousie University. Her research interests include Asian American family and kinship, racial formation and discourses of multiculturalism, cultural studies of science and technology, and digital and visual cultures.